(continued from front flap)

for determining when, where, and how often to advertise. He also discusses strategies for breaking into a market with a new brand.

The book concludes with a look at the new opportunities opening up for advertisers willing to engage in market experimentation. Jones explains how to take advantage of these opportunities, not only to increase profits in the short run but to expand our understanding of advertising and its effects. This lucid, thought-provoking analysis is a major contribution to this challenging task.

Philip A. Jones

John Philip Jones is an associate professor and chairman of the Advertising Department in the Newhouse School of Public Communications at Syracuse University. Jones's academic appointment follows a distinguished career in the advertising industry, including 25 years at J. Walter Thompson. His professional career was almost exclusively devoted to managing the advertising of brands like those discussed in this book.

What's in a Name?

There must be a personality shining through all the talk about the product. I have overwhelming evidence that one of the reasons why people buy my Mountain Grown Apples is because they take to a character called Old Jim Young, who chats with them in the advertising.

—James Webb Young
How to Become an Advertising Man

What's in a Name?

Advertising and the Concept of Brands

John Philip Jones
Newhouse School of Public
Communications,
Syracuse University

Foreword by
Don Johnston
Chairman, J. Walter Thompson Company

Lexington Books
D.C. Heath and Company/Lexington, Massachusetts/Toronto

106 780

Library of Congress Cataloging-in-Publication Data

Jones, John Philip.
  What's in a name?

  Includes index.
  1. Advertising. 2. Brand name products. I. Title.
HF5823.J718 1986   658.8′343   85-45039
ISBN 0-669-11142-2 (alk. paper)

Published simultaneously in Canada
Printed in the United States of America
International Standard Book Number: 0-669-11142-2
Library of Congress Catalog Card Number: 85-45039

The paper used in this publication meets the minimum requirements of American National
Standard for Information Sciences—Permanence of Paper for Printed Library Materials,
ANSI Z39.48-1984.

The last numbers on the right below indicate the number and date of printing.

10 9 8 7 6 5 4 3 2 1

95 94 93 92 91 90 89 88 87 86

This book is dedicated to my students, in the hope that throughout their professional careers they will remember that the value of a theory depends on the amount of empirical support it has received.

Contents

Tables and Figures

Tables

Figures

Foreword: Advertising and Brand Planning

> It sounded like an excellent plan, no doubt, and very neatly and simply arranged: the only difficulty was, that she had not the smallest idea how to set about it. _____
>
> So she sat on, with closed eyes, and she half believed herself in Wonderland, though she knew she had but to open them again, and all would change to dull reality.

The reader will shortly discover that Professor Jones begins each chapter of his rich analysis of brands and advertising with a quotation from Lewis Carroll's *Alice in Wonderland* or *Through the Looking Glass*. These volumes, written in 1864, remain startlingly relevant, even to set the tone and manner of a very sophisticated marketing argument one hundred twenty years later.

For me, the limits of the argument are set in these two quotations: for the marketing theorist the problem is to make certain that "dull reality" enlightens the theoretical; for the practitioner, the problem is to devise a workable plan which takes advantage of the best thinking available.

What's in a Name: Advertising and the Concept of Brands addresses both camps—requiring Wonderland to confront empirical data, and the marketplace to confront theoretical insights describing how brands act. At the conclusion of his argument, Professor Jones brings these elements together, makes some tentative predictions and offers a brief action plan. The professional marketer, whether advertiser or creator of advertising, should study these pages particularly carefully. The issues are clear. The challenge is unmistakable.

Those practitioners deep in the business of creating advertising are all too aware of the changing environment in which we operate. Media structure is changing everywhere. New forms with seductive promise are attracting advertiser investment away from traditional media. Yet, some of the breakthroughs in the technical revolution have already proved illusory. What change is permanent and what is merely a blip on the conventional media screen?

The emergence of super-marketers who will, and must, challenge the growing dominance of the super-retailers is already changing the agency scene. Problems of conflict and exclusivity will require these new mega-marketers either to concentrate their budgets in very few agencies, to hire a large number of smaller agencies or to start their own in-house agencies (an experiment that has never worked on a small scale in the past). The fact remains: there is an insufficient number of large agency networks to provide exclusive service for these dominant marketers.

The fallout of the recall battle, so definitively described and decried by Professor Jones, has yielded some damaging anomalies in the agency business. Increasingly, we have become embroiled in the battle of creating outstanding advertisements. Clients look for the "big idea", the "break-through execution", the winner of the Clio. Creative resources are applied to solve specific short-term problems with short-lived executions. A campaign may last as long as a year. Agencies and clients become obsessed with advertisements; the critical question of how a long-range, three- to five-year "advertising" strategy can benefit a brand is widely overlooked.

A further indication of this emphasis is the great premium placed on creative people. Agencies bemoan the dearth of creative talent; there simply are not enough top writers, art directors and producers to fill the demand for outstanding advertisements. Salaries escalate proportionately. Greater and greater time and dollars are spent looking for that award-winning advertisement.

What does it look like when it finally appears? Do consumers recognize a "big idea"? Do users of a brand respond differently, or in greater numbers? How is "breakthrough" measured anyway? The copy in these advertisements is frequently written in some mythical language, "advertising-speak", which purports to be "slice-of-life" but which, in fact, is totally alienating to the very people whose life is supposedly being sliced up.

Not surprisingly, then, readers and viewers of advertising become increasingly skeptical and cynical about the value of advertising.

With this apparent loss of consumer acceptance on one hand and growing market pressures on advertisers on the other hand, how then can you account for the fact that overall the advertising industry appears to be growing? A review of the world's leading advertising markets shows that advertising growth in the United States averaged 11 percent annually throughout the seventies. (Not all sectors enjoyed a uniform rate of growth, to be sure, but the industry grew as a whole faster than the average annual inflation rate of 7 percent.) In 12 other major markets, the nominal average growth of classical advertising ranged from just over 9 percent in Italy to over 20 percent in the Netherlands, with ten of these twelve other markets reporting a higher growth rate than the United States. Because the U.S. measures classical advertising and a large amount of below-the-line activity together, the relative strength of the advertising industry outside the United States is even more apparent. Moreover, this trend will probably continue over the longer term. Clearly, in some sense, the real world of advertising is prospering and, as the saying goes, "If it ain't broke, don't fix it."

Closer analysis of this growth, as will be seen in the more detailed discussion of packaged goods in this book, demonstrates that certain historically dynamic sub-segments are not participating in the overall growth rate. Indeed, there is not only real decline in share, there is more critically decline in potential. The importance of advertising in the minds of certain traditional advertisers is diminishing at the same time the target groups of the advertising are questioning its very relevance.

The growth in the industry is coming from new kinds of advertisers and new product categories that have entered the arena. Both the importance and the frailty of the new advertising budgets from the electronics industry in various Silicon Valleys have been well documented in the last eighteen months. Looking at the overall industry statistics, then, may not in itself be a heartening exercise but rather another means of masking what is really taking place.

The marketplace is perilous. Times change quickly. There are signs that the industry has lost its growth potential and that consumers are turning off to advertising in ever greater numbers. A very compelling case can be made that the practitioners of advertising have lost touch with the very reality of which they are allegedly the custodians. One could argue that I overstate the case for dramatic effect. To a degree I accept this point. The professional advertising community, however, will recognize the dull reality behind my allegations.

Now consider for a moment the ten largest advertisers in the year 1913:

	Advertiser	*Some of the Advertised Brands*
#1	Procter & Gamble	Ivory Soap; Crisco
#2	Quaker Oats	Quaker Oats; Puffed Wheat; Puffed Rice
#3	Postum Cereal Co.	Post Toasties; Grape Nuts; Regular and Instant Postum
#4	Victor Talking Machine Co.	Victor Records; Victrola Players
#5	Willys-Overland	Overland Coupe
#6	Colgate & Co.	Colgate Dental Cream; Colgate Cold Cream; Cashmere Bouquet
#7	Eastman Kodak	Kodak cameras; Kodak film
#8	P. Lorillard and Co.	Zubelda; Egyptian Deities; Mogul; Murad (not all household words today)
#9	Steward Warner Speedometer Co. (a bit of a surprise)	
#10	American Tobacco Company	Pall Mall; Bull Durham smoking tobacco

If we doubled or tripled this list, it would have pretty much the same characteristics. These are mostly names you still recognize, companies with known brands that command a significant market share today. As perilous as a changing marketplace can be, there must be some way to survive.

If brands have survived this long—through two World Wars, a major economic depression and (potentially most damaging of all) over twenty years of well-meaning brand managership, then something is at work which will help us overcome the problems in today's "real world." Familiar brands will continue to prosper. New brands—as long as they are demonstrably better and demonstrably different—will succeed in the marketplace. They can be brought to life, nourished and allowed to grow and survive.

Early in his argument, Professor Jones establishes a very valuable metaphor of a complex machine to describe how brands function. Another useful metaphor, of course, is to compare a brand to a person. In the preceding paragraph, all the verbs just as aptly describe a person. For years, we have known that consumers respond comfortably to the invitation to compare a brand to a person. The metaphor is helpful in this context as well. To survive as a child in an urban neighborhood today (the milieu to which the packaged goods marketplace most readily can be compared), an individual must have savvy, street smarts, a certain degree of acknowledged power, strong parentage on which to rely, and considerable luck. Most children survive and some prosper and succeed in life well beyond the most hoped-for dreams of their anxious parents.

The conditions are no different for brands—except that far fewer survive. (Whether this is the result of the obvious fact that brands have no life of their own—they are managed—is outside this discussion but not an irrelevant question.)

Key for a brand are the elements of parentage (who the manufacturer is); acknowledged power (the appropriate level of resources for the launch) and luck. What I want to focus on, however, is the importance of savvy and street smarts—knowing what it takes to survive and then using the knowledge in a flexible, tactical plan. It is in these areas where we will discover the keys to maintain and build major brands for the balance of this century and into the next.

There is a great deal about how brands and advertising work which we do not know. This volume examines the state of our knowledge in detail and Professor Jones makes a fervent and timely plea to all marketers to begin to build a better base on which to make decisions. I would agree that we need more solid and reliable information.

I would also add, however, that we must make better use of the information we already have.

Much of the accumulated wisdom and expertise lying in the files and archives of agencies and marketers is not known, understood, used or passed down to the generations of new young brand personnel. Quantities of data which are assembled about the marketplace, the consumer and social and economic trends, are simply not brought to bear on the decisions affecting individual brands. Specific brand research, diligently carried out, lies fallow because earnest, smart advertising people simply haven't the time or resources to wring it dry for every important nuance and clue. We aren't providing the marketing savvy which we have because we have no mechanism or budget to do so.

A communications revolution is at hand. At times one feels rather as one must have felt in Paris in 1789: we know the revolution is going on but we don't have the time or perspective to see who is winning. One winner will clearly be the person who can harness the accumulated expertise about a brand, its history, its properties and its marketplace and use that expertise to carry it forward.

The process of carrying it forward is the second element of the survival kit. "A plan—simple and neatly arranged—now how to set about it." Street smarts translates into the plan for survival. It is the marriage of instinct and intelligence. A brand, which requires a more explicit plan, depends no less on the instinct and intelligence of its creators. The plan must encompass all that is known about and all that is relevant to the brand:

the broad social and economic issues,

marketplace factors,

brand and category developments,

company data,

advertising data—competitive and non-competitive,

media trends and opportunities.

The plan fuses all this into a long-term strategy. A long-term strategy is not concerned with advertisements—how to make the sales target in the next quarter—it is concerned with advertising and the role it must play in the survival of the brand over the next twenty years. Only when one knows where one is going can one make the first decisions on how to get there.

(Once again, Lewis Carroll provides the appropriate quote: "'Would you tell me, please, which way I ought to go from here?' 'That depends a good deal on where you want to get to,' said the Cat. 'I don't much care where—' said Alice. 'Then it doesn't matter which way you go,' said the Cat. '—So long as I get *somewhere*,' Alice added as an explanation. 'Oh, you're sure to do that,' said the Cat, 'if you only walk long enough.'")

The development of a long-term strategy, you may respond, has always been the responsibility of the advertising agency. Isn't that what they have been doing all along? Isn't that the primary function of account management? Of course, the agency assumes responsibility for this role whenever and however it can in all client-agency relationships. The problem is that in an already fractured marketing world, the various aspects of this function have also become fractured and dispersed. Some of the responsibility lies in the agency research department, some in the client research department, some in account management, some in brand management, some in media planning, some (even) in media buying, some in R&D and some has simply fallen between the cracks because no one has the time or budget for the synthesis it requires. The demands of today's marketplace come first. The pressures which public companies feel on their quarterly earnings statements are carried into the advertising and sales departments who must "make the numbers" this quarter. The plan is not thought through or written down. The best street smarts we can give to the brand for its own survival are sacrificed on the expedient altar of time and dollar pressure.

There needs to be a new dimension in the advertising-marketing mix—a function which pulls together all that is known and, in a meaningful, relevant and helpful manner, sets it down in the common plan. This role is called "account planning". It is not really a new function. It has existed in certain J. Walter Thompson offices for over twenty years. The need for it is becoming more acute however, and this volume is, in itself, a testimony to the urgent need for some new systemic solution.

The genesis of account planning, some maintained at the time, was the "weaknesses in the training of . . . account executives" (see below, p. 270). Regardless of its cause, account planning enables the agency to do what it has always done *better*. The account planner does it better simply because he/she combines the functions which have become distorted by separation. That combination becomes the primary responsibility of a separate individual in the account team who is not its leader.

There is nothing novel in what the planner does (except that it is largely not being done by anyone). The planner provides the basis on which the advertising for a brand can be developed, executed and evaluated. The creation, maintenance and modification of the advertising strategy summarizes in a coherent model the way in which advertising in an ongoing way might help the brand to grow. To fulfill this role, the planner:

1. interprets data—which may be desk research, commissioned research or simply introspection and common sense;
2. makes advertising judgments—because strategy necessarily involves judgment about how advertising might work within the overall framework of how marketing principles in general might work;

3. communicates these interpretations and judgments to the rest of the agency team and client product group—in a way which is both objective and stimulating.

It is the combination of objectivity and involvement which makes the role of the account planner unique. The traditional split between account management and research functions prevents these two essential elements from coming together systemically. Research remains dispassionately objective (insofar as it can) and account management, heavy in the day-to-day thick of things, displays incredible involvement. Both functions remain critical (although it can be argued that the research element *per se* no longer needs to be inside the agency). Account management continues to lead the charge. It is only that they have an additional competitive weapon at their disposal—account planning.

The addition of account planning to traditional agency structures will inevitably alter how agencies function as well as how they are perceived and valued by their clients. Their service will change. The nature of their counsel will change. They will become tougher, more realistic and more demanding in their analyses and recommendations. We know this because of those instances within J. Walter Thompson where account planning has been successfully operating in the service of our clients over a significant period of time.

Will account planning overcome all the problems which Professor Jones foresees? Can account planning suddenly make it possible to undertake the kind of market experimentation which he calls us to do? Obviously, account planning is not a panacea; it merely assures us (and our clients) that we are making a conscientious effort to use the best of our expertise and resources in the most innovative and constructive way possible to solve brand problems. As long as an advertising agency can make this claim to its clients, it can fairly claim to represent the real world.

The way to provide a client with a neat and simply arranged plan to get from the Wonderland of brand strategic planning to dull reality is merely to make someone accountable for doing it, to provide the resources and information bases, and the requisite thinking time apart from, yet committed to, the specific brand problems of the moment. There are no guarantees that all problems will be solved. At the very least, however, we will be out of the business of creating advertisements and back in the business of providing advertising counsel for our clients. And, maybe the brands we are serving today will make the top ten list in the year 2013.

I commend Professor Jones's book to you. It is filled with observations and proofs which go far beyond this brief introductory observation. He provides thought-provoking analyses of what has happened to brands in the marketplace and how these events affect, modify and, in some cases, refute contemporary theoretical thinking. This insistence on allowing the history of brands functioning in real marketplaces to enlighten our knowledge is a useful and necessary lesson for us all.

For many years, John Philip Jones was a valued colleague of mine at J. Walter Thompson. He unhesitatingly applied his accumulated wisdom and expertise in the analysis and resolution of his clients' problems. He was, in the guise of an account manager, an incipient account planner in the real world. It is heartening to see him apply real-world expertise to the theoretical analysis of his craft. Is he the beginning of a new breed of academic planner?

Don Johnston
Chairman,
J. Walter Thompson Company

Acknowledgments

Many people have helped me with the argument in this book. There are more than forty persons listed below, and I am extremely grateful to every one of them. In most cases their contributions went far beyond giving me their own views and responding verbally to the ideas I had been developing. In fact, many gave me studied and stimulating written observations on early drafts of my manuscript.

Mr. Herbert Ahlgren of the Association of National Advertisers; Ms. Kim Armstrong of A.T.&T.; Professor Lord Bauer of the London School of Economics and Political Science, and Gonville and Caius College, Cambridge; Mr. Robert Berenson of Grey Advertising; Mr. Alexander Biel of Ogilvy & Mather; Dr. Leo Bogart of the Newspaper Advertising Bureau; Dr. Harold Clark Jr. of J. Walter Thompson; Mr. Robert Coen of McCann-Erickson; Dr. Watson Dunn of the University of Missouri; Mr. Russ Doerner of D'Arcy Masius Benton & Bowles; Dr. Arthur Ecker of University Hospital, Syracuse; Professor Andrew Ehrenberg of the London Business School; Mr. Jack Frantz of Grey Advertising; Dr. Jules Goddard of the London Business School; Mr. Don Johnston of J. Walter Thompson; Professor John Keats of Syracuse University; Mr. Stephen King of J. Walter Thompson; Ms. Judie Lannon of J. Walter Thompson; Dr. Peter Marsh of Syracuse University; Dr. Max McCombs of the University of Texas at Austin; Mr. Colin McDonald of Communication Research, London; Mr. Richard Miller of Best Foods; Mr. Michael Naples of the Advertising Research Foundation; Mr. David Ogilvy of Ogilvy & Mather; the late Mr. James Peckham Jr. of A.C. Nielsen; Mr. William Phillips of Ogilvy & Mather; Dr. Richard Pollay of the University of British Columbia; Dr. Lewis Pringle of B.B.D.O.; Mr. Edward Rosenstein of Saatchi and Saatchi Compton; Dr. William Ryan of Syracuse University; Mr. Robert Savard of Needham, Harper and Steers; Dr. Don Schultz of Northwestern University; Dr. Julian Simon of the University of Maryland; Dr. Vernone Sparkes of Syracuse University; Mr. Robert Steiner, consultant (formerly of the Federal Trade Commission); Dean Edward Stephens of Syracuse University; Dr. Gerald Stone of Memphis State University; Dr. Stuart Tolley of the Newspaper Advertising Bureau; Mr. William Weilbacher of the

Bismark Corporation; Mr. David Wheeler of the Institute of Practitioners in Advertising, London; and a group of anonymous manuscript reviewers working for the *Syracuse Scholar*.

I must especially emphasize the very powerful contributions of my friends Harry Clark and Bill Weilbacher, both of whom provided generous intellectual input over the course of years.

Two former graduate students gave me notably talented help: Ms. Kathleen Fitzgerald (now of the Haband Company), who worked on the scientific diagrams; and Ms. Deborah Henretta (now of Procter and Gamble) who did most of the statistical work in chapter 11.

Ms. Caroline McCarley of Lexington Books was a very imaginative and sympathetic editor.

Ms. Lynne Manuel and Ms. Vera Honis produced respectively the penultimate and final typed drafts of the manuscript, and their work was of superlative quality.

My wife Wendy typed the first three or four drafts; she is the only person capable of construing large areas of my hieroglyphic handwriting. However, her contribution went far beyond the typing, because she managed consistently to prevent me from taking too seriously my struggles with the argument. In effect she guaranteed that I survived the four and a half years of very hard work I needed to write this book.

Parts of the manuscript have appeared publicly before the book itself appeared. Chapter 2 has been published in the *Syracuse Scholar;* papers based on chapters 8, 9 and 11 have appeared in two articles in the *International Journal of Advertising* and in various Convention Proceedings of the American Academy of Advertising. I have also presented the substance of chapter 11 to meetings of the Association of National Advertisers and the Market Research Council.

Finally, I should like to remember someone who had nothing to do with this book, except in the most oblique way. He was an academic under whom I studied many years ago: the late Sir Dennis Robertson, Professor of Political Economy in Cambridge University and Fellow of Trinity College. I remember him for his gift of making accessible the most intractable abstractions of economic theory. He accomplished this by a combination of studied lucidity and natural light-heartedness. His favorite author was Lewis Carroll.

1
Introduction

Of course the first thing to do was to make a grand survey of the country she was going to travel through. "It's something very like learning geography," thought Alice, as she stood on tiptoe in hopes of being able to see a little further.

I am addressing this book to people who want to learn something about brands in the real world. Such people may already be in the marketing and advertising business as entrepreneurs, as brand managers in manufacturing companies, as executives in advertising agencies; or they may be planning to build careers in such organizations. The book should also be of value in universities, and I have every intention of using it to teach my own graduate students at Syracuse University. Academic readers are however warned that the book severely and directly disputes the validity of certain widely held notions, such as that competitive brands in a market are functionally indistinguishable from one another; that the decline phase of the so-called brand life cycle is inevitable and irreversible; and that advertising is in general a powerful persuasive force in overcoming resistant attitudes. The extent of this book's use in academe will depend on how much professors wish to protect their students from the dangerous heresies I am propagating.

This book is devoted to the marketing and especially the advertising of what are referred to most commonly as repeat-purchase packaged goods (or sometimes as fast-moving consumer goods, FMCG for short). This is rather a large field; its more important categories are packaged, canned, and frozen foods; proprietary drugs; tobacco products; toiletries and cosmetics; wine, beer, and liquor; soaps and cleaners; gum and candy; and soft drinks.[1] This mixed collection of categories has considerable homogeneity from a marketing standpoint. They all have six common general characteristics, and in most of these they differ at least in degree from other categories of products and services (such as automotive, travel, retail, direct response, financial, and entertainment). Each of these characteristics will now be briefly described as a logical starting point for the argument in this book, although the reader will find them discussed more fully in the main body of the text.

1. *Women are the most important category of buyers.*

Repeat-purchase packaged goods are sold predominantly in supermarkets. In about 70 percent of cases, the buyers are women, although such goods are of course used by all members of the family in addition to the homemaker. Despite recent change in the individual roles of women and men (which may cause the 70 percent estimate to fall), many manufacturers of packaged goods continue to refer to their target consumer as "she," and this useful convention will be occasionally followed in this book. The only other advertising category in which a female target group is comparably important is the retail one.

2. *Buyers buy repeatedly and have a repertoire of brands.*

Brands are bought not once but repeatedly, in many cases in predictably regular patterns; hence the truth of the saying that when we build brands we are making customers and not just sales. In marketing jargon, we are building a long-term franchise.

In virtually every category examined empirically, it has been found that the buyer normally buys (with varying degrees of irregularity) more than one brand. This introduces the extremely important concept of the repertoire of brands, the collection the homemaker buys in varying proportions, often (again) in predictably regular patterns.

The uniformity of such patterns will be a surprise to some readers, but they will find it plentifully illustrated by the factual data in chapter 5. This element of constancy—or the inertia of habit—in most markets for repeat-purchase goods partly explains the manifest difficulty of breaking into such markets with new brands.

It also suggests the large role for advertising aimed at reinforcement and protection for the majority of established brands. Indeed much advertising is addressed to existing regular and irregular users of such brands. We advertise to these people in order to hold as well as to increase our market share. We talk to them with the intention of reinforcing their loyalty to our brand, to compliment them on their wisdom in using it so that they will remain friendly with us, and to encourage them to use it more than before (although this is normally only possible in a special circumstance discussed in chapter 5). If we look upon advertising in this way, our approach becomes different from what conventional wisdom suggests, which is that advertising is a means of converting people, persuading them to switch from brand *A* to brand *B*. There is much evidence that brand advertising as it is practiced in the real world is substantially based on continuity and not conversion. This is quite a different way of looking at the subject. Here the phrase "looking at the subject" should be emphasized. I am talking about a fresh standpoint, a mental sidestep. In a very apposite phrase originally used in a different context, this way of looking at the subject is "an apparatus of the mind, a technique of thinking."[2]

Because of the large role of habit in the purchase decision, such decision making is often described as "low involvement." It will be hypothesized later in this book that low involvement has a bearing on the shape of the advertising response function.

These factors of repetition and multibrand purchasing are of generally greater importance with packaged goods than with most other categories because of characteristics endemic to such markets, notably the high rate of product use.

The importance of repeat purchase means that in advertising FMCG, it is not only ethical but also good business to be truthful, because if the advertising overpromises, the customer will punish the manufacturer by not buying the brand again. It is surprising that this argument appears so infrequently in debates about truth in advertising.

3. *Competitive brands differ from one another in functional terms.*

Many readers of this book will be stopped by this statement. It may very well disturb a deep-seated and rather remarkable belief held by numerous people, especially academics, that competitive brands in any market are indistinguishable from one another in functional terms. The widespread prevalence of this belief has caused products in such markets to be referred to as "parity products" or "homogeneous package goods,"[3] and product improvements in them to be described as "cosmetic changes,"[4] or "induced product differentiation" created by advertising.[5] Since this issue is important to the development of the argument in this book, it is necessary to take the time to discuss it and present some evidence before continuing with the mainstream discussion.

One point should be made first. Most consumer goods markets are oligopolies dominated by a small number of large competitive manufacturers. (This type of market organization will be discussed in chapter 2). It is substantially true that the nature of oligopolistic competition, and the relative ease with which functional improvements can be copied, are forces that cause functional innovations of new and restaged brands to be widely and sometimes rapidly diffused through markets. It is however both wrong and dangerous to infer from the force and characteristics of oligopolistic competition that all brands are (or become) functionally interchangeable. It is wrong because it flies in the face of the facts, some of which will shortly be presented; and dangerous because such a line of thinking can persuade marketers to introduce new brands which offer a mere functional parity with their competitors, with a subsequent rate of failure that is in most cases only too easily and dishearteningly predictable. Success almost always requires differentiation.

The writings of researchers, advertisers, and workers in advertising agencies—people who have a day-to-day operational knowledge of brands—make it quite clear that competing brands in any market tend to be functionally different from one another. Their evidence of differences between brands in functional terms comes mainly from blind product tests, in which the names of the brands being compared are not disclosed, in order to focus exclusive attention on their functional properties. Although such tests suffer from a number of practical imperfections, I have never come across a single manufacturer of packaged goods who does not employ them on a regular basis for evaluating consumer responses to the functional delivery of his own and his competitors' brands.[6]

Although product tests normally provide fairly clear-cut results, it is not always wise to interpret them in an equally clear-cut way. Brands with a "minority appeal" should not always be rejected by manufacturers, since these are often able to attract small groups of users interested in specific attributes, on which such brands might score well. In fact, in most markets, there is a "tail" of profitable brands with individual market shares of less than 5 percent, all of which sell steadily to relatively small numbers of consumers.

Now, what have knowledgeable practitioners got to say about functional product differences? Here are the views of five of them (six if I include myself).

James O. Peckham, a researcher with forty years of experience with the A.C. Nielsen Company, wrote:

Based on a composite trend of eighteen new and/or improved brands marketed nationally prior to the start of our study, we see that consumer purchases of these new brands are up 51 percent in the two-year period. If we examine the individual brands making up this fine sales trend, we find that they all had a "consumer plus" readily demonstrable to the consumer.

Again:

The board chairman of one of the leading manufacturers of a household product recently stated in a speech before the National Industrial Conference Board that the company's top brand had had 55 product improvements in the 29 years of its existence.

Again:

On a blind product test of your new brand versus leading brands already on the market, you should not ordinarily consider trying to build a consumer franchise unless you have a 60–40 preference—and 65–35 would be preferable.[7]

J. Hugh Davidson, a senior executive in a major international marketing company, published an empirical examination of successful and unsuccessful new products, with the conclusions that:

Fully 74% of the successes I studied offered the consumer better performance at the same or higher price. . . . My study revealed a close correlation between a brand's success and its distinctiveness.[8]

David Ogilvy, one of the most distinguished practitioners in the advertising agency field, referred to statements by the former chairman of Procter and Gamble:

Says Harness, "The key to successful marketing is superior product performance. . . . If the consumer does not perceive any real benefits in the brand, then no amount of ingenious advertising and selling can save it."

To which Ogilvy responded:

The best of all ways to beat P & G is, of course, to market a *better product*. Bell Brand potato chips defeated P & G's Pringles because they tasted better. And Rave overtook Lilt in less than a year because, not containing ammonia, it is a better product.[9]

Bill Bernbach, who like Ogilvy was one of the luminaries of the postwar advertising scene, was clear on the point:

I think the most important element in success in ad writing is the product itself. And I can't say that often enough. Or emphasize it enough. Because I think a great ad campaign will make a bad product fail faster. It will get more people to know it's bad. And it's the product itself that's all important and that's why we, as an agency, work so closely with the client on his product—looking for improvements, looking for ways to make people want it, looking for additions to the product, looking for changes in the product. Because when you have that, you are giving the people something that they can't get elsewhere. And that is fundamentally what sells.[10]

Rosser Reeves, a scarcely less distinguished figure in the field than Ogilvy and Bernbach, observed:

> The agency can induce the client to change his product, improve his product. We have done this on numerous occasions. . . . A great advertising man of three decades ago once said: "A gifted product is mightier than a gifted pen." How right he was! This is not a secondary road. It is often the first, and the best road, to travel.[11]

During my own professional career, I have studied the reports of scores, perhaps hundreds of blind product tests on my clients' brands. From this experience I found it so normal to expect different preferences for different brands that it never occurred to me or my colleagues to expect anything else. The result of a pair of such tests will be given in chapter 2. This comes from a market for manufactured food in which some of the perceptible taste differences between the brands are the result of different ingredients and manufacturing processes, but some are also there because certain manufacturers are able to get fresher stocks to the retail trade as a result of their superior shipping systems.[12]

Despite the informed opinions and the evidence quoted here, I still believe regretfully that the myth of "artificial" product differentiation[13] is so well established in the academic world that this and related notions will continue to be a picturesque feature of the literature. However, my studies of the facts leave me in no doubt that functional differences between brands are as important with packaged goods as with any other category, indeed probably more so, because of the relatively large number of competitive brands which are available in such markets, as a result of the rapid pace of oligopolistic competition.

Incidentally it might be considered reasonable to expect the proponents of the "homogeneous package goods" school of thought to subject their hypothesis to empirical examination and to publish their evidence. This, if it existed, would demonstrate in effect that consumers are fools, or at least that their clearly expressed preferences among brands are based on capricious and frivolous considerations. To the best of my observation, no such evidence has ever been presented for evaluation.

4. *Brands are enriched with added values.*

In addition to the functional rewards that consumers get from using brands, there are further benefits to the consumer which are substantially psychic. Often referred to as added values, they are built by consumers' experience of using brands, and by the advertising and the packaging. The existence of added values, will be easily demonstrated in chapter 2. Added values are important to all products and services, especially to repeat-purchase packaged goods, but their importance relative to functional benefits varies according to product category: for instance, added values are relatively more important with toiletries than with food products. Packaged goods almost certainly include those categories in which added values are of the most substantial importance.

The result of added values is that successful brands are preferred to their competitors in named product tests by a higher margin than in blind product tests since the latter screen out added values and force respondents to react exclusively to functional performance. But it is important to appreciate that added values are added on top of functional performance and do not substitute for it. A misconception of this point is the main reason why unsuccessful marketers have sacrificed fortunes in new brand ventures.

This matter is exceptionally important in the discussion of advertising. Here there is a real role for intuition and imagination, which are regarded by many people as predominantly feminine qualities, as well as for the logic, precision, and drive sometimes seen as predominantly masculine virtues.[14] The reader will note how the feminine association of intuition and imagination is generally consistent with the first characteristic of repeat-purchase packaged foods in the present analysis: the importance of women as target consumers.

5. *The field is relatively advertising-intensive.*

By "advertising-intensive" I mean that a brand's advertising, when expressed as a proportion of the value of its sales, is a relatively high figure. *Advertising Age* data, (published annually on a company and not on a brand basis) show a median figure in most of the categories of repeat-purchase packaged goods above 4 percent and substantially higher in certain categories.[15] The comparable figures in categories other than packaged goods are mostly much lower. For instance, those for the automotive, airlines, and retail categories are all about 2 percent.

The obvious inference from this observation is that advertising is a relatively important sales-generating activity in packaged goods marketing, or rather that it is perceived as such by the manufacturers, whose expenditures measured in real terms are relatively constant year by year (although there are certain well-established general long-term trends, which will be discussed in chapter 11). This consistency suggests that companies have experience-based guidelines for the marketplace effectiveness of certain levels of advertising pressure, which is in accord with my professional experience. Certain companies however have much greater knowledge of the effects of advertising weight, as a result of econometric investigations of the market-place re-sults of their advertising. This difficult procedure calls for screening out ad-vertising as a separate variable in the marketing mix, but manufacturers' increasing ability to do this is an important matter which will be examined in some detail in this book.

Although the conclusion that the field of repeat-purchase packaged goods is relatively advertising-intensive may be based on the simplest possible processes of observation and deduction, a recent analysis of six complex pieces of empirical evidence bearing on this subject reaches strongly similar conclusions.[16]

6. *The field is very large.*

Advertising investments in the various categories of repeat-purchase goods are consistently extremely large, and account year after year for more than 60 percent of the aggregate advertising investments of the hundred larg-est advertisers in the United States.[17] The size of the total category and its especial importance with large advertisers have significant additional related effects. For instance, television is the most important advertising medium for the largest advertisers (except those in the tobacco industry for the obvious reasons of government prohibition). It is not a coincidence that it is with packaged goods that television has developed its ability both to show the functional characteristics of brands by demonstrating them, and to generate non-functional added values largely through the communication of mood and emotion.

Manufacturers of repeat-purchase packaged goods have also become the most important clients of the largest and most sophisticated advertising agen-cies. Improvements in the techniques and skills of writing and scheduling advertisements almost invariably take place with packaged goods, and we are accustomed to associating most of the advances in the marketing field with names such as Procter and Gamble, General Foods and Warner—Lam-bert, and with the advertising agencies employed by such companies.

What I have attempted to demonstrate so far is that packaged goods differ in degree from most other product categories in six distinct ways. These six differences in degree are so great that they almost add up to a difference in kind. This is why packaged goods justify being examined and analyzed on their own, or at least given a special emphasis to differentiate them from the advertising field as a whole. Let us now examine how they are handled in the literature of advertising, including marketing works which embrace advertising.

Books and articles in this field fall into three categories: primary, second-ary, and tertiary works.

Primary works. These are writings by people with the highest professional credentials and are based on their first-hand experience. There are not many such works. I do not include in this category the writings of all the top professionals, but I would certainly include those of Bill Bernbach, Leo Burnett, John Caples, Claude Hopkins, David Ogilvy, and James Webb Young.[18]

Primary works are easy to read. But despite their unique and unquestioned value, they tend to be intellectually rather slight, giving a true but regrettably faint and impressionistic flavor of how advertising works in the real world. They are not therefore in themselves adequate as text books for university courses, but they are nevertheless indispensable to people interested in advertising. The works of Bernbach, Burnett, Ogilvy, and Young are informed by profound knowledge of the packaged goods field, but their treatment of it is regrettably much too cursory for anybody who really wants to learn what it is all about.

Secondary works. This extremely important category must be carefully defined. Secondary books and articles are written by both professionals and academics: the books in roughly equal proportion, the articles more by the former than the latter. I define secondary works as generally having the following four characteristics:

1. In almost every case they deal with parts of the field and not the field as a whole.
2. They are empirical rather than theoretical, and in this they publish, or republish and interpret, original source material.
3. They admit the existence of controversies surrounding the subject, and make a consistent effort to steer a path through these. In other words they are judgmental and interpretative, although the reader may not fully accept all the interpretations. But with most of the works I have in mind, the sure impression remains that the discussion is informed, embracing analysis and synthesis often of a high order, and supported in many cases by the author's direct experience in the field.
4. They are well written. This in itself is unusual, and I shall return to the question of lucidity when I make some detailed comments on my own book.

Good secondary works are relatively rare. In my belief there are about twenty books and two hundred articles in professional and academic publications which come into the category. I do not intend to list them here, but I have made extensive use of secondary works in writing this book, and the reader will see the names of many of them in my endnotes. Despite the fact that many of these books include packaged goods in their argument, there is little serious empirical (as opposed to theoretical) examination of the field, the only work exclusively devoted to the former being Ehrenberg's magnificent but narrowly focussed study.[19]

Readers would be correct in concluding that there is a respectable corpus of serious secondary literature on advertising, including marketing works with an advertising focus. They should however remember that these works represent only a minuscule fraction of all the books and papers written on the subject, the vastly greatest proportion of which come into my third category.

Tertiary works. This is a catch-all for everything else written about the field. Much is simple descriptive work. Many of the books rely on what is said in other tertiary works and the trade press. Most of the books make no attempt to be empirical, and many of the theories enunciated are highly questionable in the light of modern research. In professional and academic magazines, there is some empirical work, but it is often bedevilled with mathematical examinations (many based on inadequate data bases) of problems for which mathematical analysis is an inappropriate tool. In such works, repeat-purchase packaged goods are not looked upon as in any way special and are accorded a fairly cursory descriptive treatment if they are mentioned at all.

As far as I have been able to find out, tertiary literature is not used at all by practitioners.[20] Its use is however fairly widespread in universities.

I have tried very hard indeed to write a book which would be qualified to enter my category of secondary works. I will describe the characteristics of my book using as the framework the four criteria by which I have defined such works.

The first characteristic of my book is that it deals with a single aspect of the subject: the marketing and advertising of repeat-purchase packaged goods, and how advertising contributes to the building of brands, a process I believe to be more a matter of repetition and reinforcement than impact and conversion.

I intend that my book should be a work of practical value; and it will be fairly easy to estimate the extent of this by the simple test of how much it is actually being used by practitioners in the field. (This is not a bad criterion for evaluating the worth of anything written about any aspect of advertising). If my book is accepted by practitioners in marketing and advertising—and I have written it in close consultation with a number of them—I have little doubt that it will be found worthwhile by students.

The second characteristic of my book is that it is based substantially on facts. These facts have been interpreted, angled as it were for the light they throw on various aspects of the subject. In many instances, my supporting material is in the public domain or can at least be found with a little difficulty; the reader is encouraged to study it at leisure. Chapters 3 through 5 rely on aggregated data from the A.C. Nielsen Company and Market Research Corporation of America, sources of incomparable quality and authority. Later chapters examine many studies of the marketplace effectiveness of campaigns, some of the tests described and evaluated having been executed with the use of the most sophisticated techniques available in the United States or abroad.

However, although my book is empirical, I have lightened my writing by a selective use of anecdotes from my professional experience, anecdotes carefully chosen to highlight principles for which there is a substantial factual basis. Telling "war stories" is a favorite habit of former marketing and advertising people, and a serious attempt has been made to restrain my self-indulgence in this regard. Incidentally, since I make references to personal experience, I have chosen the unorthodox but simple policy of writing in the first person.

The third point is that the book is uncompromising in its examination of advertising controversies caused by gaps in what we know for certain about advertising and its effects. The reader will find significant debate about the following topics, about which there are and will continue to be great differences between practitioners, although it would be wrong to say that significant advances in our knowledge have not been made:

the generation of advertising ideas,

the value of the creative contributions to campaigns,

advertising response functions,

how advertising works in psychological terms,

advertising research,

the effects of the agency commission system.

In all these controversies, I have not shied away from drawing hypotheses, and even in some cases from making recommendations for policy, which I hope will generate much debate and further empirical work, because these are the only ways in which we shall seriously advance our knowledge. Writings that do not at least describe these controversies are not only inadequate, but are also seriously misleading.

My fourth point on this book concerns the style in which it is written. The subject matter is not always easy, but this is never any excuse to be turgid or obscure. No matter what may be the subject of any piece of writing, my upbringing and education have instilled in me a profound reverence for lucidity, and the belief that no pains should be spared in order to achieve it.

Only the readers can tell whether my efforts have achieved the slightest success. But I can assure them that I have not followed advice which has seriously been offered to me that books such as this should be written in a deliberately difficult or obscure way, lest students "pass them by." (This remarkable sentiment explains a great deal about academic literature in general).

What I have attempted to do in this book is to analyze and synthesize what we know about brand advertising, with the intention of instructing the curious about both what we know and what we do not know. But it must not be thought that what we have learned is enough to construct a general theory with anything like universal application. Still less is it possible to draw up laws which will predict certainly and precisely what results will follow certain courses of action. But we have learned some things with pretty fair certainty: separate or related pieces which add up to a little over a third of the total corpus of existing and potential knowledge about advertising. These elements of knowledge are individually quite small and some way removed from the all-embracing theories which we sometimes hear.

British market researcher Colin McDonald uses an extraordinarily elegant analogy to show how the study of advertising can only be empirical, and piece by piece, to examine "how patterns of response vary between markets and, on that basis, guess at what will happen in similar cases." Thus advertisements should be classified in a similar way to how an entomologist classifies insects, "where one looks for common factors linking thousands of different species."[21] McDonald is himself a major contributor to studying advertising in this way, and his name will appear more than once in this book. So will his technique, which is the classic method of inductive reasoning.

I shall, as mentioned already, be devoting quite a lot of attention to describing and evaluating what we know about the underlying patterns of consumer behavior as revealed by empirical studies. This is an essential preliminary to understanding how advertising can contribute to developing brands. Knowing how a brand fits into a market and how this may resemble how other brands fit into other markets helps us to set limits to the contribution that advertising can make to brands. But once we set, acknowledge, and understand these limits, advertising can be shown to make a large contribution indeed.

McDonald's comparison of the study of advertisements to the study of insects is strikingly apt, but the more I have dwelt on it, the more I have come to the view that it lacks the important element of movement. All markets are in a state of flux, despite what may appear to be surface stability (what I shall later refer to as "apparent stasis"). This flux is caused by the way markets are made up: of transactions resulting from a multitude of buying decisions which take place every minute of every hour of the day. I should like therefore to suggest an analogy of my own, which while it is not as unexpected and original as McDonald's, may be a little more useful in describing an untidily changing world.

I suggest that we can compare the process of marketing a brand to a large and complex piece of mechanical equipment. As with most machines, the speed of my machine bears some relation to the energy applied to make it work. We can half see and half infer (because we cannot see everything) that all parts of the machine are connected to other parts by a complex system of pulleys, levers, and cogwheels. But although we can observe much of the functioning of the machine with our eyes, and we can evaluate the input and output, the parts we can see represent only a small proportion of the total, because of things blocking our view. Some people observing the whole apparatus believe that they can explain its working in some general, overall way, following what we might call the "macro" approach (which if it oversimplifies is likely to mislead). On the other hand some people, like me, prefer to follow the "micro" or inductive approach, which attempts to build up knowledge by looking at the mechanism piece by piece. This latter approach can at least explain discrete parts and can provide the hope (although not the firm expectation) that a general theory might eventually be built up to explain the whole.

There is one important feature of the large machine: in its very center, we can make out quite clearly a much smaller apparatus which is connected with most of the parts of the bigger machine and on occasion even appears to be controlling them. We can see the small machine reasonably clearly; when we look at it, we are struck by its extraordinary precision, delicacy, even fragility. The more we look at it, the more the thought strikes us that this little apparatus was constructed by a different sort of person, by an artist perhaps, rather than by one of the engineers and craftspeople who made the larger machine. And although we can see the smaller machine whirring harmoniously, some of the visible details of its construction make no sense to the engineers and craftspeople and the rest of us observers whose education has taught us to think on rational, logical, and of course predictable lines.

It will be no surprise to the reader that the small machine within the large machine is in my analogy the advertising, one of the main sources of a brand's added values. The analogy will reappear throughout this book. As is the case with my small machine, some elements of advertising are visible (although only some of the elements that can be seen can be understood), but some things are completely concealed. Let me clarify this point.

All advertisements are by their nature visible or audible. The scripts, copy, film sequences, and pictures; the number of insertions and the number of subjects in a campaign; their scheduling and seasonality: all these are more or less available for study by the outside observer. It is moreover normally possible to make reasonable guesses at what an advertisement was intended to accomplish, although we might have in no way been privy to the advertising strategy. (In all too many cases this shows revealingly and on occasion embarrassingly). We can with little trouble compare how much money is spent on a particular campaign with expenditures on other campaigns. Finally, by studying how long individual campaigns are exposed and how much money is spent on them, we can draw realistic conclusions about their effectiveness or lack of effectiveness in the marketplace, although we cannot always explain their impact.

This point was made by James Webb Young, the most sagacious of all writers about advertising and one of the most successful practitioners of the art. He wrote:

> Advertising education must rest on the close observation and study of actual cases.
>
> The raw material for such case studies is all around you, in print and on the air. . . . Through these, by persistent accumulation of data, study, and analysis, you will begin to grasp the application of basic advertising concepts.[22]

But this technique of observation and reflection, valuable though it is, will not reveal everything, still less explain it. The central process in constructing our small machine, which is the generation of the idea behind the advertisement, remains concealed from sight. And the harder we look for it, the more maddeningly elusive it becomes.

The reader will notice that each chapter of my book is headed by a quotation either from *Alice's Adventures in Wonderland* or *Through the Looking Glass*. I have done this not so much to be whimsical, but rather from a belief that the reader might eventually find in these two extraordinary books certain clues to illuminate our elusive unknown. These clues are concerned with a rather mysterious combination of incompleteness and unexpectedness in the communication, matters which will be discussed in chapter 7.

There are however other things to consider first. Notably we must examine some of the visible parts of my large machine. And before I even embark on this task, I must say a short word about my own background. After a training in economics, I had the great good fortune to join the J. Walter Thompson Company. I left the agency early in my career but returned after two years. In all, I spent twenty-five of my twenty-seven years in advertising working for J. Walter Thompson, years mainly spent managing the advertising for brands such as those discussed in this book. Everything I write about advertising and marketing is inevitably colored by my time at Thompson, a company noted for its unrelenting tenacity in analyzing and understanding problems and opportunities before trying to solve the former and exploit the latter. The intellectual toughness of the environment of J. Walter Thompson provides good training for an academic. Many former colleagues with whom I engaged in strong although not acrimonious debate in past years, have given me their invariably enlightening thoughts on what I have written in this book. But I should also add that despite these insights and many other valuable observations on my manuscript from professional and personal friends, the responsibility for all the errors of commission and omission in this book is mine alone.

Notes

1. This categorization is used by *Advertising Age* in its annual estimates of the advertising expenditures of the hundred leading advertisers in the United States. For the most recent analysis, see *Advertising Age,* September 26, 1985.

2. This phrase is taken from a celebrated description of economic analysis by John Maynard Keynes in the original introduction to the series of *Cambridge Economic Handbooks*. D. H. Robertson, *Money* (New York: Harcourt, Brace, 1922): p. v.

3. Julian L. Simon, *Issues in the Economics of Advertising.* (Urbana, Il: University of Illinois Press, 1970), pp. 269–85.

4. Mark S. Albion and Paul W. Farris, *The Advertising Controversy* (Boston, Mass: Auburn House, 1981), p. 71.

5. *Ibid.,* p. 88.

6. These tests are thoughtfully discussed by Stephen King, *Developing New Brands* (London: Pitman, 1973), pp. 137–39.

7. James O. Peckman Sr., *The Wheel of Marketing* (privately published, 1978), pp. 50–51, 65. This primary source of exceptional importance is based on a massive aggregation of Nielsen data in a number of product fields.

8. J. Hugh Davidson, "Why Most New Consumer Brands Fail," *Harvard Business Review* 54 (March–April 1976): p. 117–22.

9. David Ogilvy, *Ogilvy on Advertising* (New York: Crown, 1983), pp. 156–57.

For a description of the operating policies of Procter and Gamble in the mid-1980s, see Bill Saposito, "Procter and Gamble's Comeback Plan," *Fortune* (February 4, 1985): 30–37. Also see John Smale and Priscilla Hayes Petty, "Behind the Brands at P. & G.," *Harvard Business Review* 85 (November–December 1985): 79–80.

10. *The Art of Writing Advertising,* ed. Denis Higgins (Chicago: Advertising Publications, 1965), p. 23.

11. Rosser Reeves, *Reality in Advertising* (New York: Alfred A. Knopf, 1961), p. 55.

12. This statement is based on first-hand evidence of a senior food chemist with extensive experience in the employ of a number of leading food manufacturers in the United States.

13. Albion and Farris, *The Advertising Controversy,* p. 88.

14. I am reminded of an aphorism attributed to Kipling (one with which I do not completely disagree): "A woman's guess is much more accurate than a man's certainty."

15. *Advertising Age,* September 26, 1985: 1–156.

16. Albion and Farris, *The Advertising Controversy,* pp. 117–36.

17. *Advertising Age,* September 26, 1985.

18. Of these famous advertising writers, Bernbach is the only one who did not leave us a book describing his views on the art. A number of his speeches can however be found by the diligent student.

19. Andrew Ehrenberg, *Repeat Buying: Theory and Applications* (New York: American Elsevier, 1972.)

20. This conclusion is based on personal observation, supplemented by information from senior executives in thirty leading U.S. advertising agencies about their own training programs.

21. Colin McDonald, "Myths, Evidence and Evaluation," *Admap* (November 1980): 546–55.

22. James Webb Young, *How to Become an Advertising Man* (Chicago: Advertising Publications, 1963), p. 12.

2

Brands: What They Are and Why They Emerged

"You will observe the Rules of Battle, of course?" the White Knight remarked, putting on his helmet too.

"I always do," said the Red Knight, and they began banging away at each other with such fury that Alice got behind a tree to be out of the way of the blows.

This chapter is concerned with defining the meaning of a brand and describing how and why brands emerged in the marketplace. It is important to spend some time on this historical progress because there are issues here beyond purely technical ones, issues which touch on aspects of social and economic welfare. The time to consider these broader matters, albeit briefly, must be at the beginning of the argument in this book.

Brands developed out of trademarks, a longstanding means of providing legal protection to an inventor's patent. But even with the earliest brands which emerged more than a hundred years ago, the branding process developed a purpose and importance beyond this simple legal role in that it suggested a guarantee of homogeneity and product quality to buyers of a brand, who might otherwise know nothing about the manufacturer of it. Even more importantly, it provided an unmistakable means of differentiating one manufacturer's output from another's, a matter central to oligopolistic competition (the type of organization most typical of consumer goods markets today).

In order to examine these points more fully so as to be able to evaluate the branding system for its implications for general economic welfare, we must make a brief incursion into economic history. The reader should be warned that there are considerable differences between my interpretation of the economic history of brands and the conventional one. Opinions vary a great deal about the broader effects of oligopolistic competition, but the majority view interprets oligopoly as an anticompetitive force, a force certainly less socially and economically desirable than the supposed alternative of atomistic competition. I take issue with this view, not on the grounds of its theoretical validity or invalidity, but on the grounds of its relevance to the real world past or present.

The argument that I shall develop in this chapter is, first, that conditions of atomistic competition never existed in many, perhaps most consumer goods markets; and, second, that oligopoly emerged as a competitive, not as an anticompetitive force. The pioneer manufacturer in most product fields was substantially a monopolist who used his brand as a device to demonstrate the legal protection of his product. The monopoly profits earned attracted competition from firms that had to grow large quickly in order to compete successfully. This process involved the launch of new brands which competed with varying degrees of directness with the original one, a process which changed the organization of the market to oligopolistic competition. If my view is correct that most consumer goods markets have during their history been only either monopolistic or oligopolistic (a very restricted range of competitive options), then our judgment about the welfare effects of oligopoly, compared with other types of market organization, is going to be quite different from our view if the alternatives were to include anything approaching atomistic competition.

It will be apparent to readers with some training in economic analysis that I am in effect attempting to stand conventional theory on its head. They will however discover that I approach economic history from an unusually empirical point of view. I should be surprised if the readers, when they finish digesting this chapter, end in total disagreement with my interpretation of the facts. A comfortable and relevant starting point is to look at some facts which any observant person would be able to collect by making a visit to a grocery store.

A Shopping Trip and Some Conclusions Therefrom

My wife and I normally shop for our groceries in Wegmans supermarket in Dewitt, a shop well known to most people who live in Syracuse. It is a large, well laid out store with an impressive range of merchandise, and although my wife and I prefer it to others in Syracuse, we know at least half a dozen stores comparable in size and style (although in our opinion not quite so good). On a recent Friday evening during one of our weekly shopping trips, I decided to spend some time in the cold breakfast cereals aisle in order to examine as many packs and check as many prices as I could before my wife got too impatient with waiting. I concentrated on the ready-prepared cereals, excluding all breakfast foods that need cooking, all prepared "complete breakfasts," and all the compressed "muesli" products made of grains, nuts, and fruit. I devoted my attention then to the familiar types which play (alas!) such a major role in the diet of the American family. I will summarize briefly my findings.

1. I counted seventy varieties of cold cereal sold under different names, with the exception of a few flavors sold under a common brand name, which I counted separately. The seventy different varieties came in 107 different pack sizes.

2. The brands appeared to be substantially different from one another in functional terms. (I counted a difference in taste or ingredients as a functional difference.) Specifically, the brands differed from one another in sweetness, in type and proportion of the various ingredients, and in shape and appearance of the product. The functional properties were clearly illustrated on the packs, and of course the surface design of the packs differed as much as their names.

3. Most brands came from one of six manufacturers: General Foods, General Mills, Kellogg's, Nabisco, Quaker Oats, and Ralston Purina.

4. The 107 different pack sizes were sold at a wide variety of prices. The cheapest pack sold for $0.43 (Malt a Meal Puffed Wheat and Malt a Meal Puffed Rice); the highest price pack for $1.97 (eighteen-pack Kellogg's Variety). The ratio between the prices of the cheapest and most expensive was therefore 100:458. (This range, of course, refers to packs of all sizes, which accounts for some but by no means all of the variation.) This range of prices was reasonably evenly spread, the median price ($1.19) being fairly close to the unweighted average ($1.23).

5. An up-to-date and efficient store, Wegmans takes the trouble to indicate clearly on the shelf-price-tickets the price per pound weight of most goods. Prices can be compared directly so the careful shopper can see at a glance what value for money the various packs are offering, irrespective of the different sizes.

I noted a price range from $0.79 per pound (Wegmans generic corn flakes) to $2.11 per pound (Quaker Puffed Wheat). The ratio of bottom price to top price was, as can be seen, fairly large (100:267), although not quite so large as in the previous analysis, for the reason already given. The prices per pound were (like the pack prices) uniformly spread, something demonstrated by the closeness of the median ($1.38) to the unweighted average ($1.36).

What lessons can we draw from this brief exercise in observation and analysis? Lest it be thought that I am going into personal competition with the A.C. Nielsen Company, let me say immediately that the object of this exercise was simply to confirm and illustrate some things I knew already.[1] But it is always useful on these occasions to have some undisputed facts available, no matter how commonplace they may be.

Before conducting my investigation, I was pretty sure in my own mind that the breakfast cereal market had five easily confirmed characteristics:

1. The market is oligopolistic, being dominated by a relatively small number of manufacturers.[2] In the 1960s, the six main firms accounted for 97 percent of total sales, the remaining 3 percent mainly accounted for by private labels.[3] The overall shape of the market is virtually the same today. The fact that there is a relatively small number of competitors, but each a substantial manufacturer, means that oligopoly can represent a heightened type of competition because it brings an advanced degree of consciousness of one's competitors and the influence of one's actions on them.

2. There are many different brands and pack sizes, each firm having a number of brands which, although in general complementary to each other, also compete to some degree. The different brands reflect different functional characteristics of the products, mainly different taste. The number of brands and varieties has increased significantly during the twenty-odd years I have been taking a professional interest in packs and prices, as confirmed by Nielsen data and Jules Backman's wellknown investigation of advertising and competition.[4]

3. All the brands on sale have significant added values. This chapter is concerned with added values, but before taking any serious steps to describe their features and importance, a number of different but related notions will have to be introduced into the argument. Nevertheless, by way of hors d'oeuvre, I can say here that added values are essentially psychological and subjective to the user of the brand and that they come in the main from two sources: a person's first-hand experience of a brand, and its presentation in the packaging and consumer advertising. Of all the brands on sale in Wegmans, we can be sure that consumers have experience of them, for the simple reason that efficient stores evaluate punctiliously and continuously the store traffic generated by all brands on display. It is also certain that such brands receive significant advertising support (a normal condition of stocking by larger stores). We can therefore reasonably assume the brands on the shelves to have added values. Another quite graphic way of describing such brands might be as "bundles of functional and nonfunctional benefits."

4. I expected the range of prices to be large and to have increased over time for a number of reasons, mainly active and continuous price competition among both manufacturers and retailers. This competition can take two forms: strategic or long-term, representing the corporate policy of the manufacturer or retailer; and tactical, by means of temporary promotional actions with specific short-term objectives. The latter are typical of many packaged goods markets (for instance, bar soaps) where a major share of total tonnage sales is made through temporary reductions, mostly indicated on the pack.[5] As a general rule, promotions are by far

the most important and aggressive expressions of price competition in oligopolistic markets. But for breakfast cereals, price promotions are uncommon; extensive and permanent price differentials are an important feature of the market.

5. Most importantly, my general conclusions from breakfast cereals apply *mutatis mutandis* to most consumer goods markets. Indeed, what I have learned from my professional experience and illustrated by my visit to Wegmans regarding price competition and product differentiation applies to most of the packaged goods that shoppers buy regularly and that account for the largest proportion of household consumer expenditure. The truth of this statement can be confirmed by checking any family's shopping list even if the reader does not have access to the vast amount of Nielsen data on the subject.

Let me also emphasize that there is nothing in any way original in these observations. I would have expected my wife or any other sensible, observant shopper to have drawn the same sorts of conclusions without even the benefit of an hour's store check.

The Economist's View of Oligopoly—and a Different Hypothesis

After the description of my visit to Wegmans supermarket with its plentiful evidence of price competition as well as significant and objectively perceptible product differentiation, it comes as rather a surprise to learn what some economic observers have to say about oligopoly. Here are two examples, neither of them outrageously extreme:

> [Under oligopoly] the characteristic form of industrial system eschews price competition as too dangerous and channels its rivalry into ever-changing strategies for winning customers away from one another.[6]

> In markets dominated by a small number of large corporations, both price and product competition decline. Such products as are on offer tend increasingly to resemble one another, and scope for consumer choice diminishes. . . . A comparison between advertising in the competitive era and today brings out clearly the virtual disappearance of price and product competition.[7]

The idea that the organization of markets changed because of a large reduction in competition is common in economic literature. On a related subject, more than one economist has associated the growth in consumer advertising with the decline of the wholesaler, a supposedly powerful participant in the market who is considered once to have maintained competition among manufacturers by subjecting them to the necessity of bidding for wholesalers' patronage.

This notion was given a degree of intellectual respectability by Neil Borden of the Harvard Business School in his important examination of the economic effects of advertising, published in 1942.[8] Borden listed conflict within the distributional chain as one of nine factors that he claimed had contributed to the growth of consumer advertising in the United States. When the debate passed from Cambridge, Massachusetts to Cambridge, England, the role of the wholesaler was given a greater, indeed a central importance among the factors leading to the growth of advertising.

The best known and also most extreme expression of this view was made by Nicholas Kaldor (now Lord Kaldor) in an influential paper published in 1950.[9] Kaldor claimed that price competition among manufacturers was once maintained by the power of wholesalers, but that manufacturers found a way of breaking out of this confinement by branding and advertising their output and "speaking over the heads of the wholesalers to the ultimate buyer."[10] This led to the growth of manufacturers until they began to dominate markets, creating the general conditions of oligopoly we see today. In this situation, the consumer has to pay higher prices because there is much less competition than in the era which supposedly preceded it; the higher prices under oligopoly are used, of course, substantially to fund advertising. The reader will note that Kaldor's argument is not devoid of political implications.

But to put this point into perspective, it is important to understand the historical progress, not so much from a purist's desire for historical accuracy (although this is not a completely unimportant reason) but more because a misunderstanding of history can lead to false conclusions which can in turn lead to dangerously misleading policy recommendations.

Neither Borden nor Kaldor produced any evidence. There have however been a number of serious examinations of the development of the wholesale trade in the United States.[11] From these studies, the unmistakable conclusion emerges that *from the beginning* it was manufacturers who were the dominant partners and wholesalers the weaker ones. Indeed, wholesalers appear to have been called into existence by the need of manufacturers to sell large volumes of production, although in most cases they were unable physically to service a multitude of retail accounts.

But as the sales of consumer goods grew, wholesalers were often unable to keep up with the demands of manufacturers, and in particular unable to make an effective job of new product introductions. Manufacturers increasingly found themselves selling directly to the retail trade, especially as the retail trade itself became more and more concentrated. (This process has continued to this day, with important effects on the balance of power in the marketing world.) Even more significant, manufacturers found it necessary to appeal directly to the public by advertising in order to maintain the impetus of demand. But the reader should note that the driving force in this first expansion of advertising was not conflict between supposedly small manufacturers and supposedly large wholesalers, but the simple and pressing need to sell rapidly the burgeoning output of mechanized production, which is essentially a large manufacturer's problem.[12] Before illustrating this point statistically, I must describe and comment on market concentration as it is conventionally described in microeconomic literature.

The concentration of markets has long been studied by economists. Karl Marx and his disciples were specifically interested in it. As shown by the Sherman Antitrust Act of 1890, the Clayton Act of 1914, and the Federal Trade Commission Act of 1914, the idea had emerged from theory and entered the realm of government policy well before the first World War. The interwar period saw vigorous development of the theoretical study of monopolistic competition in the two Cambridges.[13] The trend to concentration was assumed to move progressively from perfect competition to monopoly, unless impeded by strong legislation. In general, this development was seen to coincide with growth in the size of the market, growth of output and continuous growth in concentration being seen to proceed in step.

What is striking about the classic studies of the growth of industrial concentration is that they were concerned essentially with a limited number of special cases: transport and heavy (mainly extractive) industry, economic activities in which consumer advertising has never played a large role.[14] The hypothesis that I shall develop is that, in the markets in which advertising *has* been important (where demand had to be forced up rapidly in order to mop up increasing output), the path toward market concentration has been quite a different one. And if such a hypothesis can be validated, it would explain the dissonance between what I found during my visit to Wegmans supermarket and the conventional microeconomic description of oligopoly.

Let us now return to studying the historical growth of advertising. If we start by looking at statistical data, the most striking fact is that the first substantial absolute increases in advertising were during the decades of steeply rising manufacturing output. In the United States, although advertising appears to have begun to rise immediately after the Civil War, until 1880 it was still at a very low level in absolute terms (with an annual volume of advertising in newspapers and other periodicals the equivalent of only $0.78 per head of the population). About 1880 the increase really began.

The following tables demonstrate trends in two sets of data: aggregate consumer expenditure (which is closely related to the aggregate value of manufacturers' sales of consumer goods) and print advertising (an activity mainly directed at the consumer.)[15]

Estimated Consumer Expenditure[16]			*Estimated Print Advertising*[17]		
	$M. Current	*Index*		*$M. Current*	*Index*
1880	5,331	100	1880	39	100
1890	9,810	184	1890	71	182
1900	12,349	232	1900	96	246
1904	17,460	327	1905	146	374
1909	25,982	488	1909	203	520
1914	33,019	620	1914	255	654

There is an unmistakable relationship between the rate of increase in consumer expenditure and print advertising. This is not a mere statistical correlation. There is real cause and effect here, because the size of advertising budgets has almost invariably been governed by the volume of sales. This seems rather illogical because advertising is supposed to *cause* sales, not the other way around, but it must be remembered that advertising is a residual expense (i.e., it is committed after the fixed and more important variable costs have been paid). I am not denying that advertising is in general planned to achieve certain sales objectives, and that manufacturers have built up crude but useful experience-based guidelines to the results of different levels of advertising expenditure. But the parameters effectively determining this expenditure are the likely earnings of the brand at different levels of sales, after the payment of the fixed and main variable costs. If sales go up, advertising is almost invariably increased (normally the next year); and if they go down, it is reduced (generally immediately). This procedure means of course that the prime determinant of the amount spent on advertising, especially in the early days before manufacturers had built up their experience in using it, is the sales of the brand. With refinements, the situation remains the same today, at least for ongoing brands.

If we look at the early histories of a sample of large advertised brands, we will discover that most advertising today is for brands and even products that did not exist a hundred years ago. The basic staple commodities accounting for most household expenditure in the nineteenth century were not then advertised; nor are they today, when they account for a much smaller proportion of the household budget. The growth in standard of living in the past hundred years has led us to spend our incomes on new types of merchandise, especially on discretionary goods and services for which branding and advertising have been the characteristic marketing devices from the first day of their introduction.[18]

For example, let me take one product field as typical of the whole: the sizable market for safety razors with disposable blades.[19] Before this product was invented by King C. Gillette, the safety razor market simply did not exist.

But in the second year of production, 1905, the Gillette company's sales totaled 250,000 razor sets and 100,000 blade packages.[20] What had happened was that a total market had been created overnight, essentially by a monopoly. This was the natural result of the legal protection provided by the inventor's patent.

In the market for safety razors (as in the markets for toothpastes, deodorants, shampoos, nonsoap detergents, breakfast cereals, margarines, prepared salad dressings, frozen foods, and manufactured pet foods, to pick a few examples at random), there were simply *never* any conditions remotely resembling atomistic competition. These markets are all of enormous size and heavily advertised, accounting consistently for more than 60 percent of the expenditures of the hundred largest advertisers in the United States.[21]

What seems generally to have happened in these and most other markets for manufactured consumer goods is that an inventor had an idea for some sort of product that no one was making. The first thing he or she did after inventing and patenting the product was to name it and almost invariably to employ a trademark or brand. The word "brand" supposedly originated in the identifying marks burned onto wooden whiskey casks during the early nineteenth century, but trademarks themselves were much older than this, having their origins in the medieval trade guilds in Europe.[22]

The inventions that were to become successful caught the public favor, and advertising demonstrated to the satisfaction of the manufacturers its ability to increase sales far beyond the unsupported efforts of the retail trade. Manufacturers and final consumers almost immediately lost firsthand contact with one another, which made the use of brand names doubly essential: as a means of identifying and guaranteeing to consumers the homogeneity and quality of the advertised goods, and, in addition, to provide legal protection to the manufacturer—their original purpose. Typically, for a short while the manufacturer had a monopoly, which helped sales and profits grow. But competition would arise through fair means or foul (such as attempts to infringe trademarks). The competitors who survived were those able to achieve competitive economies of scale, so that they grew large too. This is nothing but the emergence of oligopoly as a natural result of competitive forces. Hence my hypothesis that the paths of concentration in the advertising-intensive markets for packaged consumer goods led generally *from* monopoly *to* oligopoly—the direct reverse of the path plotted by conventional economics.

What has emerged so far from this analysis is, first, a serious doubt about the relevance of the wholesaler in the growth of advertising and branding and, second, an equally serious doubt about the path of concentration in the markets where advertising is an important force: the markets for packaged consumer goods. In these markets, my hypothesis suggests oligopoly to be a competitive and not (as it is conventionally perceived) an anticompetitive force. This is a key part of my argument, and I will endeavor to develop it by looking at oligopolistic competition as viewed by economic theoreticians and also as viewed from a closer focus on the real world.

Oligopolistic Competition in the Real World

The starting point of most investigations of competition is an analysis of price in the most extreme conditions conceivable: conditions of atomistic or perfect competition. (The former term is less tendentious than the latter and will therefore be used in this discussion.) For this type of competition to operate, three conditions are necessary: a homogeneous product, many small buyers and sellers with free entry into the market, and perfect communications and knowledge between buyer and seller. These are breathtaking assumptions, and it is not surprising that they apply only in a tiny minority of circumstances: in the markets for some agricultural commodities and industrial raw materials, where there is a uniformly graded product, worldwide communications exist, and buyers can bid against one another in the produce and commodity exchanges. In discussions of most other markets, the concept is nothing more than a theoretical abstraction.

Despite this, there is however often a lingering feeling that perfect markets were once normal, or at the very least that there was once much more competition than at present, a change which has led to a loss of social and economic benefits. The worrysome aspect of such a feeling is that politicians and economists often express the wish to employ management techniques to turn the clock back, but even in such a theoretical activity, there is a difference between wanting to turn the clock back to a world that once existed and wanting to turn it back to one that never existed outside the realm of economic analysis. This is why it is so important to get the historical record straight and to understand how and why advertising actually emerged.

There is also the point, expressed with considerable logical force by Friedrich von Hayek and based on his observation of real competitive processes, that the notion of atomistic competition is a grossly flawed way of describing *any* competitive mechanism.[23] His arguments are complex and interrelated, but they hinge on the fact that the model of atomistic competition is an equilibrial state. Competitive markets, on the other hand, are almost by definition dynamic, and their dynamism is expressed in a striving to overcome *imperfections in knowledge* and, even more important, in a continuous urge to steal business from competitors by means of product *differentiation*. (The reader will remember that these central processes are excluded by the assumptions of atomistic competition.) Product differentiation is what branding, advertising, and in particular added values are all about.

The reader should by now be in little doubt about my feelings concerning the relevance of the model of atomistic competition to an examination of markets in the real world. Oligopolists, like any other businesspeople, will endeavor to price their products at what the market will bear. (This is one of the less unreasonable assumptions of microeconomic theory.) What the market will in fact bear depends on how easily the output of competitive oligopolists can be substituted for theirs. In practice, their ability to force up their prices is limited, because the elasticity of substitution between their output and that of competitors tends to be high. We know that the prices of advertised brands do not rise at a faster rate than those of other goods; there is in fact strong evidence of the *opposite* effect.[24] This is because competition among oligopolists is very real.

As anyone with the faintest first-hand experience of oligopolistic markets can testify, there is normally a burning urge on the part of oligopolists to capture their rivals' markets by functional innovation, by a rapid copying of the functional benefits of competitive brands, or by an equally rapid reinforcement of the added values of the oligopolists' own brands (not to speak of tactical price competition). There is of course a great deal of anxiety about this type of competitive situation, but this anxiety affects the oligopolists (and their advertising agencies) more than consumers, for whom oligopoly is by no means devoid of benefits.[25]

In the first place, since oligopolists are by definition large producers, oligopoly production reaps the benefit of scale economies, significantly reducing costs. Much of this point is conceded by Kaldor, although he concentrates on production economies to the exclusion of economies in purchasing (which are especially important in the food trade) and in marketing (which are important to all manufacturers once they pass a minimum size).[26] In the second place, the real competition among oligopolists commonly affords consumers a number of direct benefits connected with the dynamics of the market, such advantages including a rapid rate of product innovation and improvement, and more price reduction than is immediately obvious because promotions are the normal mechanism of price competition. (Lower prices are of course a general reflection of the scale economies of large output.)

It is not universally agreed that oligopoly provides these advantages, but there is good evidence to substantiate them, over and above personal observation. It is possible on the basis of Nielsen data to make an empirical analysis of the rate of innovation in typical oligopolistic markets. This rate is usually rapid, although the speed with which markets normally "shake down" to accommodate a successful new brand (with only marginal adjustments to the shares of existing brands) leaves a curious residual impression of overall stasis.[27] And critics would be well advised to read the statements of leading manufacturers when they speak about the number of improvements that take place in brands on a routine basis.[28] In one instance, a well-known industrialist details the number of product improvements over a five-year period in the formulae of a number of major specified brands and, examining the experience of twenty-nine different brands sold in one or another of eight different countries, demonstrates that for more than twenty brands, consumer prices had significantly fallen in real terms over a twenty-year period.[29] These were long-term and not just tactical reductions.

The amount of competition in oligopolistic consumer goods markets—those in which advertising is an important force—is also a factor that may well inhibit market concentration. Aggregated Nielsen data indicate the wide prevalence of stationary market conditions measured in terms of combined market shares of leading brands, although this apparent stasis conceals increases in some brands' shares that are balanced by other brands' losses.[30] On the evidence of Backman, there is a broad balance between the markets showing evidence of increasing concentration and those showing diminishing concentration.[31] Most important, the role of advertising can be isolated. On the basis of a number of different empirical studies, Backman concludes that there is no relationship between high advertising and either high or rapid concentration.[32] Concentration is a result of factors other than advertising; and advertising is indeed one of the more important expressions of competition, which in general acts against concentration.

The Emergence of Brands

If the first purpose of branding was to confirm the legal protection afforded by the inventor's patent, and the second was to guarantee quality and homogeneity after sellers and buyers had lost face-to-face contact, a third purpose stems directly from oligopolists' need to differentiate their products. They quite rightly see branding as a device to enable them to control their markets better, by preventing other people's products from being substituted for theirs.

It is unlikely that oligopolists have ever felt the need to rationalize these purposes; their responses are quite instinctive in most cases. It seems that in the makeup of the more successful marketing men and women there is the innate knowledge that branding is the key to protection and an important contributor to growth.

Generally speaking, oligopolists will compete on price, normally by means of active and continuous price promotions. But competition among them is not confined to price. The strength of oligopolists' brands and in particular the added values that enrich them move the field of competition from price reduction to product and brand improvement, progress in the latter tending to reduce the need for the former (although it is never eliminated). Margins are at least maintained, but not all are put into profit, because building brands costs a great deal of money. Kaldor, who makes the point clearly, calls these expenses "selling costs," although this seems a confining definition, brand-building costs being rather more precise.[33]

Before we look at the costs and prices of brands, it is essential to pause in order to define a brand simply, comprehensively, and objectively. (Objectivity is not universal in discussion of this rather emotional subject. For instance, Joan Robinson, one of the economists who pioneered the analysis of oligopolistic markets in the 1930s, argues that "various brands of a certain article which in fact are almost exactly alike may be sold as different qualities under names and labels which will induce rich and snobbish buyers to divide themselves from poorer buyers."[34] This is not untrue, but it leaves rather a lot out of consideration.)

The important distinction is between a product and a brand. A product is something with a functional purpose. A brand offers something in addition to its functional purpose. All brands are products (including brands such as Hertz or Pan American that are technically services) in that they serve a functional purpose. But not all products are brands. It follows that our definition of a brand should be something along the following lines:

> *A brand is a product that provides functional benefits plus added values that some consumers value enough to buy.*

Added values form the most important part of the definition of a brand. By way of introduction, two general points must be discussed briefly.

First, the strongest brands are often the most distinctive. But in their distinctiveness they are also generally well balanced between motivating benefits—those (generally functional) benefits that prompt the consumer to use any brand in the product field—and discriminating benefits—those prompting the consumer to buy one brand rather than another. All brands are different from each other in the obvious sense that the names and packaging are different. But distinctiveness over and beyond this is highly desirable, although a distinctiveness based so much on discriminators that it neglects motivators is a recipe for a weak brand. This all sounds extremely theoretical, but if the reader will think about successful brands in the real world with these points in mind—if he or she will think of Ajax, Birds Eye, Crest, or Dove—the idea of balance between motivating and discriminating benefits will make sense.

Second, the reader will note the emphasis in the definition on "some consumers." Tastes differ so widely that no brand can be all things to all people. Moreover, a manufacturer who strives to cover too wide a field will produce a brand that is number two or number three over a wide range of attributes, rather than number one over a limited range of attributes (which might enable it to become first choice to a limited group of consumers, the normal route to success). Many marketing professionals contend that it is more attractive to go for a limited part of the market rather than move head-on against the entrenched competition in the largest sector; the general validity of this point has been demonstrated on logical grounds, though there are exceptions to it.[35]

We now come to the matter of added values, a subject that has caused some of the greatest controversies embracing the techniques, economics, and ethics of advertising. There is no doubt whatsoever that added values play a role in almost all purchasing decisions. These values are over and beyond the prime functional benefit for which the brand or product is bought. The idea of added values is not a new one and was described succinctly by James Webb Young in a book based on his teaching at the University of Chicago fifty years ago, although only published in 1963: "The use of advertising to add a subjective value to the tangible values of the product. For subjective values are no less real than the tangible ones."[36]

What are these added values and where do they come from? Some marketing professionals claim that every factor from a brand's early history to the distribution of its competitors has a bearing on them, but while this is not completely untrue, some factors are clearly more important than others. All the most important added values are nonfunctional, although I would include as an added value the unexpected functional uses we sometimes find for some brands (such as the way Arm & Hammer baking soda can be used to sweeten a swimming pool or deodorize a refrigerator). But this is by and large an exception. Most brands have a known and restricted range of functions, and added values are the nonfunctional benefits over and beyond them.

By known and restricted range of functions, I mean for a motor car its ability to move us from place to place safely, reliably, and economically; for a suit of clothes, its warmth and appearance; for a packet of cornflakes, its taste and nutrition; for a bottle of scent, its smell; and for a power drill, its ability to produce holes of a range of uniform sizes reliably, safely, and quickly.

The added values beyond these which seem to me to be the most important are:

1. *Added values that come from experience of the brand.* These include familiarity, know reliability, and reduction of risks. A brand becomes an old friend. This introduces the centrally important notion of brand personality, which can on occasion be interpreted as the voice of the manufacturer: Betty Crocker or Old Jim Young. But it is much more frequently interpreted as the personality of the brand itself—its functional and nonfunctional features as they might be described in quasi-human terms, a device used by some advertising agencies to map a brand's position in relation to its competition.[37] But this personality must be interpreted broadly, a point I was recently discussing with the head of research of a leading Madison Avenue agency. He reminded me that his agency makes a distinction here between personality and character; the former

is a quality a person looks for in a girlfriend or boyfriend; but the latter is what is required of a wife or husband!

2. *Added values that come from the sorts of people who use the brand.* Rich and snobbish (as in Joan Robinson's definition) or young or glamorous or masculine or feminine. The reader can find examples of brands which have these user associations, most of which are fostered by the advertising.[38]

3. *Added values that come from a belief that the brand is effective.* This is related to the way in which some medicines, even placebos, work on people's beliefs, and sometimes even makes them do their job. There is indeed good evidence that the branding of proprietary drugs affects the mind's influence over body processes. "Double-blind trials demonstrated that branding accounts for a quarter to a third of the pain relief. That is to say, branding works like an ingredient of its own interacting with the pharmacological active ingredients to produce something more powerful than an unbranded tablet."[39] Belief in effectiveness also plays an important role with cosmetics, with their ability to make their users *feel* more beautiful, with generally beneficial results.

4. *Added values which come from the appearance of the brand.* This is the prime role of packaging. And lest it be thought that this matters only to brands sold to impressionable adolescents, the reader is advised to look at Theodore Levitt's well-known essay "The Morality (?) of Advertising" in which, as part of a well-reasoned discussion of added values, he recounts the following anecdote.

> A few years ago, an electronics laboratory offered a $700 testing device for sale. The company ordered two different front panels to be designed, one by the engineers who developed the equipment and one by professional industrial designers. When the two models were shown to a sample of laboratory directors with Ph.D.'s, the professional design attracted twice the purchase intentions that the engineers' design did. Obviously the laboratory director who has been baptized into science at M.I.T. is quite as responsive to the blandishments of packaging as the Boston matron.[40]

The reader may be surprised that I have omitted from the list the added values that come from a manufacturer's name and reputation. This omission is deliberate, for three reasons. First, consumers do not know who manufactures many of the brands they use. (Try and think of who make the leading brands of laundry detergent, bar soap, or shampoo.) Second, brand names are sometimes used as "umbrella" devices to help launch new but related brands (like Ivory Shampoo which follows Ivory Soap); and in examining such strategy, Nielsen provided powerful evidence that the umbrella name has little influence on the success of the new brand.[41] Third, a familiar brand name is no longer needed as a guarantee of a new product's homogeneity and quality. Branded goods are known to be homogeneous and to perform their function reasonably well. It is doubtful whether flagrant deceit was ever common, and it is rare indeed today for no better reason than the legal penalties, although some observers, including myself, believe that this attention to quality is more the result of manufacturers' policies and in particular their interest in consumers' repeat purchase, than the letter of the law or the efforts of Ralph Nader.

The contribution of added values to consumer choice is easily demonstrated by the commonly used technique of matched product tests. In these tests, a sample of consumers uses and judges brands in coded but unnamed packages, and a second and similar sample of consumers uses and judges those same brands in their normal containers. The invariable pattern is that the preferences among identified brands are quite different from preferences among those same brands in coded but unidentified containers. A leading breakfast cereal was preferred to two competitors in blind test in the ratios of 47:27:26. When the test was repeated with identified packages, the preferences changed to 59:26:15. The proportion of people preferring the leading brand was therefore 47 percent blind and 59 percent named, a difference of twelve percentage points which can only have come from the added values in the brand that were not in the product alone.[42]

The subject of added values is alluring. Readers who want to dwell on examples can extend their knowledge by observation and analysis, in the way recommended by James Webb Young.[43] But let me simply recapitulate my belief that added values arise mainly from people's use and experience of the brand, from the advertising, and from the packaging. It follows that added values are not immediately available to a manufacturer of a new brand but are built over time. A brand enters the world naked and must rely almost solely on its functional properties for its initial survival.

There is good empirical support for this belief. The majority of the large number of new brands that do not succeed fail precisely because of their functional weaknesses.[44] It also follows that old and successful brands build up a large stock of added values in the good will of their users, so a new brand whose manufacturer has ambitions to overtake them must start off with a generous margin of functional superiority if it is to make any progress. The opinion of James Peckham was discussed in Chapter 1; remember that the recommended preference for the new brand over the existing brand in blind product test should be of the order of 65:35.[45] Peckham does not describe the empirical basis for this generalization, but his views are always worth hearing. I should add that in my experience this margin of superiority in blind test is rare indeed. But so also are successful new brands.

The importance of nonfunctional added values is greatly emphasized by

John Kenneth Galbraith, who in his widely publicized *The New Industrial State* maintains with great style and plausibility that the further we get from a subsistence standard of living, the more important become both the psychological rewards of using products and the role of advertising in providing these rewards. "The further a man is removed from physical need the more open he is to persuasion—or management—as to what he buys. This is, perhaps, the most important consequence for economics of increasing affluence."[46]

But Galbraith, as he so often does, takes his argument much too far. In his view, since the oligopolist's ability to manage consumer demand is complete, a reduction in sales needs only a change of selling strategy for the situation to be corrected and management of demand reasserted. "It is the everyday assumption of the industrial system that, if sales are slipping, a new selling formula can be found that will correct the situation," he says in a passage concerned largely with the U.S. automobile industry.[47] Written in the mid-1960s, today his words read strangely indeed, after all that has happened in Detroit since then.

Equally remarkable in its own way is a passage from Theodore Levitt's widely recognized 1960 article "Marketing Myopia." "The fact that the new compact cars are selling so well in their first year indicates that Detroit's vast researches have for a long time failed to reveal what the customer really wanted. Detroit was not persuaded that he wanted anything different from what he had been getting, until it lost millions of customers to other small car manufacturers."[48] After Detroit's noteworthy inability for so many years to produce the sorts of small car that consumers have made it clear they want (and despite the spur of spectacular resultant operating deficits in the industry), Levitt's prescient words are all the commentary necessary on Galbraith's claims that such troubles can be met by a simple change in selling strategy.

The car industry is perhaps an exceptionally unhappy example of the inefficiency of the capitalist system in managing consumer demand. But these passages from two eminent academics only confirm my belief that the first step in the satisfaction of consumer demand must be the manufacture of a product with a functional performance the consumer requires and therefore might with luck be persuaded to buy. If there is management in this process, it is not quite in the sense that Galbraith means demand management. The second step in the satisfaction of consumer demand—the building of added values—is much more what Galbraith means. But added values are not a substitute for functional performance; they are, as their name implies, added on top of functional performance. And the stronger a brand becomes, the stronger the added values become, with great long-term benefit to the brand. But it is also possible to think of brands (not excluding brands of motor cars) that concentrated on added values to the neglect of functional improvements and found themselves vulnerable to competitive assault.[49] In the packaged goods field, Nielsen can provide a good deal of evidence that brands lose leadership generally because of weaknesses in relative functional performance: a failure to keep up.[50]

Because added values stem from use of the product plus packaging and advertising, building these values takes not only time but also money. It is in this sense that advertising people commonly refer to advertising expenditures as investments (money spent in order to achieve a return). This is a defensible definition, but there is one aspect of it I must clarify. I believe that advertising works by stimulating sales in the short term. This stimulates brand purchase by consumers, brand use, and the long-term buildup of added values which stems from brand use. Thus the long-term effect of advertising is via long-term use of the brand and not so much the advertising itself. There is much professional disagreement about this, with some people believing that advertising on its own has both short- and long-term effects (stimulating sales not only tomorrow but also in a week, a month, or a year's time, presumably because advertising sticks in people's conscious or unconscious minds). I personally find it difficult to accept this view on both common sense and empirical grounds. Readers who think that the distinction is a hair-splitting one are urged to consider the possibility that this matter may well have the greatest single influence on the frequency of advertising and hence on the economics of the whole advertising process.

Whether or not advertising (together with other brand-building costs) works in the short term, the long term, or both, it cannot be denied that it is an expensive process. Branded goods are almost always sold at some premium over unbranded, a practical manifestation of a brand's added values,[51] although there are limits to oligopolists' ability to push up the prices of their merchandise.[52] The question we are left with is whether people prefer a near substitute item at a low price or something different at a higher one. The higher price rules in most markets because of the real but imperfect competition among oligopolists' brands; the something different reflects the added values bought by time, by use, and by the advertising and other brand-building expenses which oligopolists can afford to pay because of the higher prices they can generally get for their brands.

This question involves a wide range of value judgments, but it is also one in which consumer behavior can be studied. And, as usual, there are some surprises.

Oligopoly, Price, and the Consumer

Let us assume that a comparable item at a low price offers an acceptable functional performance. Let us also assume that a second product at a higher price offers a somewhat better functional performance, but, most importantly, also has added values which are substantially responsible for the higher price. These assumptions are reasonable, and accord well with how buyers of generic products seem to view their purchases.[53] The question then boils down to whether people would knowingly pay the extra money mainly for the added values.

The evidence points to the fact that they *will* normally pay the premium; we need look no further than the relatively small market shares of generic brands to confirm this. In Wegmans supermarket, a packet of generic cornflakes sells for $0.79 per pound; Kellogg's Corn Flakes, in a box of similar shape and size (but not surface design) sells for $0.97 per pound (23 percent more). In Wegmans, generic cornflakes have only four box facings on the shelf compared with eighteen for Kellogg's, which suggests that Kellogg's sells a good deal more than four times as much as the generic.[54] This is the normal situation in most countries and most product fields. But why?

The fact is that human value systems encompass more than strict rationality. "No one contends that a bottle of old wine is ethically worth as much as a barrel of flour, or a fantastic evening wrap for some potentate's mistress as much as a substantial dwelling-house, though such relative prices are not unusual."[55] Advertising has not of course been blameless for the encouragement of such oddities, and advertising people should not be pleased that the "invisible hand" whose movements they influence is capable of such unexpected sideswipes.

But advertising is not the main culprit. In comparison with the influence of society as a whole (not to speak of education), advertising's importance is small indeed. Knowledgeable advertising people know that their best efforts can only either reinforce or slightly modify attitudes that are built into people's psyches. Advertising is rather a weak force when it is expected to persuade people radically to change existing attitudes. This is not commonly understood, but I and many other advertising professionals can attest to it from direct experience; it is evidenced for instance by the shockingly high failure rate for new brand introductions. In some cases, this is a result of deficiencies in the advertising; in all others, it is an illustration of the inability of advertising to overcome other inadequacies in the marketing mix.

It is also generally accepted by the more objective observers of the scene that competitive capitalism, despite all the waste and distortions it causes, offers advantages in efficiency which many of these observers believe greatly outweigh the distortions and waste. But the latter represent the world as it is, and no matter how much we may deplore consumers for their lack of education and objectivity, and their reluctance to make the sorts of rational decisions which atomistic competition and other abstractions of the real world suggest they should, there is nothing we can do about it. If Levitt's laboratory directors with Ph.D.'s are so strongly influenced by the physical appearance of the $700 testing machine, it is not realistic to expect the Boston matron or the Syracuse grocery shopper to behave more rationally.

One way in which the value system of the real world differs from that of simple models of the price mechanism is in the matter of price itself. The assumption of marketplace knowledge is, for a start, pretty wide of the mark. Studies of specific markets have found that the proportions of consumers who could recall actual prices varied widely from market to market, and nowhere was there anything like general accuracy. In one investigation of fifteen markets, "The variation in the percentage correct ranged from 44% to 80% with an average of 59%. With a 5% margin of error, the average was 65%; with a 10% margin, it rose to 73%."[56] In other words, an average of 27 percent of consumers in this particular study were unable to remember within 10 percent the actual prices they were paying.

However, despite this unquestioned (and surely not unexpected) haziness in consumer knowledge, the attempts made to construct demand curves on the basis of purchase intentions or figures of actual purchases have shown such curves to have the generally downward slope associated with classical economic theory, although degrees of elasticity vary and there are odd shapes here and there.[57] The most pronounced quirk falls at the extreme low-price end of certain demand curves, reflecting an association of low price with low quality; thus demand is in absolute terms sometimes *less* at low prices than at higher ones. There is also evidence of a price—value relationship at the higher-price end, a point made by Andre Gabor and C.W.J. Granger by means of a delightful example: "What we have in mind here is . . . the case of gin, which was not considered a gentlemanly drink and even less a ladylike one until successive increases of the excise duty brought its price closer to that of whiskey and other, formerly more expensive, alcoholic beverages."[58]

Gabor and Granger's evidence on this point is anecdotal and not statistical, but it supports the likelihood that at the upper levels of price, the value connotation reduces the elasticity of demand, although to nowhere near inelasticity. This reduction in price elasticity is serendipitous for the oligopolist, who should be grateful for it. If people buy higher priced merchandise in reasonably large quantities in the belief that it is better than a lower priced item partly by the very fact of its higher price, they will presumably get greater satisfaction from the more expensive article than they would have gotten from the cheaper one; and if this situation is deplored, people's psychological makeup is surely more at fault than the actions of oligopolists. As already suggested, the latter are not entirely blameless, but other features of oligopoly, notably the aggressive attitude of oligopolists toward one another, are not devoid of social and economic benefits. The present system has good as well as bad points, and if we are honest enough to consider the different types of economic organization in the real world as limited choices among imperfect alternatives, we can judge our present system by *realistic* criteria;

and if we are concerned to improve matters, we will be aware of our rather constricted area of maneuver.

Manufacturers have, in any event, only unconsciously encouraged perceptions of a high-price—high-value relationship, for instance by the indirect effect of added values. In building added values, oligopolists rarely touch on the argument that if something is expensive it must be good. Even on the occasions when scenes of gracious living appear in advertisements, the advertiser is often uncomfortable about them and the advertising agency is blamed for being out of touch with the real world. In this and certain other matters the agency is not always wrong, as some of the more successful agencies (and their clients) have on occasion demonstrated.

This brings us to a point which, if it is to be developed, would probably interfere with the basic structure of this book, so that this line of enquiry must be brought to an end. But having traveled some distance in the argument in this chapter, it is more appropriate now that I should try to summarize the points I have been endeavoring to make.

The Argument in Brief

This chapter has severely questioned the validity of certain theories which are widely and uncritically believed.

First, there is the idea that advertising emerged historically as a response to conflict between weak manufacturers and powerful wholesalers. An examination of historical data does not support this hypothesis, insofar as the markets for packaged consumer goods are concerned. On the contrary, it seems that the driving force in the development of advertising here was the upward pressure of manufactured production. Getting the facts right is not just a matter of historical truth; it can impinge on policy recommendations for economic management. The notion that there were once perfectly competitive consumer goods markets (to which some people may wish to return) is, I believe, substantially illusory.

Second, there is the contention that the path from competition to concentration which had been followed in many heavy industries was followed also by modern consumer goods markets. An examination of cases strongly suggests the hypothesis that such markets began as monopolies, and *oligopoly emerged as a competitive force.*

The third point (one related to my first) is that the abstraction of atomistic competition is relevant to an examination of competition in the real world. I dispute this because the very actions of competition are a denial of the assumptions on which atomistic competition is based.

I argue that oligopolistic competition (assuming the absence of any restriction to market entry or collusion between oligopolists) is always real and intense, and that it brings significant social and economic benefits despite its costs. But these costs include waste and a distortion of value systems to which all members of society (including marketing people) should address themselves.

I also argue that brands are an essential manifestation of oligopolistic competition, that they are a combination of functional and nonfunctional values (the functional ones being the more important), and that the contribution of advertising is mainly to encourage use of a brand which helps build nonfunctional added values. In the eyes of consumers, added values are often seen as the justification of the premium prices commonly charged for branded merchandise. Despite what is claimed by some of its protagonists, advertising is in general a feeble force, except when it is used to reinforce and occasionally modify existing attitudes. (In doing these things, however, it sometimes has considerable power and is one of the key influences on the building of brands.)

So much for my argument. I must however mention in conclusion a point which is implicit in everything I have said in this chapter. The things with which I have taken issue are not the methods of economic analysis per se but the misapplications of such analysis by otherwise competent and even distinguished observers. Economics began as a study of behavior in the real world; it is or should be embedded in empiricism. If it retains this characteristic, it will also retain its ability to explain social phenomena, of which branding and advertising are merely rather trivial examples. If it does *not* retain its roots in punctilious observation of the real world, it will deserve President Truman's despairing stricture that, if all the economists in the United States were to be laid head to toe on the sidewalk from the Capitol down Pennsylvania Avenue . . . they should be left there!

Notes

1. For readers unacquainted with the marketing field, the A.C. Nielsen Company is the world's largest market research company specializing in retail audits. In the United States, it is also the leading firm in the field of television audience measurement.

2. There is a technical distinction in economic literature between oligopolistic competition and monopolistic competition. Monopolistic competition means more competitors than oligopoly but with generally more differentiated products. However, I shall avoid this distinction here and use the word oligopolistic in a general sense to describe a market with a relatively small number of competitors.

3. Jules Backman, *Advertising and Competition* (New York: New York University Press, 1967), p. 109.

4. *Ibid.*, p. 77.

5. For some brands of soap, this proportion only rarely drops below 40 percent of brand sales. (This estimate is based on unpublished research).

6. John Kenneth Galbraith, *The New Industrial State* (Harmondsworth, Middlesex, United Kingdom: Penguin Books, 1978), p. 209.

7. Graham Bannock, *The Juggernauts: The Age of the Big Corporation* (Harmondsworth, Middlesex, United Kingdom: Penguin Books, 1973), pp. 72, 79–80.

8. Neil Hopper Borden, *The Economic Effects of Advertising* (Chicago: Richard D. Irwin, 1942), pp. 49–51.

9. Lord Kaldor, "The Economic Aspects of Advertising," *Review of Economic Studies* 18 (1950–51): 1–27; reprinted in *The Three Faces of Advertising* (London: Advertising Association, 1975): pp. 103–45.

10. Kaldor, *The Three Faces of Advertising:* p. 129.

11. Paul Terry Cherington, *Advertising as a Business Force* (Garden City, N.Y.: Doubleday, Page, 1913, reprinted 1919); Harold Barger, *Distribution's Place in the American Economy since 1869* (New York: National Bureau of Economic Research; Princeton: Princeton University Press, 1955); Louis P. Bucklin, *Competition and Evolution in the Distributive Trades* (Englewood Cliffs, N.J.: Prentice—Hall, 1972).

12. In case the reader thinks that Kaldor's point might relate exclusively to British experience, there is evidence that the wholesale trade in Great Britain followed the same pattern as in the United States. See Ralph Harris and Arthur Seldon, *Advertising in a Free Society* (London: Institute of Economic Affairs, 1959), pp. 9–10.

13. Two important works covering startlingly similar ground were published at the same time at the two universities: Edward Hastings Chamberlin, *The Theory of Monopolistic Competition* (Cambridge, Mass.: Harvard University Press, 1933, reprinted 1948). Joan Robinson, *The Economics of Imperfect Competition* (London: Macmillan, 1933, reprinted 1950). Chamberlin was not pleased with the coincidence of the timing. It was said apocryphally that a student could get a degree at Harvard in Chamberlin's day by abusing Robinson.

14. See, for instance, Alfred Marshall, *Industry and Trade* (London: Macmillan, 1920), book 3, chaps. 3–10.

15. The difference between the value of consumer expenditure and manufacturers' sales of consumer goods is accounted for by trade margins and adjustments to inventories. These remain more or less constant from year to year.

16. Robert R. Doane, *The Measurement of American Wealth* (New York: Harper, 1933), p. 39.

17. Frank Spencer Presbrey, *The History and Development of Advertising* (Garden City, N.Y.: Doubleday, Doran, 1929), p. 591.

18. Data in indirect but general support of this contention can be found in Borden, *The Economic Effects of Advertising*, pp. 204–5.

19. Net sales value in the United States of $359 million in 1977. *Census of Manufactures* (Washington, D.C.: U.S. Department of Commerce, Bureau of the Census, 1981).

20. *The Gillette Company 1901–1976* (Boston: Corporate Public Relations Department, Gillette, 1977): p. 4.

21. According to figures published in the late summer or early fall of every year by *Advertising Age*.

22. Borden, *The Economic Effects of Advertising*, p. 22.

23. Friedrich August von Hayek, "The Meaning of Competition" in *Individualism and Economic Order* (Chicago: University of Chicago Press, 1948), pp. 92–106.

24. W. Duncan Reekie, *Advertising and Price* (London: Advertising Association, 1979). Among the factors that inhibit rises in the prices of advertised brands is the reduction in retail margins that such brands carry: a significant scale economy.

25. This topic was explored some time ago with great perception by Frank Hyneman Knight in the title essay in *The Ethics of Competition and Other Essays* (New York: Harper, 1935), pp. 41–75. The whole discussion in this chapter is of course based on the premise that there is no restriction to entry into the market or any other collusion between oligopolists. Although in the past, entry restriction and collusion have not been unknown, it is reasonable to assume their absence in modern circumstances, largely on the grounds of the legal sanctions.

26. Kaldor, "The Economic Aspects of Advertising," *The Three Faces of Advertising*, pp. 131–32.

27. James O. Peckman, Sr., *The Wheel of Marketing* pp. 53, 60.

28. *Ibid.,* p.50.

29. Lord Heyworth, "Advertising," chairman's annual company speech, 1958 (London: Unilever Ltd., 1958).

30. Peckham, *The Wheel of Marketing*, p. 6.

31. Backman, *Advertising and Competition,* pp. 82–114.

32. *Ibid.,* p. 113.

33. Kaldor, "The Economic Aspects of Advertising," *The Three Faces of Advertising*, pp. 135–41.

34. Joan Robinson, *The Economics of Imperfect Competition,* pp. 180–81.

35. See the interesting description of the "majority fallacy" in Alfred A. Kuehn and Ralph L. Day, "Strategy of Product Quality," *Harvard Business Review* 40 (November–December 1962): 100–10.

36. James Webb Young, *How to Become an Advertising Man,* p. 73.

37. See for example Stephen King, *What Is a Brand?* (London: J. Walter Thompson, 1970): pp. 10–11.

38. One of the most famous of the earlier analyses of the brand concept made persuasive use of the notion of user associations. See Burleigh B. Gardner and Sidney J. Levy, "The Product and the Brand," *Harvard Business Review* 33 (March–April 1955): 33–39.

39. Judie Lannon and Peter Cooper, "Humanistic Advertising: A Holistic Cultural Perspective," *International Journal of Advertising* 2 (July–September 1983): 206.

40. Theodore Levitt, "The Morality (?) of Advertising," *Harvard Business Review* 48 (July–August 1970): 89.

41. Peckham, *The Wheel of Marketing*, pp. 61–64.

42. There were different consumer preferences for the various physical attributes of the three brands, so that the preference ratios of the lowest rated brands (27:26) should not be construed as evidence of parity in functional performance.

43. Young, *How to Become an Advertising Man,* p. 12. Note the author's advice about collecting case studies of print and television advertisements.

44. J. Hugh Davidson, "Why Most New Consumer Brands Fail," *Harvard Business Review* 54, (March–April 1976): 117–22.

45. Peckham, *The Wheel of Marketing,* p. 65.

46. Galbraith, *The New Industrial State,* chap. 18, sec. 2.

47. *Ibid.*, p. 212.

48. Theodore Levitt, "Marketing Myopia," *Harvard Business Review* 38 (July–August 1960): 51.

49. It may surprise some readers that added values are in any way important for "high-involvement" products like motor cars. In 1984, as a judge in the General Motors Intercollegiate Marketing Competition, I reviewed work from ten major universities. This included a reasonable amount of qualitative data which suggested that potential car buyers were well aware that the various General Motors "A Body" cars were functionally very similar to one another; nevertheless the added values embodied in the names of the different marketing divisions of General Motors represented powerful brand discriminators.

50. Peckham, *The Wheel of Marketing*, pp. 52–53.2.

51. Paul Clark, "Reaction to Recession: The Case History of Margarine," *Admap* 16 (December 1980): 612–14. Note particularly the author's remarks about premium prices.

52. Reekie, *Advertising and Price*.

53. Beth Axelrad, Bruce G. Van den Bergh, and Dean M. Krugman, "Risk, Quality and the Generic Item Phenomenon: Implications for Retail Advertising and Promotion," *Proceedings of the 1982 Conference of the American Academy of Advertising*, University of Tennessee, March 27–30, 1982.

54. This is because of a tendency for small brands to have a share of display space slightly above the proportion suggested by their market share. See Peckham, *The Wheel of Marketing*, p. 32.

55. Knight, "The Ethics of Competition," p. 56.

56. Andre Gabor and C.W.J. Granger, "Price Sensitivity of the Consumer," *Journal of Advertising Research* 4 (December 1964): 42.

57. *Ibid.*, and some unpublished examples I have in my own library.

58. Andre Gabor and C.W.J. Granger, "The Pricing of New Products," *Scientific Business* 3 (August 1965): 141–50.

3

Factors That Shape a Brand during Its Conception and Birth

"You can't look *all* round you—unless you've got eyes in the back of your head."

But these, as it happened, Alice had *not* got: so she contented herself with turning round, looking at the shelves as she came to them.

My visit to Wegmans store described in chapter 2 was a device I used to relate some of the principles of microeconomics to the everyday experience of the consumer. We are now going to visit another store in order to examine another market. Here the emphasis of the investigation is going to change: I am going to attempt by simple observation to uncover some of the facts about this market which manufacturers would need to know if they wished to compete successfully in it. The market which will be examined is cat food. I have made this choice partly because it is a product that my wife and I regularly purchase, with a relatively small repertoire of brands (the result of clear brand preferences of our household cats, something presumably determined more by functional performance than by added values!). But I have chosen this market also since available data can serve as a check on the accuracy of my estimates. The store I visited was Peter's, in the Syracuse suburb of Nottingham, another of my wife's and my favorite shopping places.

I carried out the investigation in a very simple manner: by counting the packs on the shelves, working on the assumption that the number of packs on display would lead to an approximation of the rates of sales of the various brands and pack sizes. The process took about an hour and this is what I found.

1. Brands of cat food occupy about 150 feet of shelf space. This suggests a relatively large market, although only about half the size of the breakfast cereals market, because of the relatively smaller size of the user base.[1]

2. The market is segmented into three parts (canned, dry, and moist cat food) which differ from one another in functional characteristics. Canned is the largest category; the number of packs on the shelves suggests that it represents a bit under half the total value of sales. The display of the

dry product indicates that it represents rather more than a third of the total sales value. Moist cat food accounts for the remainder: about 20 percent.

3. The largest brand in the canned sector appears to be Nine Lives (with more than 20 percent of the market), followed by Buffet, Kal Kan, and Purina. I estimated the combined shares of the four to be about 60 percent. The largest brands in the dry sector were Cat Chow, Meow Mix, Friskies, Special Dinner, and Nine Lives, which are not dissimilar in sales, and among them account for about 60 percent of the market. The moist sector seems to be dominated by Tender Vittles, which alone probably accounts for 60 percent of sales value.

4. There is a great deal of commonality in pack sizes. I estimated that at least 70 percent of sales of canned cat food are in the 6-oz. size. The dry market is dominated by the 18-oz. boxes and 56-oz. bags. The moist market is more fragmented by pack size, but a third of sales appear to be accounted for by the 12-oz. size and another third by the 18-oz. As in the breakfast cereals market, commonality of pack size is not accompanied by uniformity of price.

As in my description of the breakfast cereals market in chapter 2, there is nothing in any way original about the features just described. However, from what has been published (as of 1982) about the cat food market, my estimates seem to be pretty close to the mark. And this should act as a reminder of something extremely important, something that ought to be in the bloodstream of every marketing professional: the central importance of the retail store in consumer goods marketing. In their day-to-day work, advertising agencies invariably think exclusively of the final consumer (when they are not worrying about their client!); while on the client side, "consumer orientation" is considered the mark of the more sophisticated type of manufacturer. But both agencies and advertisers should remind themselves that the retail store is the battleground on which much of the competitive struggle takes place. An equally important point is that the most readily accessible information on both consumer purchasing and competitive activity is information gathered from retail outlets.

The way to get this information is by properly conducted retail audit research, whose mechanism will shortly be described. But even with data collection that makes as little claim to scientific accuracy as my visits to Wegmans and Peter's stores, it is demonstrably easy to get an impressionistic picture of a market, so long as the investigator observes the brands in a studied way and knows what to look for.

Much of this chapter and the next concerns generalized patterns of retail sales, and the large number of different aspects of brands which can be revealed by these patterns. I was at first inclined to treat each of these separately, with chapters devoted to describing each in detail. The five main topics I had in mind were first, the importance of innovation in packaged goods markets; and on the other side of this coin, the belief in the inevitability of decline which often accompanies belief in the importance of innovation. The second subject was factors influencing the initial and continued progress of a brand: functional performance, positioning, name, price, distribution, trade promotions, consumer promotions, and advertising. The third topic was the importance of market testing and (a related matter) the success rate of new brand introductions. The fourth was the initial growth cycle of a brand; and the fifth, the importance of restaging. But I eventually decided against the original plan of treating each topic separately because of the importance of emphasizing the interconnections.

It therefore seemed better to structure the examination by looking briefly at the more important factors operating during a brand's conception and birth, and then those operating during its growth and maturity. This led me to omit some of the topics in the above list from the present chapter, and postpone them to the next one. The extremely important matters of promotions and advertising are among the things being deferred; and I am by no means suggesting that these have no role during a brand's conception and birth, merely that their long-term continuous role makes it more appropriate to discuss them in the context of ongoing brands. Promotions are the most important expressions of continuous oligopolistic price competition. Advertising builds added values in order to achieve repeated brand use.

My purpose in these early chapters is that the reader should get used to facts about normal patterns in order to develop a deeper understanding and perhaps to acquire the quality so esteemed by the Germans, the "feeling at the tips of the fingers," a practiced ability to discern what is viable and what is not. Let us consider for instance the manufacturer who plans to enter a market with a new brand in the wake of a successful pioneer brand marketed by a competitor (a quite common strategy sometimes known as "me-too"). The newcomer should understand first of all that a mere functional parity with the pioneer will probably mean that the me-too brand will fail. On the assumption however that it is able to offer a degree of functional superiority at least to some consumers, the manufacturer will not be beaten before he begins, and a knowledge of generalized patterns will immediately give him a proper sense of how realistic (rather than how desirable) his sales targets will be. The newcomer may wish to achieve a sales level equivalent to two-thirds of the pioneer brand, but he will have learned that the normal share of market of a me-too brand after three years is only 47 percent and not 66 percent of the level of the pioneer.[2] This does not mean that he will not in any circumstances make 66 percent in three years; just that if the new manufacturer is to succeed, both his brand and the support he puts behind the brand must be very much above the normal. Knowing his resources, the newcomer can also of course conclude that the 66 percent is unrealistic and look for a viable business at a lower level of sales. But note that the firm is able to draw these conclusions, which are of direct operational value, without having sold one pack; even before inventing the product and designing the brand.

Since this chapter and the next are devoted substantially to patterns of retail sales, they must inevitably be based in the main on the work of the organization which is the best informed objective observer of the retail scene, the A.C. Nielsen Company. I am relying heavily in particular on Peckham's work, to which reference has already been made in chapters 1 and 2. His is one of those rare contributions to marketing literature to which we can constantly refer, and from which we can always learn something new.

I must however say a word first about the retail audit mechanism, so that the reader can appreciate its advantages and limitations. The most important data provided by Nielsen are estimates of consumer sales. Nielsen works with a panel of shops, and in each of these, by the simple arithmetical process of counting deliveries of goods over the checking period (normally two months), added inventories at the beginning of the period, and deducting inventories at the end, sales out of the store during the period can be accurately measured. Information is provided for all brands and pack sizes in a market. By adding the findings from all the shops in the panel, a large accumulation of data can be assembled which can be grossed up to estimate total sales in the market, the share of each brand and pack size, and how these change over time. Long- and short-term trends can be exposed, as can specific strengths and weaknesses of brands, varieties, and sizes. As well as consumer sales, Nielsen provides data on distribution and display and on retail deliveries and inventories (from which consumer sales are computed). One ever-refreshing feature of Nielsen data is that they are an observed measure of sales based on aggregated consumer behavior, and are not a monitor of people's memory or opinions, with the notorious problems which such research entails.

Yet some important limitations to Nielsen data should be borne in mind. First, the classes of stores audited by Nielsen may cover only a limited proportion of the sales of the brands in a particular product field. Remember that the retail trade is a dynamic business, and the changes are sometimes greater and subtler than imagined. This points to the wisdom of using consumer panel data to supplement those from retail audits. A consumer panel, which monitors what homemakers actually buy day by day, does not count as large a volume of sales as a retail audit, but the data collection covers purchases from all types of stores and not just the store types monitored by Nielsen. A consumer panel therefore has a wider but weaker data base than a retail audit. The two types of research complement one another.

But there is another reason why consumer panels are important. Measurement of consumer sales by retail audit is from shop sales, which are the result of an aggregation of a large number of individual consumer purchases. Internal movements inside the aggregates are concealed. The actual people buying in one period could very well be different, or the same, or partly different and partly the same as those in a second period. A retail audit cannot provide any means of tracking down these differences; it cannot analyze whether individual consumers continue to buy the same, or less, or more than before. When we further study the inner workings of our big machine (notably how the little apparatus in the middle—advertising—seems to be a motive force disproportionately important for its size), we shall need to find out how advertising influences consumers, the people to whom it is primarily addressed. For this, we shall need the sorts of research discussed in chapter 5 onward: consumer panel data in particular.

In the meantime, we shall be studying aggregated information mainly provided by Nielsen. This does not mean that in these earlier chapters we shall be ignoring the effects of advertising. On the contrary, it is possible to demonstrate quite large effects. But aggregated data will only tell us *what* is likely to happen as a result of certain advertising strategies (in particular as a result of the application of defined advertising pressures). These data will not tell us either why or how such results happened. Nevertheless, the *what* is undeniably important to us.

Let us then start with the workings of the most visible parts of the machine, in particular those parts that appear to be the most directly relevant to the establishment of a new brand. This will lead us to chapter 4, which looks at a brand growing toward maturity. Here, some of the factors discussed in this present chapter will still be relevant, but trade and consumer promotions and advertising will be coming into their own, so that it is in the next chapter that we will begin the first major discussions of these important matters.

The Importance of Innovation and the Belief in Decline

The reader will remember from chapter 1 the notion of apparent statis as an element of most consumer goods markets. By this I mean a surface stability; if not equilibrium, at least a strong tendency toward equilibrium. Viewed over short- and medium-term periods most markets appear to be stationary when we measure both total sales (with established and predictable seasonal patterns) and brand shares. New brands do not normally succeed, but the rare occasions when one does, cause little overall disturbance; competitors' shares normally settle down rapidly with a few share points clipped here and there to accommodate the newcomer.

But this picture can be misleading in two respects. First, it does not recognize the ferment of new brand activity, most of which has no lasting effect on the marketplace. Second, viewed over the long term, markets often change markedly in three separate ways. The changes appear small in the short term, but their cumulative effect is often large in the long term.[3]

1. There are sometimes substantial long-term increases and decreases in the absolute size of products or groups of products, because of the influences of technological improvement and social change. A dramatic instance quoted by Nielsen concerns convenience products. This is not a single category but a mini-aggregation of ten different product groups, from tea mixes to disposable diapers; their aggregate growth over a typical two-year period was 55 percent, which was almost seven times the increase for grocery store sales as a whole during the same period.

2. There can be large increases in the absolute sizes of *individual categories* resulting from the introduction of clusters of new and improved brands. Nielsen analyzed eighteen product classes where dynamic new or improved brands with a demonstrable improvement over the competition had been introduced, and compared these with eighteen product classes where there had been no such improvements. The categories with the innovations grew by 35 percent in a typical three-year period, compared with a growth of 7 percent in the categories without major innovations.

3. The pace of innovation within product categories causes significant *shifts of share*, with pressure on existing brands from new and innovative ones. This type of movement can be demonstrated by studies of seven different product categories over longish periods (10 to 22 years) ending in 1977. In these categories, there were 37 major advertised brands at the beginning accounting for a total of 74 percent of the market. During the years that followed, this share was pressed down to 43 percent as a result of a flurry of new brands, which by 1977 themselves accounted for a total of 35 percent of the market.

This same point can be made even more dramatically if we look at longer periods. By examining a single but typical product category of household goods over a forty-one–year period, 1936–77, it can be seen that:

1. Only two of the five most important brands in 1936 were still on the market at the end of the period, and they had severely reduced market shares;

2. Of the twelve most important brands introduced since 1949, four had disappeared by the end of the period;

3. Brand leadership had changed hands five times, the losing brands having in the main failed to keep themselves up to date.

The first conclusion concerning such changes that are apparent only in the long term, is that oligopolists innovate very widely indeed. This must be true because the changes described were brought about by the minority of new brands that succeeded; the majority of new brands always fail. And consumers respond favorably by buying the successful minority of new brands and new product types because these items satisfy their needs. Habit and inertia play a major part in purchasing decisions in the short term, but modest mutations in consumer buying behavior have substantial long-term effects because of repeat purchase.

The second conclusion is that it is mainly the pressure of competition that dictates the pace of innovation. This should be seen against a background of more general pressures on the oligopolist. One of the most important of these pressures is a virtually universal although mistaken belief in the inevitable cyclical decline of existing brands. Other pressures include the demands of technological change and the need to grow.[4] In my observation, however, the trigger for action—sometimes precipitate action—is almost invariably the competition. This expresses itself in a number of ways: in the need to preempt, bearing in mind that second and third brands in a market will achieve market shares significantly below those of the innovators; in the need for manufacturers to follow competitors' innovations for fear of erosion of existing brands; or (a common strategy with multinational organizations) in the opportunity to steal a competitor's ideas in one country and apply them in an amended form in a second country, thus preempting the originator's entry in that second country.

Without a great deal of competitive effort (much of it self-cancelling), it is extremely difficult to maintain the status quo in oligopolistic markets over long periods. I have heard more than one oligopolist quoting the Red Queen: "It takes all the running *you* can do, to keep in the same place."

British analyst Stephen King has devoted much attention to the belief in the inevitability of cyclical decline. Since it widely affects oligopolists' actions in the marketplace, it needs to be considered briefly here.

The central tenet, which is believed equally widely in business and academic circles, is that brands resemble those things studied by the zoologist and botanist, and inevitably go through the stages of birth, growth, maturity, and decline. We are talking here about long-term irreversible decline, not short-term controllable cyclical movements, which we shall consider in chapter 4. There is no shortage of examples of brands that have gone through these various stages from birth to final decline and extinction, although the actual shape of the curve up and down has varied a good deal in particular cases.[5] The empirical evidence for life cycles is however dangerous and misleading for two closely related reasons.

For a start, there is also a good deal of evidence pointing the other way: to brands that have reached maturity and maintained relatively constant permanent levels of market share in the face of competition. The large number of examples I could quote includes the leading brands in nineteen American consumer goods markets, brands which have kept their leadership for fifty years.[6] But this is not really the central point, because the question cannot be decided by weighing the examples on both sides with so many demonstrating the existence of a life cycle and so many not, for the simple reason that anyone *can cause* a brand to go into decline by simple inaction. Decline is very much within the manufacturer's control and is not by any means entirely governed by external influences.

This leads to the second and key point: the life cycle is a self-fulfilling concept, which is what makes it so dangerous:

> Not long ago, a leading manufacturer was promoting a brand of floor wax. After a steady period of growth, the sales of the product had reached a plateau. Marketing research suggested that an increase in spot television advertising, backed by a change in copy, would help the brand to regain its momentum. Feeling that the funds could be better spent in launching a new product, management vetoed the proposal. But the new product failed to move off the shelf despite heavy marketing support. At the same time, the old brand, with its props pulled out from under it, went into a sales decline from which it never recovered. The company had two losers on its hands.[7]

In this instance, the manufacturer was clearly torn by a typical conflict of priorities. There is also a sometimes obsessive fear of the competition. When in the late 1960s, Warner—Lambert was faced in Canada with aggressive new competitors (including Procter and Gamble), whose activities reduced the market share of its mouthwash Listerine, it seriously considered removing advertising support from the brand and milking it for profit, although Listerine was still significantly the market leader, was still used on the most recent occasion by a third of all mouthwash users, and still kept a clear lead over all its competitors in virtually all image attributes when the various competitive brands were rated by consumers. Warner—Lambert's attitude to the brand gives a remarkable insight into the psychological pressures of oligopolistic competition, although here wiser counsels prevailed. Support for the brand was increased and not decreased, with generally beneficial results.[8]

Much of the difficulty regarding life cycles stems from a failure to distinguish between the product and the brand. Products can become obsolete. Brands need not become obsolete if they are adapted functionally to remain competitive. (This sometimes requires launching product variations. Two important real life examples from the hypercompetitive laundry detergent market are Procter and Gamble's powder Tide and liquid Tide in the United States, and Unilever's Persil and Persil Automatic in the United Kingdom.)

It is however rather more common to find examples of the opposite: of once substantial brands which have dwindled. This should immediately prompt us to ask how many reductions in the market shares of existing brands following the launch of new brands are *caused by a conscious transfer of resources* from the old to the new. This often represents tragic misjudgment, because the growth of added values in an old brand represents a genuine investment which is all too often sacrificed through a misled belief in the inevitability of the brand's decline. To make matters worse, the new investment for which so much is sacrificed produces in many cases an unsuccessful or mediocre new brand. Remember most new brands *are* unsuccessful.

Of course one of the temptations to milk a brand (to turn it into a "cash cow") is the fact that the withdrawal of support means an immediate increase in profit. But this is temporary, because sales invariably decline, so that the brand after a time yields not only a much reduced profit, but also often a drastically reduced contribution to the general overhead.

Observation of oligopolistic markets demonstrates unambiguously the rapid pace of innovation. But for the oligopolist to survive, the qualities of balance and judgment that should lead him to nurture the old and extract the maximum return from past investments are second only in importance to the urge to participate in the forward thrust of innovation which the competitive nature of the market demands. It is by no means uncommon for an established manufacturer to have 15 percent to 20 percent of sales accounted for by brands that were not on the market five years before.[9] But the intelligent manufacturer who plans for the long term invariably accompanies this internal shift with a rising total market share, so as not to pay for new successes by undersupporting established and almost certainly more profitable brand properties. Procter and Gamble, from their observed behavior in the marketplace, is clearly an organization that accepts this philosophy. "One former brand manager notes 'the first thing they tell you is, "Forget product life cycles and cash cows!" One of the soaps has been reformulated over eighty times and is thriving.'"[10]

Five Influences on a New Brand

This section mainly concerns describing effects and interconnections. The data presented are entirely factual. They are aggregated to enable generalizations to be made. The occasional veiling of individual brands is only to preserve confidentiality.

1. *Functional Performance*

Think again of the point made in chapter 2 that a brand comes naked into the world. Without superior competitive functional performance in at least respect, it has little chance of succeeding; it will not persuade a person who buys it on a trial basis or who receives a free sample to buy it again. One of the roles of the pack design, the introductory promotions, and the advertising is to communicate this functional performance clearly and forcefully.

The pack (an extremely important advertising medium) and the advertising itself should also begin to build those added values that are vital to protect the brand's often rather fragile franchise once competitors have moved toward functional parity with it. In other words, the new brand needs the edge of added values to maintain its position when, as often happens, it loses *within months* the advantage of its initial functional lead. If when it enters the market, the brand is to be bought more than once, the decision is essentially based on its functional properties.

Nielsen once examined the fifty-three most successful new brands launched over a two-year period, finding that the most important of eleven reasons for success was clearly functional performance. In explaining the reasons for failure, functional performance was even more important. Peckham, in summarizing the data, draws an important conclusion here. He believes that the functional superiority of a potentially successful brand also provides underpinning and support for the other factors contributing to success, notably the efforts of the sales force. So if the first and most important thing, its functional performance, is recognized, synergy will lend a hand to boost its effect. But when a brand is *not* going to succeed, efforts of the sales force alone are not enough to compensate for its functional weaknesses.[11] British Nielsen data add a time dimension and suggest that functional weakness as a cause of failure is becoming even more important with the passage of time.[12]

An analysis by Davidson of 100 new grocery brands in the United Kingdom provides data which closely confirm and supplement the Nielsen findings.[13] Of these brands, 50 succeeded and 50 failed, a rate of success rather better than the general average. Of the successes, 37 offered better performance than the competition, and 22 of these offered significantly better performance. Of the failures, 40 offered the same or worse functional performance than the competition.

Competitive functional performance is not something that is important to new brands and unimportant to mature brands, because the added values that these brands have acquired over the years cannot provide a permanent bulwark against functionally superior newcomers.

The large British food manufacturer Brooke Bond Oxo has published evidence that the repeat buying of its brands correlates highly with product performance as evaluated by the blind product tests it carries out skillfully and repeatedly (itself an unusual procedure). The conclusion of the analysts who published this case is that since repeat purchase is essentially determined by consumer satisfaction concerning the functional performance of a brand, then advertising has not got much role in this process and "may find its greatest potential at the periphery of the user group."[14] This interesting suggestion will be evaluated in chapter 5, when I look in some detail at repeat purchase.

Aggregated Nielsen information supports the data from Brooke Bond Oxo on the importance of a competitive functional performance to existing brands. During the fifteen-year period 1946–61, leading brands in a third of thirty-four different product classifications in the United States lost their leadership. In two-thirds of these cases, the cause of the loss was competitive technological advances. In the six years 1965–71, well over half of the brands losing market leadership in major product fields in the United Kingdom lost it for this same reason. "It is a cardinal fact that a consumer franchise will not protect a brand against a well-advertised technical breakthrough by competition."[15]

There is a further point to be made about the functional properties of a brand. They help to describe the competition, and thus become a tool to specify the best target group for advertising: the users of defined competitive brands. What makes this such a relatively efficient planning device is the looseness of alternative (demographic and psychographic) descriptions, and their general inability to discriminate between competitive brands.

Paradoxically, users of a brand are best defined by that very fact of usage. This is not as circular a definition as it appears, because once a brand joins the homemaker's repertoire, inertia and habit begin to play a role. Repeat purchase comes about at least in part because it saves the homemaker trouble, although of course a new brand with functional superiority will always pose a threat to the brands already in the repertoire. This is why it is so important for a manufacturer of a new brand to target it specifically at existing competitive brands with the intention of elbowing them out, so the inertia will work for the new item instead of for the others (unless it is creating a new market or building one from a low existing level, both of which are now the exception and not the rule in economically developed countries).

The first question for the manufacturer of a new brand to ask is "from which brands do we want to take business?" Once this question has been answered, the firm can direct research and development efforts to the specific functional characteristics for which it must provide superior performance with the new brand. But it is impossible to provide the right answers unless it asks the right questions in the first place.

2. Positioning

There is so much talk in advertising circles about brand positioning in terms of demographic groupings of the users of brands, and more recently of their psychographic or life-style groupings, that it still causes some surprise when we look at hard data on the characteristics of actual users (for instance standardized brand penetration data such as those published by Simmons or Mediamark) and see that there is nothing like a neat differentiation of usage between any important competitive brands. They are all used in the main by the same types of people, with only differences of *emphasis* in the importance of the various demographic and psychographic groups. And as brands grow, which invariably happens as a result of growth of their user base, the overlap with other brands becomes even greater, because of the increase in multi-brand purchasing. If the buyers of Kellogg's Corn Flakes are similar to buyers of Nabisco Shredded Wheat, this can be explained by the fact that they are often the same people. During the course of a year, a large proportion of buyers of Kellogg's Corn Flakes will also be buyers of Shredded Wheat. These two unsweetened brands are positioned in the same market segment.

It follows that if Kellogg's is to introduce additional brands to compete against Shredded Wheat, it would be in danger of competing with itself by cannibalizing its own Corn Flakes. Some manufacturers will follow this strategy in the partially correct belief that to have two brands in one market segment will provide a larger total share than one brand alone, although the first brand will inevitably be cannibalized to some degree by the second. But most manufacturers will search for a slightly less self-destructive stragegy for growth.

The most fruitful policy would in fact be to introduce a new brand into a different subdivision of the market on the assumption that a market is already segmented or can be segmented by advertising and promotion into recognizably different although not necessarily completely self-contained parts. This can often be done, but the only segmentation of a market that is reasonably common in the real world is one based on *functional differences*. This in turn leads to psychographic and demographic segmentation (as people with active life styles will use deodorant bar soaps and mothers of young children will buy presweetened breakfast cereals), but the principal motivating argument for buying these products or brand groups is the functional one, as in the examples of deodorancy and presweetening.

It is possible to examine the details of quite a dramatic real-life example of a manufacturer's use of segmentation to create the opportunity for an important new brand (although copyright forces me to conceal all names). The market in question is for an important personal product bought with the greatest regularity. The market is large, static, and mature; it is also organized oligopolistically, although the leading manufacturer has a larger share than is normally the case in such markets. In 1975, the four main manufacturers (all nationally known names) had the following shares on an equivalent case basis:

Manufacturer *A*	42%
Manufacturer *B*	20
Manufacturer *C*	14

Manufacturer *D*	9
Other manufacturers	15
Total	100%

Brands in the market can be classified into four functional segments using code words *red, blue, green,* and *yellow.* Typically enough, these are not absolutely self-contained. The first two segments (*red* and *blue*) overlap with one another; in fact *red* grew out of *blue* in the 1930s. The remaining segments (*green* and *yellow*) also overlap with one another, with *yellow* having grown out of *green* in the 1970s. *Yellow* is the newest, its development initially taking place in Europe.

In 1975, each manufacturer had a number of brands and was represented in more than one market segment, but their individual patterns were different:

	Total Market Share (by Volume)	Number of Brands	Average Share per Brand	Segments in Which They Operated
Manufacturer *A*	42%	4	10.5%	*Red, Blue, Green*
Manufacturer *B*	20	2	10.0	*Red, Green*
Manufacturer *C*	14	4	3.5	*Red, Green*
Manufacturer *D*	9	2	4.5	*Blue, Green, Yellow* (with one brand in two variants covering two segments)

Manufacturer *A* was in much the strongest position, with the largest market share in total, the largest average share per brand, and the best coverage of the market segments (although this was not quite complete). By way of contrast, manufacturer *C* had four brands, each with a small market share, with three of these in fact clustered uncomfortably into one single segment. Manufacturer *A* was in such a powerful position that in any other circumstance, he or anyone else with a 42 percent market share would have been happy to preserve the status quo. But *A*'s awareness of an opportunity in the *yellow* sector supported his natural aggressiveness: such is the nature of the competition between oligopolists. And *A*'s expansion-based strategy was indeed successful, as can be seen from the market shares five years later:

	1975	Mid-1980
Manufacturer *A*	42%	46%
Manufacturer *B*	20	17
Manufacturer *C*	14	14
Manufacturer *D*	9	8

Manufacturer *A* had added 4 percent of market share, taken directly out of competitors *B* and *D*. He had in fact done this by introducing a new brand aimed at the *yellow* segment, and had managed to gain 7 percent in the process for the new brand, cannibalizing his own existing brands by 3 percent but more importantly taking 1 percent from manufacturer *D* and 3 percent from manufacturer *B*.

This is a neat, opportunistic, and successful piece of positioning. But to put it into perspective, we should go back to the point that the new and attractive market segment, *yellow,* had originated in Europe. Of our four oligopolists, three are multinationals (the exception being *B,* who lost most to *A*'s new brand). The success stemmed unquestionably from *A*'s awareness of European trends and his ability to move quickly into the United States market with a well-conceived brand, capitalizing on them.

But don't assume that manufacturer *A*'s analysis of market trends and subsequent new brand entry were a simple sequential process that anybody could have followed. It so happens that the growing importance of the fourth market segment had been known from European experience for more than ten years. And for all this time manufacturer *C* had been trying to break into this segment. Manufacturer *C,* it will be remembered, had a total of four brands, with three crowded into one market segment. *C* was acutely aware of the need to broaden his base by moving into new parts of the market. And yet the brands directed at the *yellow* segment that *C* had introduced into test since 1968 had invariably failed, despite *C*'s track record of successful innovation in Europe, considerable resources, and no lack of energy on his own part or that of his advertising agencies. The success of manufacturer *A* just says a great deal for *A*'s greater overall competence.

The odds against success in new marketing ventures are always long, and analysis alone will provide no solutions. But it is also generally true that without analysis there can be no possibility of action that leads to the solving of problems or the exploiting of opportunities.

3. Name

It might strike the reader that the choice of a name for a brand is a less substantial matter than the concerns we have discussed so far: making sure that the brand is functionally effective and is properly positioned in the market. Many people believe however that the added values of a brand are in some way embodied in its name, and that these values can be transferred to another product by using the brand name as a common property. This is the rationale for the strategy of using an umbrella name for a number of different products (a strategy often described as range extension).

The first and most obvious point is that the danger of cannibalization is likely to be greater where the products with the umbrella name are in competition with one another (powder Tide and liquid Tide), than when they are not (Ivory bar soap and Ivory shampoo).

In one published case, a manufacturer introduced a new brand on top of an existing successful entry. In the fifth year, the new brand was about a third the size of the first, which had by then been cannibalized to a significant degree, so that overall share of the two brands together was only 18 percent ahead of the company's former share with one. This is not a disastrous achievement, but a second case of a similar type shows a much better performance. Here, by the fifth year the manufacturer of the new brand had virtually doubled sales. The original brand had remained at its previous level, but the second brand had put on additional sales almost as large as these again. How can we account for this much better performance?

In view of the earlier discussion in this chapter, it will be no surprise to us that much of the difference stems from functional performance. In the less successful of the two cases, the existing brand was not improved, thus leaving it vulnerable to cannibalization, while the new brand was slightly disappointing in performance, thus inhibiting its growth. In the more successful case, the existing brand was improved so that it was protected, and the new brand performed up to expectations. Moreover, in the less successful case, the existing brand was milked in the way normally expected of manufacturers who believe in life cycle theory. In the more successful case, support was maintained for the existing brand. The findings thus far underline the principles discussed in this book. This is not however the whole story, because before getting to these causes, a more obvious one suggested itself. Very simply, in the first case the *names* of the old and new brands were similar to one another, which tended to attract an undue proportion of the second brand's customers from the first rather than from the field as a whole.[16]

But what about the more obvious *advantage* of umbrella naming: that people who use one product under a brand name can presumably easily be persuaded to sample a second perhaps different category of product using that same brand name? We are talking here about extending a franchise across product categories.

Nielsen can provide interesting aggregated information: The data base is 167 new brands in a variety of packaged goods categories, and shows their market share levels at the end of their first two years. New brands using an existing or umbrella brand name are compared with new brands using a completely independent brand name. At first glance there are big differences.

Market	Number of Examples	Median Market Share at End of Second Year	
		New Brands with New Names	New Brands with Umbrella Names
Household (U.S.)	28	6.7%	3.3%
Food (U.S.)	36	6.5	1.9
Food (U.K.)	26	14.0	7.6
Health/Toiletries (U.S)	51	2.7	2.6
Health/Toiletries (U.K)	26	8.8	8.2

On the basis of these facts, a good case can be made for using new brand names rather than existing ones, emphatically so in the household and food categories. This is however not the end of the story. There is also strong evidence that manufacturers follow an umbrella naming policy largely because they think that they can save promotional money by doing so, presumably by relying on the added values of the other products carrying the umbrella brand name. This seemingly plausible argument has tempted academic commentators to speculate, quite wrongly, on the supposed scale economies of using joint trademarks for different products.[17]

When in fact the Nielsen figures just quoted are weighted to take into account the different levels of advertising investment behind each new brand, the performance of new brands with umbrella names is brought almost exactly into line with that of new brands with new names. In other words, the generally lower level of performance of new brands with umbrella names is a result of the generally lower level of advertising investment put behind them. "[M]any marketing executives who have seen these results seem to feel that it is largely a matter of marketing psychology: realizing that marketing a new brand under a new name is tough, manufacturers gear up their marketing efforts proportionately. On the other hand, since it is commonly (and erroneously, as it turns out) believed that an established brand name is already pre-sold, less money and effort is directed at the brand and a smaller market share results."[18]

The data in these examples lead us to draw a clear but negative conclusion. The economic advantages of umbrella naming are substantially illusory in the short and medium term. Umbrella names are in general no worse and no better than completely new names. As a general rule the level of success of a new brand is much more dependent on support levels than on the name per se. It is possible that umbrella names provide greater staying power, by enabling a greater addition to added values, which is an essentially long-term process; the examples of Ivory, Palmolive, Cadbury, Kellogg's, and Kraft support this contention. But the payoff is likely to be protracted and not really discernible in the analysis of a two-year sales effect which we have just seen. In the longer term, umbrella naming is really a part of a manufacturer's corporate policy, an act of faith, and one of the basic elements on which his business is based and on which the firm might be inclined to attribute its long-term success in the marketplace.

4. Price

In perhaps two-thirds of all cases, a new brand enters an existing market at a premium price. The firm, if it feels the need, justifies this to itself and (it hopes) also to the consumer on the basis of the innovation and functional superiority of the new brand over the competition. In reality, the premium price is necessary to fund the high cost of achieving sampling by expenditures above and below the line. These expenditures must be at a high or "investment" level to compensate for the established position of existing brands with their stock of added values which have been acquired over the years. And while a new brand only rarely makes a profit during its first two years or so, deficit budgeting puts an automatic upward pressure on the consumer price. Of course, the negative effect of the premium price is often concealed by the use of temporary price reductions and other promotional methods to encourage sampling, but the wise manufacturer will be careful about the widespread use of such devices because of the destructive nature of price reductions on the consumer's perception of a brand's value.

There is also a good deal of evidence that, although new and different brands will normally command a significant price premium, this premium tends to narrow during the first few years of a brand's life. William T. Moran, formerly a senior Unilever executive, has published analyses illustrating this trend in prices of new brands of deodorants, mouthwash, cough syrups, and sandwich bags.[19] Simple observation of the retail scene can add confirmation.

There are also facts to support the contention that premium prices are reasonably well accepted as a justification for functional improvement, although consumers are hearteningly skeptical about manufacturers' attempts to charge a premium price for no obvious functional advantage at all. Davidson, whose investigation was quoted earlier in this chapter, examined 50 successful new brands and 50 failures. Of the 50 successes, more than half were sold at a premium price, and in virtually every case the higher price was accompanied by a better performance than competitive brands. Of the 50 failures, 35 were sold at a premium price, but 25 of them were accompanied by a similar or a worse performance than competitive brands.[20]

These analyses and their lessons are useful as far as they go, but this is of course not far enough to provide actionable advice for a manufacturer who wishes to launch a new brand. King, whose treatment is based partly on academic studies and partly on practical experience in the United Kingdom, suggests a useful investigative and pragmatic approach to the question of initial pricing, working on the basic assumption that the best price for the manufacturer to charge must be based roughly on what consumers will accept. The technique recommended is research into consumer attitudes based on direct and indirect questions, which will provide guidance to the feasibility of "skimming" or "penetration" pricing (aimed respectively at skimming the cream from the market by pricing high, and opening up the market by pricing much lower.)[21] On the other hand, basing prices on a derivation of production costs will tell the manufacturer whether he will cover costs at a given level of output, but it will give little idea about whether the company will in fact be able to sell that output.

It is also true that econometric techniques are helpful in pricing, although they are essentially a fine-tuning device for the period after a brand is launched. The most useful such device is a calculation of price elasticity. It is by no means impossible to estimate this within limits for ongoing brands, as demonstrated by Broadbent, whose work will be considered in chapter 4. The trouble with this type of analysis is that it is constructed from historical data, which take some time to build for any brand. But a useful procedure in a brand's early planning stage is to make guesstimates of the price elasticities of competitive brands in the market; any internal consistency could well be valuable to note.

As the reader can infer from this discussion, the role of judgment in establishing an individual price is of importance. Once a brand is launched and progressing, the sensible manufacturer will take steps to estimate price elasticity as soon as a range of data becomes available. (Sales data from different regions and in different types of store provide a surprisingly large amount of information quickly). The range of elasticities for brands is quite wide (from virtually zero to beyond -2.0),[22] and the average elasticity is quite pronounced, as confirmed by Broadbent and a number of Nielsen studies.[23]

With an ongoing brand, the manufacturer will obviously wish to protect a price premium insofar as it is practicable to do so, and there is good evidence that consumer advertising can make a major contribution here. But this brings us to the part which price plays with an established, ongoing, mature brand, a matter to be discussed in chapter 4.

5. Distribution

One key factor influencing the immediate success (or failure) of a new brand is the ability of the manufacturer's sales force to get it into distribution.

A superficial glance at Nielsen data suggests that manufacturers in general have little trouble in achieving quick distribution. This is a result of the efficiency and concentration of the American retail trade, with its relatively small number of buying points. This significant scale economy is also evidence of the muscle exercised by the sales force of the average large manufacturer.

In 1971, Peckham investigated all new brands in seventy product categories, and estimated that three-quarters of these achieved the extraordinarily satisfactory weighted distribution level of 70 percent within eight months of launch.[24] What the analysis does not show, however, is the different growth patterns for successful and unsuccessful brands. King, using British Nielsen data, draws this distinction and shows differences in degree between the two markets, in particular the absolute distribution levels in the United Kingdom, which are much lower. For example, successful brands reach a weighted distribution of well under 60 percent within the first eight-month period, and unsuccessful brands achieve much less than this. The differences between Britain and the United States are probably connected with the lower degree of retail concentration in the United Kingdom and possibly also with differences in manufacturers' and retailers' attitudes to new brand activity.

King shows us that both successful and unsuccessful brands make noticeable distributional headway during their first four months, although even in this short period the successful brands do rather better. But it is at this point that their paths seriously diverge. This distribution of successful brands continues to climb, to the 60 percent weighted level and beyond. The unsuccessful ones remain static and eventually begin to fall. Is this a reflection of differences in the effort of the sales force? Or a result of the initial acceptance of the product by the consumer, a matter influenced primarily by the brand's functional performance? The latter is almost certainly the more important cause:

> [D]istribution is a result of success. If the brand goes well in the early stages, the public demands it, retail branches hear from head office, the word get around and more retailers want to stock it.[25]

But functional performance is not important to the consumer alone. Retailers themselves, and even more importantly the sales force, are conscious of functional superiority and its contribution to a brand's success. Functional superiority will provide conviction to the salesman and draw commitment from the retailer. When Nielsen executives actually sat in as observers on seventy-eight new brand presentations to chain and independent supermarket buyers, they found the first reason for acceptance of a new brand was "evidence of saleability."[26]

Ongoing distribution is not only a concern for a growing and mature brand, as discussed in chapter 4. It should also influence the initial decision about the case size for a new brand, because too small a size brings the immediate danger of shops running out of stock before the end of the manufacturer's sales cycle. Changing the case size is obviously more difficult and troublesome once a brand is under way than at the beginning. It is at the earliest stage that the manufacturer should do its homework (which means making a careful estimate of likely rates of sale in different outlets), introduce the optimum size from the outset, and explain to the retail trade exactly why this particular size was chosen.[27]

The Importance of Market Testing

1. *Testing Mechanisms*

The manufacturer of a new brand will almost invariably test its functional performance on some consumers. Various test techniques are employed, some of them extremely sophisticated. But before being sold to the public in quantity, the brand will also almost invariably be introduced first into a test market: a restricted geographical area (or two or three areas), where the public will—it is hoped—respond to the brand and its advertising in a way representative (or not too unrepresentative) of what would happen if the brand were to be sold nationally. The procedure is in a sense an insurance policy, a way of spending a relatively modest amount of money in order to prevent the manufacturer from losing a large amount of money in the all too common event of failure. A test market also enables improvements to be made in details of the plan before national launch. The advantages of the procedure are therefore considerable, but there are two immediate tactical disadvantages: first, a test market takes time; it also alerts competitive manufacturers, who during the course of the test will have the opportunity to take retaliatory action in the classic oligopolistic fashion. Many cases have been known of competitors who have ruined test markets for new brands, because (in Stephen King's words) "If one is faced with a potentially dangerous new competitor, what better than to try to strangle it at birth?"[28]

Even more seriously, there is a fundamental structural problem about test markets, which is that they can only be representative of the country as a whole in a crudely approximate sense. This problem has been much discussed in the professional literature. Jack Gold, a senior advertising agency executive who was formerly on the client side, examined this issue by analyzing sales for a number of Mennen brands in different commonly used test areas in the United States, and grossing these sales up to give estimates of national sales, with pretty inaccurate final results.[29] (For instance, predictions from sales in a single area overestimated the national picture by at least 25 percent in about a third of all cases.) On the basis of this and many other examples, it is difficult not to conclude, in the words of John Davis, another informed practitioner: "Test marketing then tends to be statistically invalid from the start."[30]

But the more we study the niceties of the statistical representativeness of test areas, the more we depart from the way they are actually employed in the real world, which is to provide a result which might approximate in a directional way to a national outcome in order to help the manufacturer make a reasoned decision. They are also used widely for the different purpose of what King calls "pilot marketing."[31] The idea here is to allow all the details of the brand, production, and physical distribution as well as marketing to be tested in practical conditions. The brand can then shake down in a realistic fashion, and detailed problems can be solved before a national launch.

Bearing these points in mind, test marketing is not only useful. It is really indispensable. Nielsen can provide interesting data on how test markets are used in actual cases, and what sort of results they provide. In an analysis of 50 test markets in the United States, Nielsen found that the eventual national share of market came within 5 percent of the test level in 14 of the cases, within 10 percent of the test level in 25 of the cases, and within 20 percent of the test level in 40 of the 50 cases. "[L]ooking at it another way, the odds turned out to be about four to one that national performance will match test results within ± 20%."[32] This level of accuracy is nowhere near perfection, but it is a good deal better than Gold's and Davis's conclusions would have led us to expect. In general, these results can be understood in the light of the probable care and common sense used in planning, executing, and interpreting most test markets, of which Nielsen monitored a reasonably representative sample.

One important general observation which Nielsen makes is that, as a rule, conditions are *less* favorable in the national introduction than in a test area, a factor which is probably related to the retaliation of competitors. Researchers also have in their armory a number of statistical techniques to make for more sensitive interpretation of test market results. One of the most inportant is the simple arithmetical technique of standardizing test data described by Davis.[33] This means that normally in a test market, the test brand will take market share from existing brands, and retail audit and consumer panel data will provide accurate estimates of how much each existing brand loses. On a national basis, the initial shares of the competitive brands will probably be different from their shares in the test market, but the amounts they lose in test can be used to predict what they will lose nationally. This is done by standardizing or applying to the national shares the same relative losses which the competitive brands suffered in test market. As a consequence surprisingly accurate predictions of national results can be made.

There is a further aspect of testing on which Nielsen throws valuable light: the question of the time necessary for tests to provide reliable answers. From data provided by 100 tests in the United States and 41 in the United Kingdom, it is clear that the longer a test runs, the greater becomes its ability to predict the final outcome accurately. After two months, there is a very small chance indeed of a reliable prediction; after six months the chance is 50—50; after a year, the reliability is 94 percent.[34] There is of course nothing here that should surprise us, but as usual it is satisfying to have unimpeachable factual validation of what common sense leads us to expect.

2. *Success Rate for New Brands*

Anyone with the smallest practical experience in marketing and advertising is aware of the part which myth plays in a business whose practitioners sometimes make considerable scientific claims for it. Even if observers of the scene are not themselves practitioners, they will get a good idea of the part played by myths by studying the literature, certainly if they accept the view of that ever perceptive observer Colin McDonald, "what is a model but a myth with numbers?"[35]

One of the most deep-seated myths in the whole of marketing is the high failure rate of new brands, but for once, here is a myth that seems to be reasonably true. An examination of this will form a fitting end to this chapter, as well as making a bridge to chapter 4. A commonly mentioned statistic for the average failure rate of new brands is 80 percent.[36] Davidson gives his own estimate of 70 percent.[37] King reviews various empirical studies and gives different estimates of 54 percent, 60 percent, 40 percent and 49 percent.[38]

Based on 100 studies, a 1972 Nielsen investigation in the United States disclosed an overall failure rate of 55 percent, which compares closely with the British Nielsen experience. Of these 55 failures, 47 were failures in test which were not extended nationally, and 8 were national failures of brands that had apparently succeeded in test market. (Comparing these 8 national failures following test with the 45 national successes following test maarket gives us odds of about 6:1 in favor of a test market predicting national success.)[39]

There is then a good empirical basis for suggesting that at least half of new brands turn out to be near immediate failures. These brands presumably had been designed by competent and imaginative people, and the management of major manufacturing companies had been persuaded to spend money on development and test marketing. The outcome of all this effort is if anything worse than the 50—50 result of the toss of a coin. This is not an encouraging picture; and its most important cause is almost certainly a lack of functional superiority in the test brands, as is obvious from the data in the earlier parts of this chapter. Insofar as the marketing aspects of the launch plans can be blamed, most of them are in my experience unspecific about the brands used at present by the target users ("from what brands do we want to take business?") with the result that priority was not given to achieving superiority *over the functional attributes of those specific brands.* This is the heart of the problem of achieving first repurchase of a new brand, the truly nodal point in the whole path of a new brand's development.

As a result of a widespread awareness of the extraordinary failure rate of new product ventures, there has been a major change since 1968 in relative expenditures made by American business in exploration, screening, the development of new products, in comparison with commercialization of them.[40] But the key importance of comparative functional performance is still not universally understood by the marketing profession, which is the reason the matter is given such prominence in this book.[41]

The picture regarding initial success and failure of new brands is clear. But it brings us to a point of comparable importance that is discussed much less frequently; and where it is discussed, it leads to conclusions that are generally even more discouraging. Out of our 45 percent of new brands that are considered initial successes, how many grow to anywhere near market leadership, and how many limp along as neither real successes nor real failures? American and British figures provide distressingly similar answers.

Peckham made an analysis of 49 new brands launched nationally in seven product categories since 1955, and concluded that only 11 did well enough to get at least a 10-percent market share measured by Nielsen on an ongoing basis. Remembering that only half the brands entering test market are introduced nationally, then these 11 brands represent only about 10 percent of all new brands going into test. In other words, real "flyers" represent only 10 percent or so of all new ventures.[42] A recent investigation by John Madell of the British advertising agency Boase Massimi Pollitt Univas examined 730 new brand launches in the British food market, and came up with an even worse finding:

> I have chosen to define a successful new brand as one which achieved a turnover of at least 4 million pounds in 1978.
>
> This is a fairly rough and ready measure and takes no direct account of profitability. However, on the whole, most major fast moving packaged goods manufacturers would regard this as the minimum turnover necessary to sustain marketing support and show a reasonable return.
>
> Using this criterion, I found only 31 new brands had achieved this in the last ten years. In other words, only 4 per cent of the 730 new brand launches that occurred across that period.[43]

Madell's analysis adds something to Peckham's beyond the important matter of crude but general confirmation. Madell names all the brands in his successful 4 percent and these are, as could be expected, familiar to anyone who has been a regular observer of the British scene. What strikes the observer about these really successful brands is not simply a matter of their functional superiority. I am highly conscious of the added values that have been built, sometimes in quite short periods of time. Their ongoing success becomes then more a matter of brand building on a continuous, long-term basis, and the major factor which contributes to this is unquestionably advertising. This, as I have suggested, is the reason for my having deferred discussing advertising until we came to consider the brand as a growing and mature entity, a proper matter for my next and subsequent chapters.

The Argument in Brief

This chapter has concerned the retail trade and how, by research and even simple observation of competitive brands in retail stores, it is possible to obtain a clear and accurate picture of a market.

Viewed over short periods, most consumer goods markets appear to be stationary. Yet there are large long-term changes. This chapter has attempted to explain this phenomenon. Two factors are at work. The first is that most new brands fail, so that the ferment of new brand innovation leads to no *effective* change in the makeup of markets. The second point is that, even with successes, there is a strong equilibrial tendency within markets, which causes them quickly to shake down to accommodate a new brand. In the long term, however, small changes lead to large cumulative effects, and these are mainly due to repeat purchase applied to product and brand innovation. To a substantial degree also, the decline of many mature brands is brought about by underinvestment caused by a virtually universal but mistaken belief in the inevitability of cyclical decline. This is one of the most grievous myths of the marketing profession.

Five factors are most important to a brand during its conception and birth: functional performance, positioning, name, price, and distribution. These all have great weight, but the first, functional performance, has an influence on virtually all the other factors, and this makes it in effect the key to successful new brand activity.

New brands are almost always tested in the marketplace. Test mechanisms, while they have the disadvantages of being technically imperfect and giving competitors advance notice of a manufacturer's intentions, nevertheless act as an insurance policy. What makes such an insurance policy essential is the high rate of failure in new brand launches.

The most common reason for this high failure rate is functional deficiencies. Realizing this, American business has in recent years increased significantly the amount of relative effort applied to planning (as opposed to exploiting) new brands. But the failure rate remains so high that new product ventures remain the most hazardous feature of the entire marketing process.

Notes

1. Sales estimates relating to 1982 were published in *1984 Advertising Age Yearbook* (Chicago: Crain Books, 1984), pp. 248–52. The total value of the cat food market was estimated to be $1.6 billion.

The 1982 market shares of the different segments of the cat food market were: canned, 51 percent; dry, 36 percent; and moist 13 percent. (In 1982, moist was however the fastest growing sector, which means that my estimate of 20 percent may not be unreasonable for 1985).

In 1982, Nine Lives, Buffet, Kal Kan, and Purina together accounted for 61 percent of sales value in the canned sector. Cat Chow, Meow Mix, Friskies, Special Dinner, and Nine Lives accounted for 67 percent of the dry market value. Tender Vittles alone accounted for 67 percent of sales value in the moist sector.

Government estimates of the net value of sales are always some years in arrears. That for breakfast cereals was put at $2.5 billions in 1977. *Census of Manufactures* (Washington, D.C.: U.S. Department of Commerce, Bureau of the Census, 1981).

2. James O. Peckham, Sr., *The Wheel of Marketing*, p. 54.

3. *Ibid.*, pp. 51.6, 53.1, 53.

4. Stephen King, *Developing New Brands*, pp. 2–6.

5. R. Polli and V.J. Cook, "Validity of the Product Life Cycle", *Journal of Business* (October 1969): 385–400; R. Polli, *A Test of the Classical Product Life Cycle by Means of Actual Sales Histories* (Philadelphia, Pa: privately published, 1968).

6. *Advertising Age,* September 19, 1983: 32.

7. Nariman K. Dhalla and Sonia Yuspeh, "Forget the Product Life Cycle Concept," *Harvard Business Review* 54 (January–February 1976): 102.

8. Stephen A. Greyser, *Cases in Advertising and Communications Management,* 2d ed. (Englewood Cliffs, N.J.: Prentice—Hall, 1981), pp. 148–67.

9. Peckham, *The Wheel of Marketing*, p. 60.

The 3M Company requires each of its forty operating divisions to generate 25 percent of any year's sales with brands introduced during the previous five years, report Thomas J. Peters and Robert H. Waterman, Jr., in *In Search of Excellence* (New York: Harper & Row, 1982), p. 233.

10. Peters and Waterman, *In Search of Excellence,* p. 233.

11. Peckham, *The Wheel of Marketing*, pp. 19–20.

12. *Nielsen Researcher* (Oxford, England: A.C. Nielsen Company) 14, no. 1 (January–February 1973): 10–11.

13. J. Hugh Davidson, "Why Most New Consumer Brands Fail," *Harvard Business Review* 54 (March–April 1976): 117–22.

14. Peter Carter and Roz Hatt, "How Far Does Advertising Protect the Brand Franchise?" *Admap* (May 1983): 261–80.

15. Peckham, *The Wheel of Marketing*, p. 52.

16. *Ibid.*, p. 59.

17. Julian L. Simon and Johan Arndt, "The Shape of the Advertising Response Function," *Journal of Advertising Research* (August 1980): 23.

18. Peckham, *The Wheel of Marketing*, p. 63.

19. William T. Moran, "Why New Products Fail," *Journal of Advertising Research* (April 1973): 5–13.

20. Davidson, "Why Most New Consumer Brands Fail."

21. Stephen King, *Developing New Brands,* pp. 161–67.

22. Simon Broadbent, "Price and Advertising: Volume and Profit," *Admap* (November 1980): 532–40.

23. Peckham, *The Wheel of Marketing,* pp. 21–25.

24. *Ibid.,* p. 8.

25. Stephen King, *Advertising as a Barrier to Market Entry* (London: Advertising Association, 1980): p. 14.

26. Peckham, *The Wheel of Marketing,* p. 13.

27. *Nielsen Researcher* (September–October 1972): 7–9.

28. King, *Developing New Brands,* p. 172.

29. Jack A. Gold, "Testing Test Market Predictions," *Journal of Marketing Research* (August 1964): 8–16.

30. John Davis: *The Validity of Test Marketing* (London: J. Walter Thompson, 1965).

31. King, *Developing New Brands,* pp. 169–70.

32. Peckham, *The Wheel of Marketing,* p. 67.

33. Davis, *The Validity of Test Marketing,* pp. 8–12.

34. *Nielsen Researcher* (January–February 1968): 4–7.

35. Colin McDonald, "Myths, Evidence and Evaluation," *Admap* (November 1980): 546–55.

36. This figure is mentioned on a number of occasions by A.S.C. Ehrenberg and G.L. Goodhardt in their Seventeen Essays *Understanding Buying Behavior* (New York: J. Walter Thompson and Market Research Corporation of America, 1977–80).

37. Davidson, "Why Most Consumer Brands Fail," p. 117.

38. King, *Developing New Brands,* pp. 1–2.

39. Peckham, *The Wheel of Marketing,* pp. 67–68.
Note that the odds on a test market predicting national success as given here (6:1) are more favorable than the odds quoted in the text near note 32 (4:1). The reason for the difference is technical, in that the quotation referred to near note 32 in the text calculated the number of times test market predictions came within 20 percent of the eventual national outcome. These could be 20-percent overestimates or 20-percent underestimates. In the later quotation, the underestimates have been ignored, to give better odds on predicting success. They have been ignored for the simple and practical reason that if a national outcome exceeds test market prediction, this does not indicate an unsuccessul test!

40. Booz, Allen and Hamilton, *New Product Management for the 1980s* (privately published, 1982).

41. Two examples, one from the professional and one from the popular press, show this.

    1. "An annual trek through the product development practices of thirty to seventy (sic) firms has given the University of Michigan Graduate School of Business Administration a unique opportunity to assess the 'state of the art'." The report of these treks discloses that the "state of the art" does not include any form of recognition of the importance of functional efficiency for a new brand.

(C. Merle Crawford, "Product Development: Today's Most Common Mistakes," *University of Michigan Business Review* 29, no. 1, (January 1977): 6.

2. In the *New York Times,* March 3, 1985, the head of a major advertising agency, a securities analyst, a Miller distributor, a marketing professor, and a bartender commented on the new Miller High Life Beer advertising campaign. The first four people were concerned exclusively with the marketing and advertising reasons for Miller's problems and how these had influenced the new campaign. Only the bartender referred to the functional performance of the beer: "I think High Life is very bland. It has no significance at all. No character. It is a little watery." The difference between this comment and the statements of the other four observers was raised in a letter by a James Rudolph published in the *New York Times,* April 7, 1985.

42. Peckham, *The Wheel of Marketing,* p. 53.2.

44. John Madell, "New Products: How to Succeed When the Odds Are Against You," *Marketing Week* (February 22, 1980): 20–22.

4
Factors That Shape a Brand during Its Growth and Maturity

"An uncomfortable sort of an age. Now if you'd asked my advice, I'd have said leave off at seven—but it's too late now."

"I never ask advice about growing," Alice said indignantly.

This chapter concerns growth; and it is substantially concerned with the long term. But we must reach the long term via the short term, and there is often a severe dissonance between long-term and short-term objectives when it comes to planning the growth of a brand. It is important for the reader to appreciate this dissonance before I get into the main argument of this chapter.

In fall 1984, while conducting qualitative research among advertising decision makers on media selection, I interviewed the marketing vice-president of a fairly large American-based international food company, one whose advertising budget exceeds $60 million. The conversation moved, much to my interest, to the relative value of above-the-line (theme advertising) and below-the-line (promotional) expenditures, and the long-term trends in the marketplace, which seem to be demonstrating strong relative movements from the former to the latter. (This important topic will be examined in chapter 11).

During this interview, there was an immediate affinity between our views. Afterwards he wrote me a letter. Its points are acute, having extra force because they come from a successful advertiser. (A manufacturer is a much more objective observer than, say, an advertising agency or media executive, whose views might be colored by the self-interest of dependence on clients' advertising expenditures.)

The real problem is the same one which pervades other aspects of corporate behavior today: an overemphasis on the short term with short term defined, at best, as "this year," just as often "this quarter."

Trade deals generate *measurable* volume *now*. It can be seen, tabulated, and included in current financial statements. Advertising, on the other hand—and marketing practitioners and scholars such as you and I know this well—cannot be tied directly to volume, except possibly over the long term (two to five years), and even then only imprecisely.

So when we need extra volume this quarter, or this year, whatever the reason, we do not increase advertising, we increase trade deals. And since short-term budgets tend to be filed, we naturally shift relative monies from the imprecise area of advertising into the more easily measured area of trade deals.

Note the emphasis on the problem of reaching sales goals, a problem caused mainly by competitive pressure. Note also the long-term value implicitly attributed to advertising. It is indeed not difficult to demonstrate that a syphoning of funds from advertising to promotions may increase sales, but it does so at the expense of long-term damage to brands. Persuasive empirical evidence exists.[1] In my judgment however, such evidence is not likely to have much influence on individual advertisers, no matter how strong and enlightened they may be, in the all too common pressures of the marketplace, specifically when tonnage targets are in jeopardy but simply have to be met. Advertising is normally a matter of strategy aimed at the long-term obective of increasing the number of customers and their loyalty to the brand. Promotions are essentially a matter of tactics, aimed at increasing sales in the short term. With the increasing strength of the retail trade, the ferocity of tactical battles will not lessen in the future.

Readers should dwell on these issues as they consider the initial growth of a brand, a topic which serves as an introduction to my discussion of promotions and advertising.

Initial Growth

The first problem which a manufacturer faces with a new brand is to achieve consumer trial. Various techniques are used to bring this about: in the main, consumer promotions of different sorts, although advertising also has some part to play. As a result of the initial activity, a consumer base is built: people who have tried the brand once. The critically important stage now is first repurchase. It should again be emphasized that the brand must offer some type of functional superiority in order to achieve repurchase; the consumer will be aware of how well the brand performs after having used the first package. But naturally, not all trial purchasers will make a repeat purchase. First, because in functional performance a new brand cannot be all things to all people, any brand will have functional weaknesses as well as functional strengths. It follows that the brand will not be bought again by those people who were more disappointed by the weaknesses than satisfied by the strengths. It is also likely that some people are going to be wedded to their existing brands, which may have added values that are particularly strong and personally relevant to these consumers, so that the new brand will need to offer considerable functional superiority indeed to compensate.

The largest increases in the sales of a new brand will be those accompanying the growth in its distribution, although when the brand has achieved a high level of distribution, growth must then come from increasing sales in the average store. It is, incidentally, surprising how low a level of sales is achieved by even a major brand. In a fairly large supermarket, three-quarters of all brands sell a maximum of twelve packs per week; a third of them sell only four packs or even less.[2]

As a brand becomes accepted by the consumer, distribution grows at a continuous and often rapid rate. As we saw in the previous chapter, it is by no means uncommon for a new brand to achieve a 70-percent weighted distribution level after about eight months. But the growth is often slower than this. In observing the growth of distribution, we can normally discern a relationship between distribution and sales which can help us to predict the eventual sales level when the brand has reached its long-term stability. This is a modelling procedure, and the mathematics are no more complicated than the standardization of test market data described in chapter 3.

The first thing to do is to look at a new brand's sales and weighted distribution in test market, and compute the ratio between them. This shows sales volume per percentage point of weighted distribution. With sales of 61,000 units and weighted distribution of 41 percent, this ratio is 61,000:41, or 1,490 units per percentage point of weighted distribution. This is more simply expressed as 1.49 thousand units per distribution point.[3]

As the brand grows, so the sales and distribution grow, and we can calculate this ratio of sales to distribution for each period. We will immediately see that this ratio steadily increases. In other words, sales are going ahead faster than the number of shops stocking our brand, because the sales per shop are increasing due to the growing popularity of the brand. The actual progression of the ratio over the course of the first year in our example is as follows: 1.49, 1.51, 1.76, 2.13, 2.27, 2.50. As the ratios are calculated for further periods, the rate of increase is seen however to be slowing up. Here are the figures for the second year, with a calculation of the increase over the same period in the previous year, showing how this progressive increase is being reduced:

Second Year	Period 1	2.65	(78 percent above a year before)
	Period 2	2.26	(50 percent above a year before)
	Period 3	2.48	(41 percent above a year before)
	Period 4	2.88	(35 percent above a year before)
	Period 5	3.02	(33 percent above a year before)
	Period 6	3.28	(31 percent above a year before)

We now have a series of data from which three specific predictions can be made.

1. The future ratios of sales to distribution can be predicted on the basis of the declining rate of growth, projecting forward the trend in increases over the year before (the figures on the right of the preceding table).

2. Distribution growth can be separately forecast, or at least targeted. It is after all substantially under the manufacturer's own control, in that it is directly influenced by promotional and sales force activity.

3. By applying the projected ratio to the targeted distribution, we can make a forecast of sales. This tool is of day-to-day value to the brand manager. (This book and indeed this chapter contain others.)

Another pronounced pattern about which generalizations can normally be made is the primary growth cycle for a brand. We are talking here about a medium-term period (of an average length of two years or so) and a sales pattern showing a peak of initial sales followed by noticeable decline. This decline can partly be explained by the loss of some initial users: those who are not sufficiently convinced of the new brand's functional superiority to repurchase it. It is also partly the result of a slowing in the growth of new trial users following the normal reduction in promotional and advertising expenditures from an initial peak to a more normal ongoing level. And it is also commonly the result of competitive retaliation. The reader will note that this primary growth cycle (something finite, predictable, and to some extent within the control of the manufacturer) is a totally different concept from the long-term supposedly uncontrollable life cycle in chapter 3, where it was argued that final and irreversible decline is normally the result of a manufacturer's policy of draining resources out of a mature brand because of a belief in the inevitability of its eventual extinction.

The concept of the primary growth cycle is relatively straightforward and it is a useful tool to help us plan the recycling that is normally necessary to maintain a brand's long-term strength, thus prolonging its mature life. At the end of this chapter, we will take a look at the recycling process, but let us first examine the primary growth cycle. The data quoted are based on a Nielsen examination of a large number of newly introduced brands in scores of different product categories.[4]

Nielsen's observation of these brands suggests that the normal pattern is for a brand to grow to its peak and then decline to a relatively stable level of 80 percent of that peak. The primary growth cycle is defined as the time between the brand's introduction and when it drops to this 80 percent level. The first thing to examine is the length of the cycle. The average figure calculated from an examination of 86 cases in 28 months, with a spread from less than a year to more than four years, the average brand taking slightly longer to peak (15 months) than to decline to the 80 percent level (13 months).

Four points can be made about this cycle as it affects different types of brands.

1. There is a direct relationship between a brand's share of market and the length of the cycle. The brands with the longest cycle are those with the highest achieved market shares.
2. Brands in the health and beauty fields have longer primary cycles (an average of 34 months) than brands in the household and food fields (averages of 23 and 24 months, respectively).
3. Brands with long primary cycles tend to have high levels of advertising support and innovation, but a low level of new brand activity in their markets.
4. Brands with short primary cycles tend to be in large, crowded markets with a high degree of new brand activity, but a low degree of innovation and relatively low advertising support.

These characteristics point to the likelihood of the cycle becoming shorter over time, as markets become more densely crowded with brands and as it becomes increasingly difficult for new brands to gain large market shares. Additional analyses demonstrate that this has indeed been happening, with cycles falling to as little as eighteen months in many cases. An interesting sidelight is that in a less developed market like the United Kingdom, the share of market of a new brand is on average two to three times greater than in the United States. This suggests that overall economic development may be leading to progressively lower average market shares and shorter primary cycles.

Because of the characteristics of the primary growth cycle, the operational lesson from this analysis is the importance of regular restaging, and that plans for the first restage must be developed in the period following the initial launch of a brand. Increasingly long lead times will be required to develop and implement product innovations and all the other changes that restages always call for, while the inital growth cycle itself may be growing shorter.

A rather different illumination on the primary growth cycle is provided by a classic investigation of British test market experience by John Davis.[5] Davis examined forty-four test markets, both successes and failures. Although he does not make direct comparisons with Nielsen's analyses which are mainly American, his observed primary growth cycle:

1. is of much shorter duration (as little as eight months in most cases);
2. shows a pronounced drop from peak to relative stability (on average about 40 percent);

3. is associated with generally lower levels of distribution than in the United States (a point discussed in chapter 3).

The differences from the mainly American experience of Nielsen are not too easy to explain. Some of these differences must stem from the fact that Davis's examples include a large number of test market failures, which probably cause both the extent and speed of the drop to be exaggerated. The Nielsen data appear to exclude early failures, although some of the analyses do not make this absolutely clear. It is also probably true that the differences between the American and British findings are a reflection of the differences between the two markets, with the likelihood of a greater general volatility in Britain, as is evidenced by the larger initial market shares there.

The thing that makes Davis's study so interesting is a supplementary investigation into the levels of the drop from peak to stability. Davis's conclusion has not been tested in the United States, but there is no intrinsic reason to believe that it would not operate here. What he suggests is a *consistency* in the extent of the drop from peak to stability for individual brands, as they are moved from test to national distribution. In other words, no matter if the initial peak is different between the test and the national launch, the ongoing level can be predicted.

Here we have the making of another simple model in which it should be possible (on the assumption that American and British experiences are similar) to forecast the extent of the drop to the ongoing national sales level on the basis of the percentage drop in test market when that is applied to the initial national peak sales level.

Five Influences on a Growing Brand

It is time now to look at some more visible parts of our large machine. As in chapter 3, the approach will be analytical rather than descriptive, as we take our first look at trade and consumer promotions and at consumer advertising. After this, we will enjoy a new perspective on two factors discussed in the previous chapter, price and distribution. This chapter will conclude with a brief look at the restaging process, which brings us back yet again to the factor of functional performance, the first and most pervasive of the factors influencing a brand's initial success and continued growth. But now, functional performance will be shown to work much in tandem with advertising.

1. *Trade Promotions*

Trade promotions, which normally take the form of either explicit or indirect rebates to wholesalers and/or retailers, are costly but are generally considered important both for a new brand and an ongoing one. They are an essentially defensive tactic dictated by what competitors are doing. Their main effect is a loading of inventories in wholesale and retail establishments. The success of trade promotions in achieving this makes them popular with manufacturers' sales forces, who use them as a lever to sell what they believe to be significantly higher-than-average volumes of merchandise. In contrast to consumer promotions, which act on the consumer to pull goods through the distributional pipeline, trade promotions are aimed at the trade, to push the stocks through this same pipeline, mainly by encouraging retailers to put the goods on display and perhaps pass on some of the benefit of the promotional rebates in reduced selling prices to the consumer.

There is little doubt that trade promotions can have a demonstrable short-term effect in moving goods out of the factory, but two considerable qualifications must be made about them.

In the first place, they are extremely expensive in absolute terms. Indeed, the whole matter of promotional as compared to advertising expenditure calls for some comment. Nielsen estimates the average proportion of a manufacturer's marketing budget that goes into various trade promotions to be of the order of 23 percent, a larger figure than that for consumer promotions (18 percent) or consumer advertising (15 percent). This gives a promotion—advertising ratio of 41:15 (the residual 44 percent representing all other marketing costs, which are mainly sales force salaries and expenses).[6] Expressed more simply, this ratio is 62:38. Such an estimate gives rather more weight to promotions than did most of my former clients, although they all tended to spend more money below than above the line. An estimate by Donnelley Marketing of 56:44 is more in accordance with my own clients' practices.[7] Interestingly enough, Procter and Gamble used to be well known for spending more money on advertising than promotions as a general rule. However, the pressures of business conditions in the 1980s have caused a change in this policy, so that even Procter and Gamble now spends almost 60 percent of its total budget on promotional activities.

From some points of view the traditional advertising—promotion distinction is artificial. Robert Prentice, a consultant to the Marketing Science Institute, makes a good case for creating a new category entitled "consumer franchise building" expenditures, which should include advertising, sampling, certain coupons (manufacturers' coupons that include a selling message), demonstrations, and service material (such as recipes). In his opinion, these expenditures should account for 55 percent of the advertising and promotion budget; I do not disagree with him except for wondering if his figure is low. This analysis suggests, incidentally, that if his 55 percent is to include such expensive items as sampling and most manufacturers' coupons, the advertising element alone is likely to come down to something as low as Peckham's figure of 38 percent.[8]

What makes promotions so expensive is that they are substantially a means of price reduction which, either at retail or consumer level, must come out of the manufacturer's contribution to overheads and profit, basic production costs being the same whether or not the goods are rebated. A 10-percent trade rebate can commonly mean a 20-percent reduction in contribution. In these circumstances, the manufacturer would need to increase sales by 25 percent simply to cover the costs of the deal and break even.

This brings us to the second important point about trade deals, which is that although it is by no means impossible for a trade deal to boost sales by 25 percent in the short term, this may not be quite what it seems, because much of the spurt may represent a pulling forward of sales that would have been made anyway during a later period. The all too common effect is therefore to transfer goods from the manufacturer's to the trader's inventory without bringing about much noticeable increase in sales through the pipeline to the consumer. Additionally, there is frequent evidence of trade promotions syphoning business away from varieties of a brand (like flavors of a food) that do *not* carry the offer, to those varieties that *do,* leaving total sales more or less unchanged.[9]

These unquestioned difficulties prompt us to ask why manufacturers continue with these expensive and sometimes destructive tactics. The answer must come back again to the nature of oligopolistic competition, which forces them to go on with an activity that is in the last analysis nothing more than implicit price competition. And as retailers grow in strength vis-à-vis manufacturers, the pressure on the latter to grant substantial, increasing, and even permanent overriding discounts will unquestionably become greater, with interesting effects on the balance of power in the marketing world. Indeed, a recent analysis of trade promotions based, among other things, on information from marketing managers and promotional specialists in manufacturing companies, indicated strongly that "trade promotion expenditures are rising at the same time as their productivity is declining."[10]

As with consumer promotions (as we shall shortly see), trade deals tend to be a more effective device for a growing or stable brand than for a declining one, for which they can result in catastrophically low levels of offtake in the periods following the promotion. An overall estimate by Nielsen, based on hundreds of case studies, suggests that the median increase in sales resulting from a trade promotion is a 5-percent uplift over a four-month period, the equivalent of approximately a 1½-percent gain in a year's sales of a brand. This figure could well be reduced by the transfer of sales from the period after the promotion, not to speak of competitive retaliation. For a brand with a stable 16-percent market share, the net gain in share is likely therefore to be 1½ percent (or less) of 16 percent, or a quarter or even less of one percentage point of market share.[11] It would be interesting to know how many manufacturers would willingly pay the cost involved to achieve this measurable but extremely modest result, if they were not forced to do so by the competitive climate in the markets in which they were operating.

Display is an important motive for trade promotions. Sometimes promotions are specifically geared to achieving it. This is about the only way in which trade promotions can be said to act on the consumer, and most manufacturers are conscious of the problems that arise for growing brands, because of the strong tendency for larger brands to receive *fewer* shelf facings than their market share justifies, while smaller brands receive more. This is for simple mechanical reasons, shelf stocking being generally done in multiples of a case, which provides rather a large minimum display for the smaller brands, thus squeezing the display space available for the larger ones.[12] But even if increased display results from promotional actions, there are problems that could cloud the effects. For a start, very few lines are on mass display in a supermarket at any time, perhaps twenty in any week out of a total of many thousand different items. This means that the display of the brand on offer is neglected at other times. Peckham writes: "One district manager I know kept a two-year record of his sales separately for stores which occasionally featured and mass-displayed his merchandise and also for comparable sized stores which stocked his brands normally. You know what he found: the annual sales trend was better in the stores with normal but year-round support."[13] Much of the effect of mass display must be to enable users of the brand to fill their own store cupboards, so that these promotions bring about a neat transfer of inventories from manufacturer to retailer and from retailer to customer, with a most modest increase in final consumption.

The value of a brand's display is of course influenced by its pack design, which must be neatly balanced between what is required by the brand's endogenous characteristics (packaging being a means of communicating functional performance and added values) and what is required to make it stand out on the shelf from possibly more aggressive rivals. Not all brands have aggressive personalities. It will of course encourage considerable dissonance to use powerful colors and lettering for the packaging of brands whose underlying character calls for a quieter outward impression.

One further type of trade promotion, cooperative advertising, deserves brief consideration, although evidence of its prolonged beneficial effects on the standing and sales of brands is just as scarce as with other types of trade promotion. A distillation of Nielsen experience suggests that although cooperative advertising is often associated with increasing sales of mature brands, it is difficult to disentangle the specific effect of cooperative advertising from other stimuli that may be contributing to the increased offtake, not least the manufacturer's own consumer advertising.[14] As with other types of trade promotion, it is doubtful whether manufacturers would allow themselves to be forced into this sort of activity were it not for the presence of competitors who would step in if they were to drag their feet. We should remember also that with the strength of the retail trade, cooperative advertising provides some protection to small manufacturers from being delisted, an ever present danger for the third, fourth, and lower brands in a market. The advantage of cooperative advertising may then lie in its influence on the retail buyer rather than the ultimate customer, especially since the average cooperative advertisement, with its hard-selling, relentless, almost exclusive price orientation, can add little indeed to the average brand's store of added values.

One simple but necessary recommendation is that manufacturers should keep much fuller and more carefully compiled records than many of them do at present of the results of their trade promotions (and their consumer promotions too). Trade and consumer data should be included in both cases. As some additional return for the huge investments on these activities, manufacturers should assemble a constantly growing portfolio of promotional ideas that work (or do not work), including how well they perform and why.[15] To my knowledge, Procter and Gamble is the only firm which has done this consistently.

2. Consumer Promotions

We have already seen from Nielsen's broad data aggregation that consumer promotions take a smaller proportion (18 percent) of the average manufacturer's marketing budget than trade promotions (23 percent). Consumer promotions are nevertheless a large and dynamic influence on a brand, with an importance that differs according to whether the brand is expanding or contracting and also according to the type of promotion itself.

The logic of consumer promotions is that they provide an incentive (normally price-oriented) for the consumer to sample a brand. Sales will rise sharply, always going down after the end of the promotion, but (the manufacturer hopes) still settling at a slightly higher level than before, as some buyers like the brand enough to add it to their repertoire. This might be called the ideal pattern, and only if this happens can promotions be said to be building the consumer base. In most circumstances, however, the main emphasis is only on short-term sales. Nielsen provides empirical illumination, with conclusions of considerable operational importance. In studies of 83 different promotions, the brands with an *increasing* sales trend can be shown clearly to follow the ideal, with sales before the promotion indexed at 100, sales during the promotion at 110, and sales in the period after the promotion at 107. Brands are of course more commonly in a stationary position in the short and medium term; in these cases, the Nielsen data show sales in general coming down to the prepromotional level at the end of the promotion. With brands with a *declining* sales trend, however, the sales in the period after the promotion are usually lower than those in the period before it, presumably a reflection of general disappointment in the brand's performance, and evidence of erosion of, rather than addition to the customer base.

Consumer promotions can be seen then as a sampling device, something extremely important for a new brand and an extra dynamic to the short- and medium-term sales trend of an established brand, speeding the success of the growing ones, but hastening the failure of those going down. The empirical basis of Nielsen's generalization is European as well as American, with the sole difference that promotional sales peaks tend to be higher in Europe, a point connected with the greater volatility of the less sophisticated markets.[16]

As with trade promotions, consumer promotions are essentially defensive, competitive tactics for an ongoing brand; the manufacturer finds himself forced into them to protect his position. Like trade promotions, they are expensive, so they are a deduction from the manufacturer's contribution to overhead and profit. A sales gain would have to be large indeed to compensate for the reduction in revenue necessary to fund the promotion. There is substantial merit in the argument of British analysts King[17] and Roberts[18] that price rebates (the most popular type of consumer promotion[19] as well as virtually the sole type of trade promotion) should not actually be considered as marketing expenditures at all. They are after all hardly investments in the sense of money staked out in order to achieve a return. They are reductions in income, or a variant on the theme of price competition. The more regularly they are carried out by manufacturers, the more they take the form of long-term price cuts, which are effectively subsidies to existing buyers, in whose eyes the brand is likely to be devalued, a counterproductive side effect.[20]

This is really another way of saying that consumer promotions do not help declining brands. Growing brands, with their increasing base of contented repurchasers and accumulation of added values, have less need to be rebated, with the concomitant danger of debasing the value of the brand in the opinion of its users. One slight qualification to this generalization is that consumer promotions can to some extent buy time for a normally successful brand under immediate threat from new brands with product improvements. But the role of promotions here is a "holding" or short-term one, to provide a breathing space for the manufacturer to improve his own brand's formulation in line with the new market entrants and thus protect his own long-term position.

Some types of price promotion are more efficient and beneficial than others. Some types of nonprice promotion can even noticeably add to a brand's stock of added values, although promotions that combine a short-term sales stimulus with added values are rare. There is sometimes a genuinely creative element here, but I have not found creative groups in advertising agencies to be generally interested in generating promotional ideas, although those same people may do the most distinguished work in developing consumer advertising campaigns.

Of the different types of price promotion, couponing (apparently the most rapidly growing although not yet the largest type in volume terms) has distinct advantages over direct rebating by the use of such devices as price-off packs, banded packs ("buy three and get a fourth pack free"), and other explicit way of flagging cheapness. Absolutely the most effective, but also the most expensive promotional device is house-to-house sampling in conjunction with a coupon for follow-up purchase. Procter and Gamble's use of national sampling in Great Britain two decades ago for Fairy Liquid dishwasher has become a marketing legend; Fairy Liquid has never subsequently lost its market leadership. In an example quoted by Peckham, a new brand launched in half the United States with a home sample and coupon achieved a market share of 5.3 percent in the fifth check period. It was launched with a conventional introductory price-off in the other half of the country and achieved 3.1 percent in that same period.[21] But this Nielsen analysis does not give details of the vastly greater costs of the sample and coupon.

The particular advantages of coupons are fourfold. First, regular buyers are limited to one reduced-price pack, so that the element of subsidy to existing buyers is reduced. Second, a coupon does not erode brand values by introducing the idea of cheapness quite as explicitly as printed bargain packs. Third, with rebate packs, the customer tends to resist paying the normal price again after the rebate has come to an end. And fourth, competitive retaliation is not triggered quite so directly by couponing as by rebating.

All the generalizations made here about consumer promotions are solidly based on facts. Evidence is also available that diminishing returns set in rapidly with promotions for even well-established and growing brands. Peckham recommends, again on the basis of his long experience, that consumer price rebates should not be used more often than once every twelve to eighteen months. Yet, despite this rapid fall in efficiency plus the longer-term danger of devaluing brands in the eyes of consumers, manufacturers are sometimes led by competitive pressures to self-destructive orgies of rebates. Stephen King documents one well-known case of an established brand, Kimberly—Clark's Delsey toilet tissue in the United Kingdom, which was to all intents and purposes destroyed by continuous promotions funded by stopping all consumer advertising.[22] I have known from personal experience one complete product field in which competitive price cutting extinguished the profit for all manufacturers. This took place in a small country, Denmark, but the market was a large one: washing powders.

Nevertheless, in spite of these extraordinarily dramatic and by no means isolated examples, consumer promotions of the most direct and ultimately most self-destructive variety continue seemingly unchecked by any second thoughts by even the most academically well-trained brand managements. This can only be because consumer promotions, like trade promotions, enable the manufacturer to buy short-term tonnage irrespective of the longer-term consequences.

But not all consumer promotions are like this, especially those for new brands and those with rising sales trends, and most particularly those few consumer promotions with sensible long-term as well as short-term objectives. Nielsen's estimate of the effect of the median consumer promotion is that it lifts sales by about 5 percent over a six-month period (or about 2½ percent on an annual basis). Scaling this down to account for competitive retaliation could provide a net gain in market share on an annual basis of a third to a half a percentage point for a 16-percent brand.[23] As we have seen, this is a slightly better average rate of return than a normal trade promotion provides, although it is also an expensive way of buying tonnage. But in addition it offers at least the opportunity of augmenting a brand's store of added values. The use of the more creative rather than the more strident types of consumer promotion is a matter of businesspeople's balance and judgment.

3. *Advertising*

Much the most important aspect of advertising—and one receiving a good deal of attention in this book—is the creative content of campaigns, an essentially qualitative consideration. But there is also another aspect on which I shall spend much time in this chapter: the quantitative element, or the effects of the weight of money put behind campaigns. There are relationships here between advertising volume and sales which will be looked at in some detail. This is a productive study, although it took considerable time for the advertising industry to come round to examining these relationships. Early explorations of campaign effectiveness concentrated almost exclusively on campaign content, using simple techniques derived from direct response. Even Albert Lasker, one of the small handful of really powerful personalities to come out of the advertising agency business, once admitted that "it took him years to learn that mere volume of advertising could be as important as the copy message."[24] In this statement he perhaps goes too far, but volumes in themselves have a quantifiable effect, which I shall in due course illustrate.

One thing to bear in mind is that advertising does not account for as large a share of the average manufacturer's marketing expenses as trade and consumer promotions. This does not mean that the effect of advertising is eventually not large. Its effect is as large as it is because over and beyond its short-term influence there is an additional long-term overtone. Because advertising contributes in this way to building the customer base, I made the point in the analogy of the large machine that the small apparatus in its middle appears to have an effect disproportionate to its size. But in the early stages of a brand's life, the cumulative effect of advertising on brand use has not had time to be built. Indeed from strong evidence in the British market, "shop display and word-of-mouth are thought to be much the most important channels of communication for a new brand," with advertising a much less important influence.[25] Over longer periods however, advertising moves steadily to a position much more comparable in importance to the functional performance of the brand. Indeed, as discussed in chapter 3, advertising has the important role, during the growth of a successful new brand, of building added values quickly in order to protect it once competitive brands have been improved to reach functional parity with it.

Nielsen and other sources provide a good deal of information on the generalizable relationships between volume of advertising and volume of sales for ongoing brands. We should however be careful about reading too much into these, because (as we saw in chapter 2) the prime determinant of the absolute size of the advertising appropriation for an ongoing brand is normally the absolute level of sales. This means that it is misleading and possibly dangerous to interpret the relationship between absolute advertising volume and absolute sales volume as cause and effect, except in rather special circumstances.

There are three such circumstances. The first is the case of new brands, for which the advertising appropriation is always established at an "investment" level, influenced by the ongoing expenditures of competitive brands, and determined by the client's and agency's considered judgment on what needs to be spent to ensure a successful launch in a competitive marketplace. The best Nielsen evidence of the success of such launch expenditures comes from thirty-four new brands, indicating a marked degree of response to advertising pressure. "New brands having the highest share of sales also have the highest share of advertising and, conversely, those having the lowest sales shares are at the bottom of the share-of-advertising list." The degree of advertising investment in the new brand can be described by its share of all advertising in the market (share of voice); Nielsen evidence suggests that this needs to be a good deal higher than the anticipated brand share for success in the market.[26]

The second circumstance is when advertising budgets are set with the help of econometric techniques, for instance using knowledge of the brand's advertising elasticity coefficient (discussed later in this chapter). But this is a relatively rare procedure, and there are not enough cases available to enable us to draw any generalized conclusion about advertising volumes so determined and resultant sales volumes.

The third circumstance is when a careful comparison is made between year-by-year changes in advertising and year-by-year changes in sales. This focuses on short-term adjustments that are not necessarily dictated by projected sales increases and decreases, although total advertising expenditures in the medium and long term continue to be governed by the brand's earnings and therefore its sales. The change in advertising for a given year (measured in comparison with a norm) is calculated from the advertising budget, which is set and agreed upon before the beginning of the year. In the majority of circumstances, the sales result in that same year does not influence the level of advertising, most of which is spent before the year's overall sales have been made anyway. (But a good sales performance will probably cause the budget to be increased the next year, while a poor performance will cause a cutback next year or even in the last quarter of the present year.)

Such a comparison of changes in the two variables make it reasonable to expect a causality from advertising to sales, and not vice-versa. Credibility is increased by the ability of the assumed relationship between the two variables to predict the effects on sales of advertising increases and decreases.

Before we begin to examine a number of readings of this relationship between change in advertising and change in sales, let us return to the concept of measuring a brand's advertising by its share of voice. There is a simple mathematical aspect of this share which must be cleared out of the way. This stems from the fact that not all brands in a market are advertised; in a typical market there could be ten important advertised brands, plus twenty others in fairly broad but patchy distribution which are sold only on price and promotions, these being almost invariably the smallest brands. Now, in such a market, ten brands account for all the advertising, but thirty brands account for the sales. Therefore, the average *advertised* brand will have a larger share of advertising than the average *brand's* share of market, because there are ten of the former and thirty of the latter.

These are 1979 figures for a major packaged goods market (the market used to describe positioning in chapter 3). The ten largest brands are ranked by market share.

Brand	Share of Market by Volume (%)	Share of Advertising (%)
G	3	8
H	3	5
J	4	6
K	5	6
L	6	8
M	7	10
N	8	11
P	10	10
Q	15	12
R	17	13
Other brands	22	11
Total market	100	100

Certain things are clear about this table. First, seven of the ten brands follow the normal pattern which I have just explained, in that for each the share of advertising exceeds the share of market. The amount by which the one exceeds the other depends on the degree of investment spending. Brands *G* and *N*, for instance, are relatively new and aggressive brands, which the reader can see reflected in their advertising expenditures.

But it will immediately also strike the reader that there is something different about the three largest brands at the bottom of the table. For *P* the two shares are equal; but for the two largest of all, *Q* and *R*, the share of advertising is significantly *smaller* than the share of market. This is an almost universal tendency with big brands, and a demonstration of *measurable scale economies* which can be calculated in terms of advertising expenditures. This phenomenon receives general confirmation in Lambin's analysis of 107 European brands.[27]

These scale economies are very real, yet there is a limit below which it is dangerous to reduce the advertising budget. For the largest brands, this limit has to be carefully judged. This can be demonstrated by an examination of five years' figures for brands *Q* and *R*.

	Brand Q		Brand R	
	Share of Market by Volume (%)	Share of Advertising (%)	Share of Market by Volume (%)	Share of Advertising (%)
1975	18	11	18	11
1976	17	9	17	10
1977	17	11	16	9
1978	16	8	16	12
1979	15	12	17	13

The reader can see from this table how the manufacturer of brand *R* kept the brand in generally better repair than the manufacturer of brand *Q*. The latter's share of advertising was on occasion reduced a little too low for safety, and losses of share resulted. Brand *R*, on the other hand, was advertised at a slightly higher level. It is a much older brand than *Q*, and as a result of the manufacturer's marketing skills, has yielded enormous profits over a long period. The brand is a household name, and its profitability must be considerable indeed, with a 17 percent market share financed by a 13 percent advertising share. But from the evidence of the table, expenditure on *R* is rather carefully evaluated, and the manufacturer is not so greedy for profit that he eschews large absolute advertising investments. The 13 percent in 1979 represents an expenditure well in excess of $10 million—money well spent.

Brand *R* is in fact an excellent example to demonstrate the general invalidity of the life cycle theory.

Brand *Q* is an equally instructive example, although for a different reason. Brand *Q* comes from the same manufacturer as brand *G*. The briefest glance at their advertising expenditures will show clearly where the funds for *G*'s investment have come from. The manufacturer has in fact maintained high investment spending for five years on *G*. Its 1979 market share of 3 percent must have been disappointing and some way below what was necessary for profitable operation. So here we have yet another example of the classic pattern of a disappointing new brand *G* funded in the main from a large and successful brand *Q*, which is now also suffering from this unproductive syphoning of expenditure.

We now come to a formal exposition of the long-term relationship between advertising changes and sales changes. This will be done by means of the important concept of the *dynamic difference,* designed ("discovered" is perhaps a better word) by Unilever analyst Michael Moroney, the author of a well-known text book on statistics.[28] His book does not mention the dynamic difference, because this device has been used over the past twenty years on a more or less confidential basis by Unilever marketing companies. But ten years after Moroney's original work, it so happened that the model was independently discovered by James Peckham of A.C. Nielsen. Many of the Nielsen findings have now been published and I shall be quoting these extensively, while at the same time continuing to pay tribute to Moroney's original work, to which I was personally first introduced during a private seminar run by Moroney himself in the early 1960's.

The mathematics of the model are deceptively simple. The reader is however advised to think about them carefully and to go back over the description until it is understood. The model itself employs a simple two-dimensional diagram in the form of a cross. The data applied to the diagram are based on readings for one brand for two-year periods. What is measured is the *change* between the second year and the first.

On the horizontal axis, we measure the advertising level change. This is represented by the difference between the share of advertising in year 2 and the share of market in year 1 (the dynamic difference). The principle behind it is that the share of market in year 1 should dictate a "normal" advertising expenditure level. In fact this would be a slightly subnormal expenditure because, as we have seen, most brands have a share of advertising rather greater than their market share; hence, if their advertising share is only the same as their market share, they are spending below the norm. This difference is however substantially technical, because we are examining *changes* and not absolute levels.

On the vertical axis, we measure the difference in the brand's market share between year 2 and year 1. The reason for the diagram being cruciform

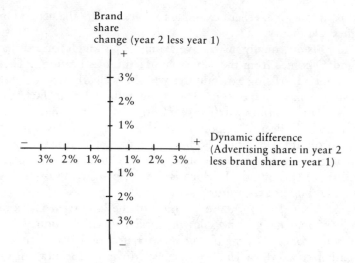

is that movements can be either positive or negative, the positive and negative parts being on different sides of the point of intersection.

Now, for each individual brand, a number of years' experience can be plotted. Based on the experience of more than three hundred brands in five countries, a line can be fitted in about 70 percent of the cases.[29] The line will rise from left to right if the regression has a normal fit. It will not necessarily cut the center of the cross. And most importantly, the lines will be quite different for each brand in a market, a total market looking then something like this:

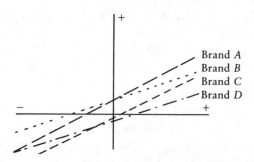

Peckham makes clear, on the basis of substantial empirical evidence, that the pattern "is different for every brand in much the same way as human thumbprints differ."[30]

But what does the diagram mean? It exemplifies five major points.

1. The relationship between advertising and brand shares is essentially long-term, needing perhaps five years of data to establish. It can be used for long-term predictions.

2. The slopes for individual brands have the same general shape, rising from bottom left to top right. This should reassure the more skeptical advertisers and afford their agencies fewer sleepless nights, because these slopes indicate a general rule that increases in advertising pressure are associated with increases in market share, and reductions in advertising pressure with reductions in market share. As indicated, the model fits in 70 percent of the cases examined by Nielsen.

3. The model can be of considerable predictive value to a manufacturer. The company must of course be able to estimate what the total advertising expenditure will be in its market in the next year in order to determine its own share. But on the assumption that it can do this reasonably efficiently, the firm can predict with fair accuracy what market share will result from a given advertising investment. It will also be apparent to the reader that the responsiveness of market share to change in advertising pressure is measured by the slope of the curve. The steeper the slope, the higher the degree of response. Nielsen, by using the model in a total of five hundred actual cases, made accurate predictions of market share changes following advertising pressure changes in 76 percent of the cases in the United States, 71 percent in the United Kingdom, and 68 percent in Germany. Even if they were not precisely accurate, the model's predictions were in the correct direction in 92 percent of the United Kingdom, 86 percent in Germany, and 83 percent in the United States.

4. One important conclusion concerns the best established and most profitable brands. For these, the dynamic difference slope cuts the horizontal axis to the left of the point of intersection, in this way:

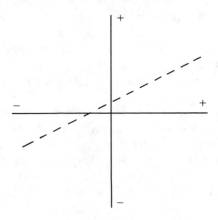

In effect such a brand is able to hold its market share constant even though its share of advertising is reduced below its market share level. This is precisely the situation for brands Q and R in our earlier example; their expenditure could afford to be well "below the odds," yet it was possible in many years for them to hold their market shares. The dynamic difference model provides here a precise quantifiable expression of those brands' added values, which can be seen to provide a benefit that for other brands without such added values costs substantial advertising dollars. This important demonstration and conclusion will be the foundation of an argument concerning pressure reduction experiments I shall make at the end of this book, one addressed directly to large advertisers.

5. The last point is not so positive, and it brings me back to the matter of campaign quality. The fact is that the dynamic difference is based on a constant relationship between advertising content and advertising effect. The model examines a number of years in a brand's life. In the 70 percent of cases in which the model fits, the quality of the campaign can only have made a noneffective or at least uniform contribution throughout. This must be so, because the model establishes that the direct relationship is between market share change and change in *quantity* of expenditure, with no reference to the quality of the advertising effort.

The person who believes in advertising cannot be happy that such a situation is normal in the real world, because he or she would find it deplorable to accept that advertising is solely or even mainly a matter of brute force. The reader will remember from chapter 1 that the small but important apparatus in the center of the large machine in my original analogy was apparently constructed by an artist and not by an artisan. What an artist is interested in is originality and economy of force, not just the application of force per se. The disheartening feature of the dynamic difference (although it is a simpler, more valid, and operationally more useful mathematical model than a number of the others used in the advertising industry) is that it is validated in the 70 percent of "normal" cases by demonstrating that what should be the most important factor in the whole advertising process—the quality of the campaign—makes a neutral contribution from year to year. This only goes to show that in most markets and most countries, the advertising process is a dull affair.

This is however a criticism of the advertising scene, not of the model, because an extra dimension can be added to the dynamic difference to help us quantify the effect of campaign changes. Work carried out in the United Kingdom by Jeremy Elliott of J. Walter Thompson suggests how to do this. The following diagram describes the dynamic difference regression for Kellogg's Rice Krispies for the years 1971–77. It can be seen that the line provides a reasonably good fit for the seven market observations. The line is of course upward sloping, and cuts the horizontal well to the right of the point of intersection of the axes. The brand is therefore without built-in advertising-related scale economies, since it needs increases in the share of advertising above the market share to maintain the status quo.

But in 1978, the campaign was changed. The new campaign, according to a number of other econometric measures, was highly successful in the marketplace. This success can also be expressed on the dynamic difference model by providing a new observation clearly incompatible with the old regression. This immediately suggests the possibility of an upward movement in the dynamic difference line (although it would need more years of data to confirm the permanence of the new relationship).

Another, rather dramatic way of using the former regression to evaluate the effect of the new campaign is by estimating that the 1978 sales increase would have needed a dynamic difference of ±8.5 points of advertising share in excess of brand share, if the former advertising–sales relationship had still been in operation. The difference between such an advertising investment and what was actually spent on the brand is equivalent to approximately a million dollars at 1978 media prices—a sharp reminder of the cash value of the creative content of an advertising campaign. It is also a reminder of the value of

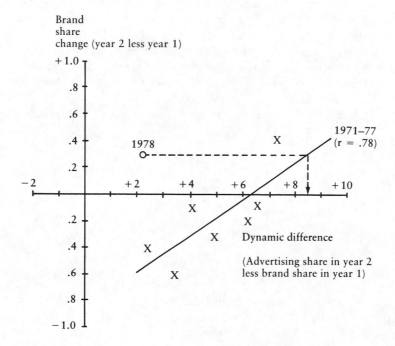

the dynamic difference model and its versatility in accommodating and quantifying the importance of an unexpected variable.[31]

This is by no means the end of my consideration of advertising weight. Indeed, there is another way of expressing a brand's response to change in pressure: by direct estimates of advertising elasticity. But this procedure is best viewed when compared with estimates of price elasticity, because there can be interesting links between the two. This is the substance of the next section of this chapter.

4. Price

Remember from chapter 3 that although it is difficult to estimate the price elasticity of a new brand for lack of historical data, it is common practice to do so for an ongoing brand. We are measuring here the immediate or short-term effect on consumer offtake of an increase or decrease in price; the elasticity is a calculation of the change in offtake resulting from a 1-percent change in price. Manufacturers normally have a lot of information to help them with the calculations because they can use regional as well as national retail audit figures. National data alone are sometimes enough, even a simple series like the following Nielsen data for a real brand. In this particular instance, we can judge by eye that the brand has a pronounced price elasticity.[32] Note that as the price premium is reduced, the market share goes up, while in the single year in which the price premium is increased, market share goes down markedly.

The price in this example is expressed as price premium above other brands, because by doing this we can eliminate the overall influence of inflation, which can be assumed to affect all brands in a more or less similar way.

	Price Premium (cents)	Market Share (%)
Year 1	7.3	19.9
Year 2	5.6	21.1
Year 3	3.9	23.6
Year 4	6.6	20.0
Year 5	5.8	22.8
Year 6	5.1	25.5
Year 7	5.0	26.6
Year 8	4.6	26.5
Year 9	3.9	28.1

Empirical studies tend to show quite a high degree of price elasticity for most brands within the limits explored. This qualification is important, because it can be dangerous to extrapolate the figures too far. However, since the operational value of price elasticity is to help to make marginal price adjustments, the limited span of the data does not matter too much. Simon Broadbent, former head of research at the London office of Leo Burnett, has published the following distribution of elasticities for 105 brands (some taken from other published studies) which all show some uniformity, suggesting that they are probably reasonably typical figures.[33]

Price Elasticity Range	Number of Brands
0 to −0.49	22
−0.50 to −0.99	20
−1.00 to −1.49	26
−1.50 to −1.99	16
−2.00 and over	21
Average −1.32	105

As a general confirmation of the relatively high degree of price elasticity for most brands, it has been estimated by econometric techniques that anything between 65 percent and 85 percent of the short-term variability of sales of most consumer brands can be explained by price alone.[34]

Another important related concept is the break-even elasticity, or the amount by which volume offtake could be reduced before a 1-percent price increase reduces *profit*. In an examination of twenty-three brands handled by the London office of the then D'Arcy, MacManus & Masius, the agency's operations director, Andrew Roberts, tabulated the distribution of both their actual price elasticities and their break-even elasticities. His actual price elasticities show a reasonably broad spread with an average figure of −1.67, a marginally higher figure than Broadbent's. But Roberts's calculation of break-even elasticities yields a most important conclusion: "Overall, these results suggest that half of the brands are seriously underpriced."[35] In this important number of examples, the price could be raised without any great effect on offtake, and the higher price would of course go virtually entirely into increased profit. Naturally, most of the brands to which this applies have the lower levels of elasticity. Thus, although price elasticities as a whole tend to be quite pronounced, the range is so great that there are many brands at the inelastic end that provide their manufacturers with significant opportunities for profit improvement by price increases.

These analyses should provide most manufacturers with food for thought, and encourage them to take a hard, objective look at their present prices and the way they are set. But there is more that can be done yet, because advertising is also an activity to which the elasticity concept can be applied. What is measured here is the short-term sales response to a change in advertising pressure (again within fairly narrow limits). The elasticity measure is the percentage change in offtake following a 1-percent change in advertising. The reader should note that the relationship here is direct, with an increase in the one leading to an increase in the other (unlike price elasticity, where the relationship is inverse).

Broadbent's data for eighty-four brands show a range that is probably typical of the field as a whole.

Advertising Elasticity Range	Number of Brands
0 to 0.09	27
0.10 to 0.19	27
0.20 to 0.29	12
0.30 to 0.39	5
0.40 to 0.49	4
0.50 and over	9
Average 0.20	84

As is obvious from this table, advertising elasticity tends to be less pronounced than price elasticity. But the break-even advertising elasticity is generally quite close to the actual advertising elasticity, so that in most cases manufacturers do not have the opportunity to boost profit simply by increasing advertising within the present parameters of a brand's price and profit.

The operational value of Broadbent's and Roberts's work is the way in which price elasticity and advertising elasticity can be treated together, with the intention of guiding manufacturers toward optimizing their profits. This parallel calculation is an especially good way of estimating the extra profit provided by a price increase, and the further extra profit provided by applying some of the first extra profit to increased advertising. All that Broadbent and Roberts claim for the technique is the ability to set directions with limited objectives. But even in this, they are talking of profit optimization in a greatly more calculated and precise way than is done at present in the vast majority of businesses. It is regrettable but generally true that manufacturers and their advertising agencies make insufficient use of historical information in their own possession. This is mainly because of lack of experience in handling such data; they simply are not conscious of its potential operational value. This lack of experience is compounded by shortages of time and statistical skills.[37]

There has also been a good deal of work in the United States in the exploration of advertising elasticity. A range of elasticities for a number of unspecified American brands has been published by Nariman Dhalla, formerly of J. Walter Thompson.[38] Dhalla's range of twenty-one short-term elasticities is not dissimilar to Broadbent's, with an average of 0.23 (compared with Broadbent's 0.20). But what makes Dhalla's analyses especially interesting is that he calculates for each short-term elasticity a long-term or cumulative elasticity as well. This is generally a good deal higher than the short-term figure, especially for cigarettes, liquor, gasoline, and proprietary drugs. What Dhalla is saying is that advertising has a measurable cumulative effect on sales in the long term over and beyond its immediate effect on sales in the short term. "Advertising may lead directly to sales; and many new buyers, being satisfied with the brand, may repeat the purchase. Or, the advertising stimulus, instead of winning fresh converts, may increase brand usage per customer; and this habit may persist far into the future."[39] This is a neat expression of the beneficial effect on sales, first, of favorable consumer experience which comes from use of the brand, and, second, of the added values which come from the advertising.

A consideration of such long-term effects brings me to my final and most dramatic demonstration of the use of market data to illustrate the workings of advertising. This analysis relates strictly to price. The technique, which was pioneered by Tom Corlett of J. Walter Thompson, London, and confirmed by further empirical work by his colleague Jeremy Elliott, demonstrates a clear operational distinction between the short and long term. It will be remembered that the dynamic difference, although it is built from a series of short-term changes, is really an examination of a long-term relationship. The advertising elasticity, on the other hand, is a short-term concept. What Corlett's work demonstrates is a short-term situation and how this changes in the longer term.

Corlett's starting point was to build a demand curve for a brand. He chose a major British brand in a reasonably large packaged goods market. (I was for a time the brand's account director, so I have first-hand experience of the case.) This calculation was possible because the brand is sold at various price premiums above other brands in different regions, with resultant differences in the brand's market share, so that a range of data could be provided for a time period of defined length. The demand curve follows the normal descending slope we would expect from a study of microeconomic theory.

The price is expressed as the premium over other brands, thus eliminating the effects of inflation (the practice followed by Nielsen in the example quoted at the beginning of this section). This also means that what is measured on one axis (the price of one brand compared with others in the market) is entirely consistent with what is measured on the other axis (the sales of one brand compared with others in the market).

The second stage in Corlett's work is the construction of a similar demand curve for a later period, after the exposure of advertising. I can attest to the fact that the campaign had initially been judged highly successful on the basis of all available objective measures: ex-factory sales, market share, attitudinal and other qualitative research, and popularity polls. But the best demonstration of the campaign's success is Corlett's analysis of the brand after the campaign's exposure, because his demand curve has moved quite significantly to the right:

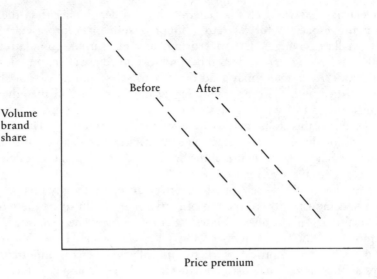

Volume
brand
share

Before   After

Price premium

This clearly shows that, after the advertising:

1. At a given price premium, the brand could now command a quantifiably greater brand share.
2. At a given brand share, the brand could now command a quantifiably greater price premium.

This enables us quite simply to make estimates of marginal sales revenue added by the campaign. These estimates can also be compared with the cost of the campaign, to indicate its marginal profitability to the manufacturer.[40] Jeremy Elliott shows a similar movement of the demand curve in his description of the Kellogg's Rice Krispies case.[41] And Eskin's work in the United States, although more complex, has similarities of method.[42]

5. Distribution

The reader will remember from chapter 3 that even for a new brand with growing distribution, shops running out of stock can be a problem that can cause widespread switching away from a brand to its competitors during the period just before the end of its sales cycle. With an ongoing brand, although the absolute level of distribution is generally steady once the distributional base has been built, the disappearance of retail stocks remains a real and continuous problem.

This can put consumers in a dilemma. They will normally buy a substitute brand if the brand they are looking for is not available. This will happen in 58 percent of cases, according to Nielsen data. If the size they seek is not on the shelf, they will buy another size of the same brand in 52 percent of cases, and buy a different brand altogether in a further 30 percent of cases. Retailers should realize that in the case of the missing brand, 42 percent of customers will leave the store with no purchase in the product category. In the case of the missing size, 18 percent will leave.[43] These represent absolute losses of business, in most cases to other stores.

This dilemma is by no means uncommon. Extensive Nielsen data describe the product categories in which homemakers are more loyal, and those in which they are less loyal to the brand they are looking for during any particular shopping trip. Among the categories in which homemakers will not readily accept a substitute are dentifrice, instant coffee, floor wax, and detergents. Among the categories in which substitutes are more readily acceptable are toilet tissues, crackers, ready-to-eat cereals, and canned beans. During the course of a year, homemakers will buy a number of different brands, but on many individual shopping trips they will be looking for a particular brand (perhaps for use by a particular member of the family), and will not buy another if this is not available. Interestingly enough, Nielsen shows a degree of correlation between the long-term level of advertising investments and the product fields in which customers are unwilling to substitute. This is but one example of the many beneficial side effects of advertising.

However retailers running out of stock remains a stubborn problem, with dangers of marginal but real losses of business. A normal out-of-stock level is considered to be 3 percent. With computerized stock control linked to the checkout, there is no real reason for manufacturers and retailers even to accept as much as this. But 6 percent and more is by no means uncommon. With the resultant level of sales loss (which is as much as 6 percent of case sales over a year in a specific and typical Nielsen example), manufacturers even more than retailers will continue to pay a significant penalty for their inability to solve what is in essence a relatively simple mechanical problem, and one which it is in the interests of manufacturers and retailers alike to solve.

Beyond the Primary Growth Cycle

Now that we have reviewed the factors that matter most to an ongoing brand, we can point our attention toward the future and the path that a brand will normally take if it is to be a long-term contender in a market. Whether its long-term sales trend is going to be upward, static, or even declining, its path will commonly ebb and flow in accordance with regular planned and announced improvements, a process known as restaging or recycling (commonly known in Europe as "relaunching"). This is the normal and indeed necessary strategy for companies in competitive markets. There is strong Nielsen evidence from both the United States and Great Britain that recycling is a much more efficient means of increasing market share than attempting to prolong brands without the novelty and incentive for consumer reappraisal that recycling provides. In fact, for a brand which is *not* restaged, odds are about three to one that it will not increase its long-term market share.[44]

A restage covers a shorter period than the primary growth cycle for a brand, perhaps one year compared with two for the primary cycle.[45] This does not mean that a brand is recycled every year, but the recycle stage, which occurs perhaps once every three or four years, itself lasts for about a year. In view of the lead time for the necessary changes in product, packaging, and advertising, planning is needed at least a year in advance of the beginning of the recycle. As suggested at the beginning of this chapter, the manufacturer of a new brand will need to be thinking about the first restage as soon as an initial launch is under way.

Although with restaging, there is still a continuously important role for functional improvement, advertising now joins functional performance in the front-running position, becoming one of the two dominant influences on the development of a brand, cementing the loyalty of trialists, and working with other stimuli to extend the consumer franchise. By this time the added values will have begun to accumulate.

Nielsen data from the history of 320 different brands make it clear that 61 percent of the vehicles for recycling are connected with advertising. We are talking here about the 41 percent of recycles that involve product innovation plus increased advertising investments and new campaigns, a further 10 percent involving merely increased advertising expenditure, and a further 10 percent again involving more expenditure and new campaigns. The question of a new campaign for a restage is a matter of careful judgment. While the task of advertising during the primary growth cycle is mainly to contribute (together with consumer promotions and packaging) to meeting the first object of consumer trial, these introductory advertising campaigns often quite rightly contain first indications of the added values that will become more important during the subsequent life of the brand. The added values to be built up in the long term will also be expressed in the pack designs, which should be planned sensitively to promise more for the brand than functional performance alone.

During a brand's long-term development there will be a continued and growing advertising emphasis on those added values that soon become its unique property. With progressive restaging, product improvements can be evaluated alongside the established and accepted battery of functional and nonfunctional benefits that the brand provides. Recycling is thus the opportunity for the manufacturer to bring a brand now and again quite sharply to the attention of existing users and potential new users alike. These people will probably by now know quite a lot about the brand, but this is the opportunity for the manufacturer to encourage them to look at it with fresh eyes and be made aware that it is not falling behind in functional performance, but instead is being improved to meet the challenge of newer brands.

Restaging is however not only a means of introducing functional improvements. It is also extremely useful for the introduction of new variants (types, flavors, colors, and so forth) which if the manufacturer judges the situation well, can add market share to a brand without cannibalizing its existing sales. The word *new* is of great value in all matters of communication (packaging and display as well as advertising) in which the consumer is encouraged to reappraise a brand. *New* has always had a special connotation in advertising circles; most experienced copywriters attest to its continued value and the way that it should be used for as long as possible after the beginning of a restage.[46] There is also a group of related words (*now, announcing, introducing, improvement,* for example) that offend the fastidious because of their overuse. But successful creators of advertisements harden their hearts to such niceties. David Ogilvy is such a one: "Don't turn up your nose at these clichés. They may be shopworn but they work."[47]

The Argument in Brief

The initial sales of virtually all brands of packaged goods follow a similar pattern in that they rise to an early peak, and then settle down to a lower, steadier level. The rise is partially influenced by increasing distribution, but more heavily by increasing sales per shop, an indication of consumer repeat purchase. Simple models based on test market experience can be applied to the earliest retail audit data measuring national sales and distribution, and these can be used to forecast the path of sales during the period (which averages rather more than two years) before a brand reaches its stable national level. This period is tending to shorten as markets become more crowded and competitive. This puts increased emphasis on the importance of early plans for restaging.

Trade and consumer promotions account for more money than advertising, out of the average manufacturer's total expenditure above and below the line. There is a significant dissonance between the short-term demand for promotions to increase sales, and the long-term (but normally less insistent) demand for advertising to increase the numbers and loyalty of consumers. This dissonance is frequently expressed by budgetary adjustments during the last quarter of any year, under unplanned and often crisis conditions, to enable tonnage sales targets to be met. The pressures to increase promotions are increasing over time because of the growing strength of the retail trade.

Advertising, expressed as a share of advertising voice in a market, can be viewed in parallel with the market share of an individual brand. For large brands, the market share normally *exceeds* the advertising share; for smaller brands, the opposite is true. This general relationship is strong evidence for the existence of advertising-related scale economies for large brands.

This chapter has examined the influence of advertising share on market share, allowing for the possible contamination of the reverse influence of the sales level on the advertising level. In the cases of about 70 percent of ongoing brands, there is an apparent relationship (from advertising to sales) which is both linear and causal. The dynamic difference regression describing this relationship can be used for two purposes: first, to predict the effect on market share of a change in advertising weight within the regression; and second, to demonstrate the financial productivity of any campaign change having effects beyond its parameters.

The marginal extra productivity of a new campaign can also be estimated approximately by the use of the moving demand curve technique. Another productive device, the use of advertising and price elasticities, can be used not only for sales maximization, but also for sales optimization to maximize profit. Although the data needed to compute these elasticities are difficult to put together, the technique of manipulating them operationally is relatively simple to understand and apply. The other mathematical techniques discussed in this chapter are in general easier to compute, and they are also simple in their application.

Notes

1. See, for example, Don E. Schultz and William A. Robinson, *Sales Promotion Management* (Chicago: Crain Books, 1982), pp. 469–80; and Robert M. Prentice, "How to Split Your Marketing Funds between Advertising and Promotion," *Advertising Age* (January 10, 1977): 41–44.

2. James O. Peckham, Sr., *The Wheel of Marketing*, p. 13. The data came from a study produced by *Progressive Grocer.*

3. *Ibid.*, p. 10.

4. *Ibid.*, pp. 55–56, 64; *Nielsen Researcher* (May–June 1967): 3–7.

5. John Davis, *The Sales Curves of New Products* (London: J. Walter Thompson, 1965).

6. Peckham, *The Wheel of Marketing*, pp. 2, 34.

7. F. Beaven Ennis, *Marketing Norms for Product Managers* (New York: Association of National Advertisers, 1985), p. 81.

8. Prentice, "How to Split Your Marketing Funds between Advertising and Promotion": 42.

9. Peckham, *The Wheel of Marketing*, pp. 33, 35.

10. John A. Quelch, "It's Time to Make Trade Promotions More Productive," *Harvard Business Review* 61 (May–June 1983): 130–36.

11. Peckham, *The Wheel of Marketing*, p. 48.

12. This point was raised in chapter 2 in connection with the displays of generic cornflakes and Kellogg's. See chapter 2, note 54.

13. Peckham, *The Wheel of Marketing*, p. 31.

14. *Ibid.*, p. 30.

15. Quelch, "It's Time to Make Trade Promotions More Productive": 135–36.

16. Peckham, *The Wheel of Marketing*, pp. 38–39.

17. Stephen King, *What Is a Brand?*, p. 5.

18. Andrew Roberts, "The Decision between Above and Below the Line," *Admap* (December 1980): 588–92.

19. *Nielsen Researcher* (July–August 1973): 4.

20. Peckham, *The Wheel of Marketing*, pp. 41–48.

21. *Ibid.*, p. 43.

22. King, *What Is a Brand?*, pp. 5–7.

23. Peckham, *The Wheel of Marketing*, p. 48.

24. James Webb Young, *The Diary of an Ad Man* (Chicago: Advertising Publications, 1944), p. 230.

25. Stephen King, *Advertising as a Barrier to Market Entry*, p. 15.

26. Peckham, *The Wheel of Marketing*, p. 73.

27. Jean Jacques Lambin, *Advertising, Competition and Market Conduct in Oligopoly over Time* (New York: American Elsevier, 1976), pp. 127–29.

28. M.J. Moroney, *Facts from Figures* (Harmondsworth, Middlesex, United Kingdom: Penguin Books, 1951).

29. Peckham, *The Wheel of Marketing*, pp. 80–91.
The regression can be described algebraically or geometrically. The latter has been chosen because it makes for easier exposition to the reader who is unsophisticated in mathematics.

30. *Ibid.*, p. 84.

31. Jeremy Elliott, "Kellogg's Rice Krispies: the Effect of a New Creative Execution" in *Advertising Works: Papers from the I.P.A. Effectiveness Awards* (London: Holt, Rinehart and Winston, 1981), pp. 86–87.

32. Peckham, *The Wheel of Marketing*, p. 22.

33. Simon Broadbent, "Price and Advertising: Volume and Profit," *Admap* (November 1980): 536.

34. Tom Corlett, "Anyone for Econometrics?" *Admap* (August 1978).

35. Andrew Roberts, "The Decision between Above and Below the Line": 592.

36. Broadbent, "Price and Advertising: Volume and Profit": 536.

37. Simon Broadbent, "Practical Economics and Computing at Brand Level," *International Journal of Advertising* 2 (January–March 1983): 3–15.

38. Nariman K. Dhalla, "Assessing the Long Term Value of Advertising," *Harvard Business Review* 56 (January–February 1978): 87–95.

39. *Ibid.*, 87.

40. Tom Corlett, "How to Make Sense of Market Analysis," *Campaign* (May 26, 1978).

41. Elliott, "Kellogg's Rice Krispies: The Effect of a New Creative Execution," pp. 84–85.
Both Corlett and Elliott put the price on the horizontal axis and quantity on the

vertical, the opposite to how they are plotted in the geometry of price theory. But this idiosyncrasy does not affect the analysis.

42. Gerald J. Eskin, "A Case for Test Market Experiments," *Journal of Advertising Research* (April 1975): 27–33.

43. Peckham, *The Wheel of Marketing*, pp. 16–18.

44. *Nielsen Researcher* (May–June 1967): 6–7.

45. Peckham, *The Wheel of Marketing*, pp. 57–58.

46. This period has been set rather arbitrarily at six months by the Federal Trade Commission. Samm Sinclair Baker, *The Permissible Lie* (Cleveland: World Publishing, 1968), p. 24.

47. David Ogilvy, *Confessions of an Advertising Man* (New York: Atheneum, 1963, reprinted 1984), pp. 105–06.

5

The Mature Brand and the Consumer—The Nature of Repeat-Buying Theory

"The rule is, jam tomorrow and jam yesterday—but never jam *today*."

"It must come sometimes to jam today," Alice objected.

"No, it can't," said the Queen. "It's jam every other day: today isn't any other day, you know."

This chapter concerns uniformity and regularity. The reader may be surprised that such words could ever be used to describe matters as naturally erratic and subject to the vagaries of competition as the marketing and advertising of a brand. The previous two chapters were devoted to the most important factors that shape a brand from its conception to its maturity; and while there is a respectable number of consistent and generalizable underlying patterns, these are far short of anything deserving to be described as uniform and regular.

This chapter will demonstrate that the mature brand which has joined the user's repertoire and has its niche in a stationary market, acquires some of the stasis of that market. When this happens, the role of advertising changes from aggressively promoting growth, to a more restrained protection of the status quo.

There are many circumstances when a manufacturer may indeed not wish to increase the sales and market share of his brands. Four of the most obvious are:

1. If the marginal extra profit yielded by the extra sales is less than the advertising and other costs required to achieve these sales;

2. If the growth in the market share of one brand carries the danger of clipping a share point or two off other brands the firm markets, with the result that overall share is not much increased;

3. If the resultant total increase in company market share will make the firm

vulnerable to investigation to the Federal Trade Commission (or its equivalent in other countries);

4.   If the company has other priorities for funds and management time.

The larger a manufacturer becomes, the more these circumstances will operate; the greater will be his stake in the market and his interest in its preservation; and the more the firm will act protectively—especially in product, marketing, and advertising strategies—in order to maintain the existing situation.

The reader may wonder whether the regularity and uniformity to be described shortly might in any way be created by manufacturers' strategies. In my opinion, the answer is no. Manufacturers' strategies, in particular those for their advertising, do not have strong force in a world of free choice. They cannot create demand or alter beliefs, although they are quite effective in reinforcing what is there already. This fundamental limitation is the ultimate reason why so many new brands fail: manufacturers are inefficient at discovering things that have real potential interest to consumers, but they cannot build business with anything less.

Consider one aspect of uniformity and regularity: consumers' response to advertising stimuli. Where the influence of an advertisement can be isolated from the other variables in the marketing mix, there is an invariable regularity of patterns—if advertisements *A, B,* and *C* yield different results from one group of consumers, they will almost certainly yield the same differences from other groups of consumers. The evidence for this statement comes from the field of direct response. Indeed, I have worked with an advertiser whose operation provided firsthand evidence that consumers in one *country* respond to advertisements in a way closely similar to consumers in another country.[1] Facts of this sort are normally lacking in debates on the controversial and much misunderstood subject of international advertising.

If readers remain skeptical about this uniformity of response to campaigns (or about the separate question of whether direct response can provide a reliable measure of trends and tendencies in nonspecialist fields), they should consider the vast worldwide use of well-known advertising strategies and campaigns in the most substantial and competitive consumer product fields. And while there is a scarcity of hard facts on the testing of such procedures in an experimental, scientific way, the overwhelming *opinion* of advertisers and agencies, based on their direct and often extensive experience, is that such strategies and campaigns are probably effective in most circumstances. And they work with a sometimes surprising uniformity of effect in countries that are far apart geographically as well as in culture, income, and sophistication.[2]

Response to advertising is not however the main concern of this chapter. We are concerned here with patterns of consumer buying, and their relevance to a brand's advertising strategy. An individual's purchasing behavior may at first glance appear erratic and haphazard. But the more we study such behavior over time, and the more we look at the aggregate behavior of large numbers of consumers, the more regular and predictable it all appears to be.

Previous chapters used retail audit data to study total volumes of sales. These data of course are the result of the accumulation of many individual buying decisions. But we have not begun to study the purchasing process itself, only its overall effects. We have seen for instance that changes in advertising pressure can lead to differences in sales. But the problem with using these data is that they tell us the "what" but certainly not the "how." If we wish to explore the "how," we must work from the assumption that the consumer sees the advertising and responds in some way. To examine this process, we are forced to look at parts of the mechanism of our large machine that are well below the surface. And in order to make such an examination, we shall need different research data from the aggregated data we have used in the analysis so far.

We shall now need to look at the purchasing behavior of individual consumers over time. We can only do this by studying data, continuously collected with the use of diaries by panels of consumers, that expose what brands are bought on what occasions by whom.

There is a second problem with concentrating on aggregated data, one which will be important when we study specifically the effects of advertising exposure. Aggregated data can create a misleading appearance of a direct association between a brand's advertising and its sales, when in fact the advertising and the sales might both be separately influenced by an unconnected third factor. A well-known example of this is the presence of children, which causes a household to use more of certain brands and also to watch more television. It is therefore often misleading to attribute high sales of brand *A* to heavy television advertising for that brand. The household using brand *A* heavily may also be exposed to considerable advertising for competing brands, just because the television may be on for longer periods than the average. There is therefore no certainty that it is the brand *A* advertising which has the decisive effect.[3]

These problems are avoided if we concentrate on the study of individual consumers' diary records. If we are examining the influence of a brand's advertising on its sales, we can relate individual buyers' purchasing to their exposure to advertising, and thus establish real rather than spurious relationships. Diary studies, because of the way they track data through time, are sometimes described as longitudinal. They produce large quantities of data which are extremely cumbersome to handle. Researchers have however developed the techniques and the patience to interpret the information, and this chapter is illustrated virtually exclusively by data collected by this means.

Let us start by looking at typical purchasing patterns. Remembering the points made in chapter 1 that the average homemaker buys a brand not once but repeatedly, and that she or he normally buys more than one brand in any product field. Individual purchasing patterns when viewed longitudinally can look something like the following. The letters refer to specific brands and to real homemakers. There are different patterns which occur regularly, and these can be described in the following ways:

Cyclical: AEAEAEA

Trend: AAACCAACBABBB

Conversion: AAABBBBBB

Spasmodic peak: EEEEEBBBBBEEEE

The patterns are commonly much more complex, with one type superimposed on others, as in the following example of one homemaker's purchases of different brands of tea: BOOcGBOCOBGBGABBGBBcBGBCBBGGBBB This customer "shows a trend towards brand *B* and a cycle in buying brand *G*, which recurs on average every 4.4 times."[4]

This complexity may surprise readers not familiar with reasons why homemakers need to buy a number of different brands. At least three factors are at work. First, there is the need for more than one functionally different brand for different purposes; brand choice is determined here by the homemaker's judgment of the different brands' functional performance for these different purposes. Second, the consumer is normally buying for other members of the household and for visitors, who in turn have different functional needs. Third, homemakers want variety as such, a factor that makes it easier than it might at first appear for a manufacturer to get people to try a new brand once. These three explanations, provided by the British analyst John Treasure, are amplified by a battery of data demonstrating the degree of multibrand purchasing in different markets. Treasure examines fifty different product fields over a six-month period and finds multibrand purchasing in every one of them, although the number of buyers who buy more than one brand varies greatly from a low of 17 percent for starch to a high of 87 percent for butter and margarine. Typically 50 percent of buyers in a market buy two brands or more.[5]

But only rarely do homemakers split their patronage equally between brands. "For most housewives a brand either accounts for a high proportion of her purchases or for a very low proportion . . . although there may be several brands on the housewife's shopping list, she tends to have one particular favorite."[6] This introduces the notion of the homemaker's major and minor brands, which will be important to us when we consider advertising strategy. But to put a major brand into proper perspective, it must not be thought that it is by any means a dominant purchase in any product for normal homemakers. On the contrary, an individual's combined purchases of other brands will almost always be greater than purchases of her or his major brand. A homemaker is likely to have a single major brand in a product field plus a handful of minor brands, and these various brands will all be bought at different regularities. "A major characteristic of frequently bought goods is that consumers vary greatly in how often they buy them."[7]

However, despite the complexity and seeming irregularity of purchasing patterns, there is a large degree of underlying consistency; to illustrate this I shall be referring extensively to the work of Andrew Ehrenberg, the British academic now recognized as the most informed student of the *facts* of consumer purchasing behavior and a major contributor to our understanding of the role of advertising in influencing this behavior. I shall be referring to the underlying theory described in his classic monograph *Repeat-Buying: Theory and Applications*[8] and to data from various American markets published in *Understanding Buying Behavior,* a series of essays he wrote in cooperation with his colleague G.L. Goodhardt. The data base is wide, covering more than thirty product fields, leading brands in each field, different pack sizes, the United States and various European countries, a thirty-year time span, various demographic subgroups, and periods of time ranging from one week to twelve months.[9]

The work of Ehrenberg and other analysts on this enormous data base disclosed patterns of consumer behavior consistent enough to form the basis of mathematical models. With their use, predictions of behavior patterns in other markets were compared with observed behavior, and prediction and reality generally more or less coincided, thus providing further validation for the models. This procedure was carried out so extensively that we are able without exaggeration to talk of generalizable patterns.

The underlying assumption to these generalizable patterns is that the market in which they hold must conform to the stationary conditions described in chapter 3. As a specific illustration of these conditions, I shall describe some other features of the real market I used for the discussions of brand positioning in chapter 3 and advertising weight and share of market in chapter 4.

In this particular market, the data show an 8-percent advance in total volume in the five years 1974–79, or an average growth of under 2 percent per annum. In the most recent two years, the total size of the market did not change by a fraction of a percentage point. As far as individual brands are concerned, the reader will remember from chapter 4 that the market shares of the ten leading brands totalled 78 percent in 1979. Their combined shares in 1974 had totalled 72 percent, but in 1974 only nine of the ten had been on the market. The tenth brand, introduced in the intervening period, reached a market share of 7 to 8 percent in 1979. None of the remaining brands however gained or lost brand share by more than a point or two, except for brand Q, which as described in chapter 4 lost three points of share, from a high of 18 percent in 1975 to a low of 15 percent in 1979, mainly because its manufacturer did not sustain the necessary volume of advertising support.

This typical market then exhibits only modest mutation over the years, and nothing resembling strong trends which in Ehrenberg and Goodhardt's definition would make a market nonstationary. Stationary assumptions not only provide the underlying conditions for the models, which describe normal patterns. The models have a further use, because exceptions that they sometimes throw up can be explained in terms of nonstationary elements. For instance, if consumer purchasing of a brand does not appear to be happening as predicted, this is probably because there is something abnormal about that brand: it is following to some degree an upward or downward sales trend. It is normally possible to isolate the reasons for this trend, assess the relative importance of such reasons, and thereby draw actionable conclusions.

Consumer Sales Defined in Consumer Terms

We are now in a position to get much closer to what sales actually represent than the earlier aggregate figures, which were based either on a manufacturer's shipments or retail audit estimates. We need to do this to get closer to consumers and details of their behavior in order to understand more adequately how this behavior can be influenced by advertising. A single example of the available choices would be to increase sales either by getting new people to buy once, or else by getting existing buyers to buy more often. We cannot tell which is the better alternative until we understand more about consumers and their buying habits.

In consumer terms, sales of a brand in any period can be calculated from the following equation:[10]

sales = number of households in the country
     x proportion of households buying the brand
     x number of purchase occasions per buyer
     x number of packs per purchase
     x weight or price per pack.

Looking at one fairly important brand in the U.S. breakfast cereal market, Nabisco Shredded Wheat, we can estimate sales over a particular four-week period at 3 million pounds. This is calculated from our equation in the following way:

sales of 3.0 million lb. = 85.4 million households in the United States
x 0.034 (the 3.4 percent who bought in four weeks)
x 1.3 purchase occasions per buyer
x 1.05 packs per purchase
x ¾ lb. (12 oz.) per pack.

Of the five elements on the right side of the equation, two are more or less constant, varying little between brands (or between time periods of the same length in the short and medium term). These are the size of the household population and the average number of packs per purchase. In some although not all markets, there is a uniformity of pack sizes. The other two factors are the penetration (proportion of households buying a brand) and the number of purchase occasions per buyer. These do vary between brands, especially the proportion of households who buy (the brand's penetration). Consumer panel diaries provide the data on which estimates for any specific brand can be made, like those in the above calculation.

As explained, the equation relates to a four-week period, but a similar figure could be worked out for any purchasing period, although the shortest worth looking at is normally a week. Remember, purchasing behavior takes more regular forms as we consider longer periods of time. Behavior which may seem erratic on a week by week basis looks very regular when looked at over months, quarters, or years. We shall therefore confine ourselves to longer periods of four weeks, thirteen weeks, and fifty-two weeks.

Returning to the equation, we can see that sales in a period can be determined from the penetration and the purchase frequency, on the assumption that we also know the three other factors, which is normally possible in practice, since they are mostly constants. Ehrenberg's models can now be used to extend our knowledge. From the facts of penetration and purchase frequency, it is possible to predict frequency distribution, repeat buying, and multibrand buying. This is enough information to enable us to understand consumer purchasing in a market clearly and precisely. Here are the five key variable factors:

Penetration: percentage (normally of households) buying at least one pack of a brand,

Purchase frequency: number of purchase occasions per buyer,

Frequency distribution: number of buyers who buy a brand at different frequencies (once, twice, and so forth),

Repeat buying: percentage of buyers who continue to buy the brand,

Multibrand buying: percentage of buyers who also purchase another brand or brands.

All these factors must relate to time periods of the same length. But the mathematical models whose workings will be illustrated function equally well no matter what time period is chosen. We can compare week with week, month with month, quarter with quarter, or year with year.

Note that the word *penetration* has the special and precise meaning of the percentage buying at least one pack of a brand in a particular period. Confusingly enough, the word is used in at least three other senses in marketing literature. In the Ted Bates advertising agency it is "the number of people who remember your current advertising;" the unpenetrated are those who do not remember.[11] In the automobile market, it means the market share of a single make of car. It is also sometimes used to mean the percentage of people who have ever bought a brand.[12] The reader must be careful not to be misled by these different meanings, but to concentrate on the precise meaning used in the present context: the proportion of buyers in a stated and limited time period.

Of these five factors, the key ones are *penetration* and *purchase frequency*. Their importance is such that all other variables in some way stem from them. In fact the main use of the mathematical models is to make projections of the other factors on the simple basis of estimates of penetration and frequency in one period.

Predictive Models in Action

This chapter concerns typical applications of the models described by Ehrenberg. Mathematically sophisticated readers should note the technical background and the algebra by which he discusses these models.[13] Any mathematical formulae I use will be severe simplifications which can be understood by the most nonmathematical reader.

There are three main models used by Ehrenberg. First is the negative binomial distribution (NBD), and second, a simplified version of this, the logarithmic series distribution (LSD). These relate to the purchasing of a single brand in a stationary market. They have a strong empirical base and have been extensively validated. "Given the value of the brand's penetration and average purchase frequency in some specific 'base period' like a particular quarter of a year, the models can predict all the detailed aspects of buying frequency in that time period and also in any other periods of any length."[14] Third is the Dirichlet model (named after a nineteenth century German mathematician) dealing with multibrand buying. It fits well with the observed data, but the empirical base and the amount of validation are not as extensive as with the NBD/LSD models. The Dirichlet model can predict penetration and average purchase frequencies for different brands on the basis of the market share of each and certain characteristics of the product category as a whole: the percentage of households who bought any brands in the category in the period in question, the average frequency of purchase of the buyers, and the average frequency of purchase of the average brand.

I am now going to examine some applications of these models. The data relate to real and typical brands. But understand that the models are not just illustrative. They are capable of providing precise estimates for any brands and markets in which a reader may be interested, and can provide the appropriate data inputs.

The original analyses frequently provided two sets of data—the theoretical data provided by the model and the observed data provided directly from consumer research (collected and tabulated in order to verify the predictions of the model). The two series are mostly closely similar to one another. But when I have had a choice of data, I have invariably selected what was observed rather than what was predicted, and this is what we shall mainly see in the following tables. This procedure does not imply any lack of confidence in the models' predictions. Rather, I always see a value in approaching as closely as possible to the real world.

1. Penetration

Penetration varies a good deal between brands, and indeed most clearly differentiates one brand from another when we try to explain sales differences.[15] But it remains consistent for any one brand in different time periods, so long as they are of equal length.

	Four-Week Penetrations (%)				
	Kellogg's Corn Flakes	GM Wheaties	Nabisco Shredded Wheat	Quaker Cap'n Crunch	Post Sugar Crisps
Weeks 1–4	11	6	3	3	2
Weeks 5–8	11	7	3	3	2
Weeks 9–12	10	6	3	4	2
Weeks 13–16	11	7	5	3	2
Weeks 17–20	11	6	4	4	3
Weeks 21–24	12	6	4	4	3

The very uniformity of these figures is however rather misleading, because the people who buy a brand in one period are *not* all going to be the same as those who buy it in the next. The table must not be misread as implying that they will. In fact, as we move from the first to the second period, some buyers will drop out (they will mostly only be lost temporarily, not forever), and some new buyers will come in. The penetration in two periods (we might say "net penetration") will therefore always be greater than that in one period. Of course this (net) penetration grows with the length of the period examined.

Penetration Growth

	Kellogg's Corn Flakes	GM Wheaties	Nabisco Shredded Wheat	Quaker Cap'n Crunch	Post Sugar Crisps
Percentage of households buying in:					
1 week	3%	2%	1%	2%	1%
1 month	11	6	3	3	2
1 quarter	22	12	7	6	5
1 year	41	23	17	16	14

From this, readers can easily see how the net penetration for each brand is progressively growing; but they can also make out that it is growing at a somewhat diminishing rate. If the growth had been at a uniform rate, the penetration figures for Shredded Wheat for example would have been 1, 4, 13, 52 (in direct proportion to the number of weeks) instead of the actual 1, 3, 7, 17. This deceleration in growth is caused by a slowing down in the percentage of new buyers in each new period. The percentage of buyers who have bought before must therefore be increasing. This is a reflection of the reappearance of the infrequent purchaser who, to paraphrase the White Queen, buys jam last month, next month, but not this month.

2. Purchase Frequency

There are five important points to be made about average purchase frequency.[16] In the first place, it tends to be low. Over the course of a year it is rarely more than about six purchases for even large brands of packaged goods, and it is commonly much smaller than that. (The single notable exception to this rule is purchases of brands of cigarettes, but this market exhibits a number of exceptional patterns.) This fact of low purchase frequency is another way of saying that most major brands do not account for the majority of people's purchases. No matter how attached a housewife is to her major brand, she will buy a larger total quantity of other brands.

The second point about average purchase frequency is that, surprisingly enough, although it varies between markets, it does not vary very much *between brands in any market,* as seen from the following average quarterly purchase frequencies for presweetened breakfast cereals.

	Average Purchases per Buyer in 13-Week Period
Sugar Frosted Flakes	2.2
Life	2.7
Cap'n Crunch	2.4
Froot Loops	1.9
Sugar Crisps	1.8
Lucky Charms	2.1
Trix	1.8

In this market Sugar Frosted Flakes has a much larger market share than Trix, yet the average buyer of Sugar Frosted Flakes buys only slightly more often than the average Trix buyer. But if the difference in the number of purchase occasions will not explain the differences in market share, the relative penetration of the two brands will. The quarterly penetration figures are 12 percent for Sugar Frosted Flakes and 5 percent for Trix; this relationship between penetration and market share is what makes penetration the key variable in describing consumer buying behavior.

The third feature of a brand's average frequency is that it varies very little between periods of equal length.

	Average Purchases per Buyer of Nabisco Shredded Wheat
Weeks 1–4	1.3
Weeks 5–8	1.3
Weeks 9–12	1.3
Weeks 13–16	1.3
Weeks 17–20	1.3
Weeks 21–24	1.3

The consistency in these frequency figures resembles the consistency in the penetration figures for equal length periods.

My fourth point suggests a parallel between average frequency and net penetration, because, like penetration, average purchase frequency grows over time, but at a diminishing rate.

	Average Purchases per Buyer of Nabisco Shredded Wheat
In one week	1.1
In one month	1.3
In one quarter	2.0
In one year	3.8

However, the rate of growth is here very much slower than the penetration growth (where, it will be remembered, the comparable figures were 1, 3, 7, 17). This is a reflection of penetration growth taking place through the entry of increasingly infrequent buyers.

My fifth and last point about frequency concerns its direct relationship with the penetration variable. In fact, when a brand reaches a high absolute level of penetration, this is likely to be accompanied by an *increase* in the purchase frequency. This double effect is something akin to an economy of scale, and indeed there is more than one type of scale effect associated with high penetration. I shall coin the phrase *penetration supercharge* to describe these effects, whose importance will be considered later in this chapter.

3. *Frequency Distribution*

The normal frequency distribution of purchases of a brand is (as common sense might lead us to expect) extremely skewed. The pattern is a regular one. Given normal penetration levels, much the largest figure will be in the "no-purchase" category. As we progress upward in terms of purchase frequency, there is a relatively high figure in the "one-purchase" category but thereafter the figures trail away.[17] The following distribution is for purchases of Nabisco Shredded Wheat in one quarter. Although the data come from the observed readings, the predicted readings are (as usual) close to them. The predictions were drawn up on the basis of two simple inputs: the brand's penetration in the quarter (which the reader will remember from the discussion of penetration growth, to be 7 percent—to be precise, the figure is 7.3 percent); and the average purchase frequency of 2.0 (from the discussion of frequency in the previous section).

Frequency Distribution of Purchase of Shredded Wheat: Number of Purchases in 13 Weeks	
None	92.7%
One	4.3
Two	1.1

Three	1.0
Four	0.2
Five	0.4
Six or more	0.3

The widespread existence of this type of skewed distribution has led to the formulation of the so-called "80:20 rule," which is normally an excellent approximation of the concentration of heavy purchasing in any market. This can be expressed in one of two ways: either in the form that "the 80-percent lightest and 20-percent heaviest users of a brand each accounts for about half of its sales;" or that "if buyers are divided into three groups, the 50-percent lightest, 30-percent medium, and 20-percent heaviest buyers, then these groups often account for about 20 percent, 30 percent and 50 percent of sales respectively."

It is salutary to realize from a table like the previous one that even fairly large brands have such low levels of purchase: a third of all Shredded Wheat purchasing in this thirteen-week period was done by buyers who bought only once. There is also a significant technical point connected with this "once-only" figure: although in most respects frequency distribution patterns are regular, and observed distribution coincides with the model, the model frequently underestimates one figure, the amount of single purchasing (probably in most cases trial purchasing). In the same way, the model commonly slightly underestimates long-period penetrations because it fails to take account of the frequent presence of trial purchasers appearing for the first time. This is a nonstationary element—the model cannot therefore cope adequately with it—but it opens a most interesting avenue for exploration, because it is the very element that leads to brand growth. Net penetration growth almost invariably takes place by the addition of a small number of low-frequency buyers; the manufacturer hopes that some of these can be persuaded by the added values of the brand, reinforced by its advertising, to use it more often. We shall shortly look at this point in detail.

4. Repeat Buying

It is a relatively simple matter for the models to predict the percentage of purchasers of a brand in one period who will repurchase in a subsequent period. It is also simple to predict their frequency of purchase in that second period.[18]

If again we use Shredded Wheat as our example (with its 7.3 percent penetration and average frequency of 2.0 in one thirteen-week period), the model predicts that 58 percent of the buyers in this quarter will repurchase in the next. (The actual observed figure was 59 percent.) Making the normal assumption that there will be no significant change in the total number of purchasers between the two periods, then in the second quarter 59 percent of purchasers will be repeaters from the first quarter and 41 percent will be new purchasers (much the majority being very infrequent purchasers from earlier periods). Thus the increase in net penetration in the second quarter will be by the addition of 41 percent: from the actual net level in the first quarter of 7 percentage points to a new net level of 10 percentage points in the two quarters. (This was the actual observed figure.)

From the discussion of frequency, the reader will remember that the higher levels of penetration in a particular period are associated with higher general levels of purchase frequency in that period (a phenomenon contributing to the penetration supercharge, the tendency of a large brand to have a higher frequency of purchase than a small brand). But the effect does not stop there, because higher penetration is also associated with higher repurchase rates in the next period. If a brand is in the 5-percent to 10-percent penetration range (Shredded Wheat for example), an average purchase frequency of 2.0 will predict (as we have seen) a repurchase rate of 58 percent. But if a brand's penetration is as high as 20 percent, predicted repurchase goes up to 60 percent with further increases in frequency causing predictions of even further increases in repurchase. Again, this is a scale effect for a brand expressed in consumer terms.

Among repurchasers in a second period, frequency of purchase will tend to be higher than in the earlier one, in the Shredded Wheat case, at 2.52 purchases compared with the earlier period's 2.0. But among *new* purchasers in the second period, average frequency will be at a much lower level, an approximately constant level of 1.4.

Sole purchasers (people who use only one brand and are therefore by definition repeat purchasers if they are regular buyers of the product field at all) are normally a small group, especially if we confine the definition to buyers of just one brand over a reasonably long time period. Again using Shredded Wheat as our example, only about 18 percent of buyers are sole buyers over the course of one month, 6 percent over a quarter, and less than 1 percent over a year. When these purchasers are analyzed by their frequency of purchase, they appear no different from the much larger number of multibrand purchasers, so that there is no particularly heavy usage to justify special attention being paid to these buyers. Therefore, for operational purposes, the small group of sole users is generally neither large nor attractive enough to justify any special marketing effort to exploit it.

5. Multibrand Buying

From the definition of multibrand buying (more than one brand will be bought in a given period), it follows that the rate of product purchasing must be higher than the rate of brand purchasing, and this will be more marked in long than short time periods.[19] For instance with breakfast cereals, the average Shredded Wheat buyer will purchase 1.1 packs of the brand in a week but will buy an average of 1.9 packs of breakfast cereals as a whole. Over the course of a year, the average Shredded Wheat customer will buy about 4 packs but from the product field as a whole will buy as many as 42 packs. In fields where there is less variety than breakfast cereals, the homemaker's weekly purchase of one brand will represent the total of product purchasing; but the consumer soon begins to buy other brands, so that after a time the normal relationship of greater product buying than brand buying begins to assert itself.

Product purchase rates are similar within markets or within defined functional market segments. In a market such as gasoline in the United Kingdom, which has no functional segmentation by brand, the average buyer of each of the major brands will make the following number of product purchases (purchases of all brands) in a four-week period:

Esso	5.8
Shell	5.8
National	6.2
Mobil	6.1
BP	6.1
Texaco	6.0

Similarly, where there is functional segmentation by brand (as in the American breakfast cereal market), the average annual purchases of all products in the same segment will be similar. *But they may be different in different segments.* Here are the annual figures for the presweetened segment:

Cap'n Crunch	55
Life	55
Sugar Crisps	55
Froot Loops	54
Lucky Charms	60

But for buyers of unsweetened brands, the figures are:

Kellogg's Corn Flakes	34
Rice Krispies	39
Grape Nuts	37
Shredded Wheat	42
All Bran	38

The internal consistency between each of these sets of figures is obvious. A moment's thought will give us the reason why purchase levels are significantly higher for the presweetened segment than for the unsweetened one: the larger size of the average household using sweetened cereals due to the presence of young children.

An important feature of product purchase rates is that although they are generally consistent from brand to brand, there is a tendency for them to be slightly lower for larger brands. We have seen that there is an opposite tendency for *brand* purchase rates, in that these are higher for larger brands. Thus, *the buyer of a larger brand will show generally greater brand loyalty than the buyer of a smaller brand,* because she or he will be making more purchases of the larger brand out of a smaller total number of purchases in the product field as a whole.

Having looked at the differences between brand buying and product buying, we can now examine the duplication of buying between brands. This is yet another aspect of buying behavior that shows regularity and consistency, at least within markets (or between functional market segments). This consistency is in fact so great that the relationship has been formulated into a rule called the *duplication of purchase law.* This states simply that the buyer of one brand will buy a second brand in direct proportion to the penetration of the second brand. For example, over thirteen weeks, 11 percent of Kellogg's Corn Flakes buyers will also buy Shredded Wheat, 11 percent of Kellogg's Rice Krispies buyers will also buy Shredded Wheat, and 11 percent of Kellogg's Bran Flakes buyers will also buy Shredded Wheat. The duplication figure between these different brands and Shredded Wheat remains fairly constant, and this duplication is essentially related to Shredded Wheat's penetration, which is of course a single figure, 7 percent.

The duplication is not however exactly the same as Shredded Wheat's penetration, but rather a *multiple* of it, about 1.5. This figure is called the *duplication coefficient* and remains reasonably constant over a whole market, about 1.5 for breakfast cereals in the United States, but only 1.2 for gasoline in the United Kingdom.

Significantly, the higher values of the duplication coefficient (including exceptionally above-average figures we sometimes see for two or three brands in individual markets) relate to groups of brands which consumers regard as particularly similar to one another. The brands have a lot of users in common because of their similarity. The values we are talking about here are much higher than those we have seen so far for gasoline and breakfast cereals, where the average duplication between brands is effectively uncorrelated. But there are exceptions even within these markets, such as between Kellogg's Raisin Bran and Post Raisin Bran. For these two brands, 35 percent of Kellogg's buyers buy Post (3.5 times the Post penetration and much higher than the market duplication coefficient of 1.5). This high degree of duplication is simply explained in terms of the two brands' functional similarity. But the reader should also bear in mind that the duplication between these two brands is by no means complete, because although 35 percent of Kellogg's buyers buy Post, 65 percent of them do not, so that as a general rule, homemakers' purchasing patterns are much less self-contained than preconceptions of market segmentation would have us believe: a point to which we shall shortly return.

Four Myths

We shall now use empirical studies and mathematical models to illustrate some commonly held conceptions (or misconceptions) about how markets work. Three of these illuminations are general and apply over the whole marketing field; the fourth is a special case with a limited empirical foundation, although judgment suggests it to have a quite general application. (The reader is urged to examine the source material for more detailed explanations.)

1. Demographic and Psychographic Positioning

Ehrenberg's work confirms chapter 3's points on positioning and the weaknesses of demographic and psychographic measures as means of segmenting markets and determining brand positions.[20]

As the reader knows from this chapter's discussion of multibrand buying, there is little evidence in the real world of any clear-cut segmentation by *consumers*. There is however often a segmentation of brands on the basis of their functional performance. In the market for ready-to-eat cereals, what clustering takes place is of brands having particular functional characteristics, such as:

The two bran flakes, Kellogg's and Post;

The two raisin brans, again Kellogg's and Post;

The range of presweetened brands: Sugar Frosties, Froot Loops, Cap'n Crunch, Trix, Sugar Crisps, Lucky Charms, and Life;

Rice Krispies and Cheerios (both expanded products).

But even such unusually clear functional segmentation will not enable a manufacturer to reach anything like exclusive groups of new consumers. "Instead, there is a general mass market, with buyers of each brand buying the other brands in about the same proportions. Superimposed on this is the high substitutability of brands of the same sub type."[21] Finding a market segment where such substitution takes place can however provide opportunities to a manufacturer as alert as the one discussed in chapter 3, who was imaginative and aggressive enough to launch a new brand which achieved a 7-percent brand share (four percentage points of which came from competitors). The secret was to target potential consumers in terms of their brand usage. This was not exclusive usage, but it was large enough for the firm to come in and seize (and build) a substantial business.

2. *The Hard Core of Loyal Buyers*

There is a prevalent idea that when sales of a brand decline, they reach and maintain a rock bottom level which represents the use of the brand by a hard core of old and loyal users.[22] I have observed at first hand manufacturers who have developed and implemented marketing strategies based on this idea on more than one occasion and in more than one country. The underlying assumption is that the loyal group repurchases the brand at an above-average rate (hence the above-average loyalty). Although their numbers may dwindle, they make up for this decline by their high level of repurchase.

Empirical studies illuminate this question in two ways. First, the word loyalty itself can be seen to have a special meaning. What we know of the buyers is that these people are not so much *less loyal* to the brand as *less frequent buyers* of it. Although they may not buy in one particular period they will return in later periods, since most brands have a long tail of irregular purchasers who are not lost forever (as we shall see when we examine the "leaky bucket" hypothesis). Second, when we look again at the average frequency of purchase of a brand and the frequency distribution around this average, we will note the remarkable and predictable similarity between such averages and such distributions for different brands.

There is therefore no empirical basis whatsoever for the notion of a hard core of loyal buyers, whether these are for a declining brand, store brand, generic brand, or any other type. The only brands which have a regularly above-average rate of purchase are those brands with high absolute levels of penetration. This has nothing to do with any special characteristics of the brands, but is simply a result of their high penetration per se.

Generally speaking, when a brand declines, this is the result of falling penetration, and when sales reach rock bottom level (which occasionally happens for such brands), this is because the penetration has been stabilized. Frequency of purchase has not come into the matter at all.

3. *The "Leaky Bucket"*

There is also a prevalent theory, which is even subscribed to by that normally impeccable observer Peckham, that the users of a brand, like the contents of a leaky bucket, are constantly dripping away, disappearing from the market in significant numbers, accounting perhaps for the loss of a fifth of a brand's sales during the course of a year.[23] Such losses would make it necessary for the manufacturer to devote much attention to recruiting new users simply to compensate for the natural wastage.

We have seen in the analysis of repeat buying that 59 percent of all Shredded Wheat buyers in any one quarter will come back to buy it in the next quarter. The average repurchase rate for *any* brand of breakfast cereal is 54 percent (46 percent not repurchasing). If there were a "leaky bucket," we should expect the normal repurchase to waste away to nothing after a few further quarters. If, for instance, it were to decline by 46 percent on a continuous basis, the repurchase by the original buyers would be very low in less than a year, and would be close to disappearance in eighteen months:

1st quarter	100%
2nd quarter	54
3rd quarter	29
4th quarter	16
5th quarter	8
6th quarter	5

But this just does not happen in practice. The actual repurchase in the fourth quarter is not 16 percent, but three times that, or an observed figure of 48 percent.

This means that as a general rule infrequent buyers remain infrequent, but do not drop away altogether except in marginal cases (which might eventually be reflected in a slight erosion in a brand's market share, a nonstationary element). This erosion will in any event not happen if the slight loss in repurchase is matched by a modest compensating entry into the market of new trialists (as discussed in the case of Shredded Wheat's frequency distribution). The way in which market share will actually trend up and down is in most circumstances a reflection of these modest marginal changes in penetration between periods. And although these are real movements, they are not of an order of magnitude to justify manufacturers diverting effort simply to influence them.

4. Promotional Sales Increases and Seasonal Uplifts

We now come to the meaning of two types of short-term sales increases, those caused by promotions and seasonality, which are commonly thought to be brought about by increased usage by existing users.[24] It is not possible to generalize widely from the data, although judgment suggests strongly that the patterns discussed here are widespread.

In a successful consumer promotion for a brand of laundry detergent in Britain, sales increased during one February by 30 percent, thereafter coming down in the way expected of all consumer promotions for stationary brands. The promotion employed a banded pack, offering more powder for the same price, a type of offer thought to be much more interesting to existing users of the brand than to new users.

On the basis of January sales, Ehrenberg's model predicted that without the promotion, 210 packs per 1,000 households would have been sold in February, and of these, 60 would have gone to people who did not buy in January. In fact, the promotion boosted February sales to 272 packs per 1,000 households, and 101 of these went to households that had not bought in January. Thus, contrary to expectations, the promotion appealed to a considerable degree to new trialists. But if this suggests some long-term effect for the promotion, this was denied by the almost immediate re-establishment of normal repeat-buying rates as soon as the promotion was over. The promotion gained some extra sales, mainly from new trialists, but these people did not appear to have selected the promoted brand to join their repertoire. The effect of the promotion in this case was to increase penetration by the entry of some extra once-only buyers, but this was of little long-term value to the brand.

A similar conclusion was drawn from an instance of a seasonal sales increase for a brand of packet soup in the United Kingdom. The sales level was 480 packs per 1,000 households during the three winter months of peak sales, compared with 360 packs during the three summer months of lowest sales. Food manufacturers believe that the winter increase in soup sales is always due to people using more soup, rather than new buyers coming into the market. But the facts of this case showed the opposite to be true. The model predicted that repeat buying by off-season purchasers would account for 320 sales per 1,000 housholds in the peak season. The remaining 160 purchases (the seasonal uplift) has to be coming from new purchasers. "Getting winter-only buyers of soup also by buy in the summer is a different task than getting all-the-year-round buyers to buy *more* in the summer."[25]

How Brands Grow

After considering and digesting all this evidence, in particular the examples of consumers buying in regular and unchanging patterns, readers are probably wondering what in fact is the mechanism that causes the market share of a brand to increase or decrease?

Two clues in this chapter will help us understand changes in market share. First, a brand's penetration is the consumer measure that has the greatest influence on a brand's sales; big brands always have a higher penetration than smaller brands. Second, in the discussion of frequency distribution, the point was made that models of stationary market conditions slightly under-estimate the amount of once-only purchasing by brand trialists. The percent-age movements need only be marginal to represent substantial numbers in absolute terms. This is how stationary markets become a little less stationary.

But might the emergence of one-time trialists upset the normal patterns of skewed frequency distribution? In practice, the re-establishment of the nor-mal frequency distribution is more likely to be achieved with a growing brand by the trialists remaining infrequent purchasers; *but with some of the former infrequent purchasers becoming more frequent purchasers.* Everybody moves up a rung. Some nonusers become minor users; some minor users become major users. Thus the same normal frequency distribution will now hold for the higher level of penetration. Remember in chapter 1, I said that advertising can contribute to an increase in the frequency of purchase *only in a special sense.* This is the sense I meant.

When a brand is declining, the opposite happens. Some major users be-come minor users, and some minor users become nonusers. The brand even-tually settles down to the same frequency distribution pattern at a lower level of penetration. British analyst Tom Corlett first worked out this hypothesis to explain growth and decline in consumer terms; it accords with common sense.[26] I have in addition a well-documented unpublished case of a medium-term decline of a major brand of packaged goods on the British market, which is explicable precisely in the terms just outlined. In this case, the anal-ysis of the trouble enabled the manufacturer to take successful corrective action.

The powerful tendencies toward equilibrial regularity in markets give a brand an inbuilt momentum once it crosses that first and most difficult hurdle of early establishment of penetration and repeat purchase. Once a brand be-comes a "goer," the tendency toward regularity is as much in its favor as it was an obstacle to be overcome during its initial market entry.

How Advertising Strategy Should Be Influenced by Repeat-Buying Theory

After readers have grasped the meaning of the abstract concepts described in this chapter and the rather complex relationships between them, and after they have accepted the overall importance of the continuity and regularity of behavior so plentifully illustrated here, further reflection should suggest that what has been described ought to have a major influence on the way a man-ufacturer draws up advertising strategy. I shall identify twenty factors of vary-ing importance.

Factors Influencing the Choice of Target Group

1. Demographic and psychographic measures are imprecise descriptors because:
   a. There is generally a large common usage of functionally different brands within demographic and psychographic categories.
   b. Users of different brands are often actually the same people because of everyday multibrand purchasing. This factor becomes more important as any brand grows in size.
2. A target group can be precisely described in terms of brand usage. But a decision must be made about how much the manufacturer is targeting his own users (for repeat purchase), how much he is targeting users of competitive brands, and *which* competitive brands are being targeted. Generally speaking, the larger the advertised brand, the greater the emphasis that should be placed on existing users.
3. Figures for penetration tend to be large. Over a year, for instance, the size of the penetration is much bigger than the size of the market share. This is because of the continuous growth of net penetration, through the increase in the numbers of infrequent buyers. These factors suggest that:
   a. While the route to increasing market share is mainly via increasing penetration, this strategy should be accompanied by a secondary strategy.
   b. A brand has enormous numbers of infrequent buyers, so that the secondary strategy should be addressed to them, to increase their purchase frequency.
4. Data from another source than Ehrenberg suggest that advertising has a consistently greater effect on users of a brand than on nonusers.[27] This is probably connected with the fact that users of a brand notice its advertising because of selective perception.
5. Over periods of six months to a year, there are effectively no sole buyers of a brand except in the case of cigarettes. There is therefore no such thing as absolute brand loyalty.
6. Heavy users of a brand represent a small proportion of total users. (Twenty percent of users use half the volume, according to the 80:20 rule.)
7. Purchasers of a brand, when measured by how often they buy, are distributed in a skewed fashion, but the average purchasing level is in general low. (With a typical brand, a third of all purchasing in a thirteen-week period is made by people who buy only once.)
8. Overall levels of brand purchasing are also low. Nielsen shows that in a fairly large supermarket, three-quarters of all brands sell only a dozen packs a week.[28]
9. Points 6, 7, and 8 are mutually supporting, and suggest that the best target group for a brand (heavy users of the product category and brand)

represents a relatively small proportion of the homemaker population (in many cases under 25 percent). This in turn means that the advertising only has to influence a relatively small number of people to have an effect. Unfortunately no way is known of finding these people accurately and without waste by using media selection as the means of locating them. (This is because of the overall lack of selectivity of television, although magazines are not quite so inefficient.) Therefore they must be located by means of the content of the advertisement (the creative appeal, which should be sharply angled to catch them).

10.   Point 3 suggests that the secondary target group (irregular users of the brand, who should be persuaded to increase their purchase frequency) is probably much larger than the primary target group. Irregular users should also be located by the creative appeal of the campaign, although the larger size of this group means that attempts to locate it by the use of media are less wasteful than with the primary group.

Factors Influencing the Argument and Tone of Voice of the Advertising

11.   Since much advertising effort is directed to the maintenance of the status quo, the tone of voice of such advertising should be quiet, protective, and reinforcing. Selective perception means that a brand's advertising will be noticed by existing users, which means that it is not required to be strident to attract attention. In parallel with this, the budgetary policy should be un-aggressive in order to shore up profit. The evidence on advertising weight presented in chapter 4 suggests strongly that the advertising of larger brands tends to be more cost-efficient than that of smaller ones.

12.   Regular product use means that homemakers are familiar with the motivating arguments (those aimed at primary demand in any market). Brand advertising should concentrate on discriminating arguments emphasizing especially the brand's added values.

Factors Influencing the Role of the Advertising

13.   The role of the advertising directed at the primary target market should be to increase penetration. This is a tough task for a large brand, and consumer promotions should work alongside the advertising to accomplish this. This whole argument is consonant with the Brooke Bond Oxo experience described in chapter 3, with its recommendation that the most fruitful area for development is "at the periphery of the user group."

14.   The role of advertising during seasonal sales peaks should be for the temporary increase of penetration rather than usage.

15.   The role of promotions in most circumstances should also be to

increase penetration rather than usage. If a brand's sales trend is slightly up-ward, a permanent increase in penetration could take place, although this would likely be proportionately smaller than the temporary increase in sales.

16.   There is no permanent loss of users in stationary market conditions. There is no "leaky bucket." Advertising should not therefore be addressed to people who are thought to be quitting a brand.

17.   There is no hard core of loyal buyers. Advertising should not there-fore be addressed to such a group.

General Considerations

18.   Multibrand buying means that homemakers will continually ap-praise competing brands. This is yet another confirmation of the importance of maintaining competitive functional performance. Multibrand purchasing is the norm between functional segments as well as within them. Segmenta-tion is virtually never brand-exclusive.

19.   There are scale economies for large brands connected with the "penetration supercharge," economies explained essentially in terms of con-sumer usage. This means that such brands should be punctiliously nurtured and certainly not sacrificed on the altar of the life cycle!

 a.   Brands with a high penetration tend to have a higher purchase fre-quency within a purchasing period. This can be quite large within long purchasing periods.[29]

	Brand A	Brand B
12-month penetration	46%	12%
Average observed purchase frequency:		
in 1 week	1.0	1.0
in 4 weeks	1.8	1.5
in 12 weeks	3.7	2.5
in 24 weeks	6.0	3.3
in 48 weeks	10.1	5.0

 b.   Brands with a high penetration tend to have a higher repurchase rate and higher repurchase frequency in the next purchasing period.
 c.   Brands with a high penetration tend to have slightly lower than av-erage *product* purchase rates. Since they also have slightly higher *brand* purchase rates, this means that they generate greater than av-erage brand loyalty.

20.   Data on penetration, purchase frequency, frequency distribution, repeat buying, and multibrand buying can be collected for a brand and its competitors from analysis of a couple of years of consumer panel data, which

many manufacturers may already possess but not fully use. These data will provide a more enlightening basis for developing strategy than the superficial information most commonly used.

The Argument in Brief

Patterns of buying in stationary markets (such as are normal in the world of repeat-purchase packaged goods) disclose a remarkable degree of underlying uniformity and regularity. These can be described with the use of the mathematical models constructed by Ehrenberg and other analysts from a wide data base, with virtually universal application to such markets.

In order to understand a brand fully, we need to know a number of facts about its consumers and its competitors. These include penetration, purchase frequency, frequency distribution, repeat buying, and multibrand buying. Knowing the first two of these variables is normally enough to enable the remaining ones to be predicted from the models.

A knowledge of the facts of purchasing behavior has considerable operational value. For instance, it enables us to examine the validity of commonly held received beliefs about markets. It can also help us understand how brands grow, normally by an increase in the number of once-only purchasers, which is enough to disturb the existing stationary pattern of a market. Such an increase is often accompanied by an increase in the frequency of purchase by existing buyers, which in turn leads to a continuation of the normal pattern of frequency distribution, although the brand as a whole is now slightly larger.

The facts of consumer buying carry many implications for advertising strategy. Some of the most important are that, with many brands (certainly large ones), a good deal of advertising effort should be directed at the maintenance of the status quo in a market. The primary target group for advertising should normally be heavy buyers of a product field (many of them users of the brand advertised). The secondary group should always be users of the brand (but infrequent ones), the purpose of the advertising being to increase their frequency of buying. In many circumstances, both creative and budgetary policies should be protective and unaggressive.

Brands with high penetration and market share benefit from the scale economies associated with the penetration supercharge. This is itself a strong reason why manufacturers should nurture such brands, and not encourage decline by inaction, notably by allowing investments to dwindle.

The facts of consumer purchasing behavior can be assembled relatively easily for any ongoing brand and its competitors. This procedure provides a data base for developing strategy that is more direct, stimulating, and productive than the rather jejune information normally used for this important purpose.

Notes

1. My experience dates from 1966–67, when I was responsible for coordinating European advertising for the Famous Artist Schools, a substantial direct response advertiser. The campaign ran fully in six European markets and experimentally in two others.

2. My main clients in the international field have been Chesebrough—Pond's, Gillette, Nestlé, PepsiCo, and Unilever (with whom I was involved with about two dozen different brands). Outside the FMCG field, I worked with the Champion Spark Plug Company, Ford Motor Company, and Pan American.

3. Six specific examples are quoted by Colin McDonald, "What Is the Short Term Effect of Advertising: The Relationship between Frequency and Advertising Effectiveness" in *Effective Frequency,* ed. Michael Naples (New York: Association of National Advertisers, 1979), pp. 86–88.

4. Michael Barnes, "The Relationship between Purchasing Patterns and Advertising Exposure" in *How Advertising Works* (London: J. Walter Thompson, 1974), p. 55.

5. J.A.P. Treasure, title essay in *How Advertising Works.*

6. Barnes, "The Relationship between Purchasing Patterns and Advertising Exposure," p. 57.

7. A.S.C. Ehrenberg, and G.L. Goodhardt, Seventeen Essays on *Understanding Buying Behavior,* pp. 5.14, 5.5.

8. A.S.C. Ehrenberg, *Repeat Buying: Theory and Applications.*

9. Ehrenberg and Goodhardt, *Understanding Buying Behavior,* pp. 1.3, 5.15.

10. *Ibid.,* pp. 6.2–6.3.

11. Rosser Reeves, *Reality in Advertising,* p. 10.

12. Ehrenberg and Goodhardt, *Understanding Buying Behavior,* pp. 6.12, 6.5.

13. Ehrenberg, *Repeat-Buying, Theory and Applications,* chap. 7–8; Ehrenberg and Goodhardt, *Understanding Buying Behavior,* essays 11–12.

14. Ehrenberg and Goodhardt, *Understanding Buying Behavior,* p. 12.1.

15. Ehrenberg, *Repeat-Buying Theory and Applications,* pp. 33–40, 305–7; and Ehrenberg and Goodhardt, *Understanding Buying Behavior,* pp. 6.7, 7.7.

16. Ehrenberg, *Repeat-Buying, Theory and Applications,* pp. 37–40; and Ehrenberg and Goodhardt, *Understanding Buying Behavior,* pp. 6.7, 7.4, 8.5–8.7, 11.7, 12.14.

17. Ehrenberg, *Repeat-Buying, Theory and Applications,* pp. 56–59; and Ehrenberg and Goodhardt, *Understanding Buying Behavior,* pp. 10.5–10.6, 12.10.

18. Ehrenberg, *Repeat-Buying, Theory and Applications,* pp. 17–29, 180–83, 303 (which contains a useful table of average repurchase frequencies); and Ehrenberg and Goodhardt, *Understanding Buying Behavior,* pp. 3.4–3.8, 12.4–12.5.

19. Ehrenberg, *Repeat-Buying: Theory and Applications,* pp. 183–92; Ehrenberg and Goodhardt, *Understanding Buying Behavior,* essay 9.

20. Ehrenberg and Goodhardt, *Understanding Buying Behavior*, essay 4.

21. *Ibid.*, p. 4.9.

22. *Ibid.*, essay 3.

23. *Ibid.*, pp. 2.14–2.15. See also James O. Peckham, Sr., *The Wheel of Marketing*, p. 80. This source is a good example of the occasional problem associated with using aggregated retail audit data.

24. Ehrenberg and Goodhardt, *Understanding Buying Behavior,* essay 2.

25. *Ibid.*, p. 2.13.

26. Tom Corlett, "Consumer Purchasing Patterns: A Different Perspective" in *How Advertising Works*.

27. "Major Advertiser Ad Tel Scheduling Study 1974" in *Effective Frequency*, pp. 44–56.

28. Peckham, *The Wheel of Marketing*, p. 13. The data came from a study produced by *Progressive Grocer*.

29. Ehrenberg, *Repeat-Buying: Theory and Applications*, p. 38.

6
Advertising Research—A Digression on Recall

"What sort of things do you remember best?" Alice ventured to ask.

"Oh, things that happened the week after next," the Queen replied in a careless tone.

Before proceeding with the mainstream argument in this book, and in particular to the important matters of advertising quality and campaign effects, I must make a digression to describe methods of evaluating advertising, all of which require market research. This chapter mainly concerns one particular type of research: recall testing.

Market research was originally made possible by the discovery of techniques of sample selection, and is virtually the only scientific tool available to marketing and advertising practitioners. Over the years there have been continuous improvements in the way it is carried out, particularly, in the recent past, in methods of analyzing data. But while we cannot deny the increasingly important contribution of research to marketing and advertising, we must also be aware of four endemic concerns with all research: in ascending order of importance, the sample, the sample frame, causality, and the questions. We must also remember that research is to be an aid to judgment, not a substitute for it.

1. The Sample

The reliability of research results depends on the size and representative nature of the sample. A great deal is known about both sample selection and the margins of error. It is nevertheless common practice to use small samples of about one hundred for quantitative surveys and even smaller ones of about twenty for qualitative investigations. While such samples can be usefully employed, researchers do not always make it explicitly clear that the range of error is extremely wide; and in the case of qualitative investigations, that the data are not capable of any type of quantitative extrapolation at all.[1]

2. The Sample Frame

This means that we should decide whether we are questioning the right type of people: are we selecting the sample from the correct universe? This decision is often heavily judgmental; for instance, in researching advertising, should we talk to users or nonusers of a brand? If this is in turn decided by the target group described in the brand's advertising strategy, it begs the question of whether that is in fact the most suitable group for the marketing plan and therefore for the research.

3. Causality

There is a fundamental question, which is particularly important with continuous tracking studies, of which of two variables is the cause and which the effect. Does *A* cause *B,* or does *B* cause *A*? Or are they both perhaps caused by *C*?

4. The Questions

This is the worst problem of all, because people are only rarely capable of responding to possibilities outside their range of direct experience. (It is sometimes said that if the development of household lighting systems had depended on market research, houses would be lit today with highly sophisticated paraffin lamps). The problem is exacerbated by researchers' almost universal habit of framing questions in ways that may be easy to apply and tabulate, but often provide a blocked conduit when it comes to providing insights into consumers' beliefs and attitudes. All too often, instead of asking people a range of direct and oblique questions for them to answer in their own way, researchers make startlingly bald statements, many concerned with matters of trivial or at least questionable importance, and expect people to respond, according to varying degrees of agreement or disagreement, on a five- or seven-point scale. The user of such research should beware.

In discussing these central problems, I have ignored common solecisms in the description of research findings, since the mathematically skilled user of research will immediately notice these. One of the most common and irritating mistakes is the habit of percentaging data on the basis of totals much smaller than 100. The person who does this needs to be reminded that he or she is in effect making projections. Before such projections can be accepted, we need evidence that when the smaller total is projected up to the larger, the internal composition of the figures is not going to be changed in important ways.

This chapter will concentrate on one specific variety of research: the measurement of advertisement recall. I am going to examine the measures used to test the effectiveness of individual advertisements, later briefly discussing recall measures used to evaluate the cumulative effect of campaigns. Research into individual advertisements is most commonly and succinctly (but not most elegantly) described as copy testing. Depending on the technique, such testing can take place either before an advertisement is exposed, after it has been exposed on a trial basis, or after it has been exposed before a substantial audience. Of all types of advertising research, recall testing has the longest history, and the widest popularity, certainly in the evaluation of finished campaigns.[2] It also has a most pervasive aura of controversy surrounding it.

The earliest types of advertising research were developed by George Gallup and Daniel Starch in the 1920s. They were originally and continue in the main to be concerned with print media. The "reading-and-noting" method, originally developed by Gallup, has been used in a regular syndicated service by Starch since 1931, and is run in Great Britain by the British Gallup organization. The research aims to find out whether members of the public can recognize advertisements in specific issues of newspapers and magazines that they claim to have read. They are taken through the appropriate issue and asked about each advertisement in it. Recognition is assessed at three levels: first, whether the advertisement in question has been noted (whether the respondents remember having see it); second, whether they associate the advertisement with the advertiser's name; and third, whether they have read at least half the copy. Starch, it should be emphasized, is concerned with *recognition* of something supposedly seen in the recent past.

The method used by Gallup and Robinson in the United States is based on a different and more searching technique. Here, the publication is not opened for inspection, and people who have read it are asked whether they can remember (and what they can remember about) advertisements for particular brands, with emphasis on sales points. This technique can correctly be described as recall rather than recognition, although the methodological problems that apply to an extreme degree to recognition also apply to some extent to the various types of recall. (Gallup and Robinson's work provides typical examples.)

For many years, Starch was looked upon as a service that provided—if not diagnostic insights—at least a general confirmation that particular campaigns were working. The findings were rarely regarded as critical discriminators between advertisements, but were widely read by creative people in agencies, who used them in a general way to improve their skills.

In the late 1950s, I was a young executive in J. Walter Thompson, London, working on the advertising of two generic commodities, butter and cheese. (The role of the advertising was to stimulate overall consumer demand in order to boost the producer price. The campaigns were funded by levies on each ton of imports and home production.) During my time on these accounts, some of our most interesting campaigns were editorial in style and devoted to recipes. In our media buying we took particular pains to ensure that they appeared on women's pages in national newspapers.

These campaigns consistently achieved remarkable reading-and-noting scores. Some of our smallest advertisements (four inches across two columns) received levels of copy readership normally expected of advertisements ten times as large. The copywriters were suitably gratified, but this research evidence did not prevent the campaigns from being abandoned—on the grounds of their supposed dullness—before they had run their full course. This decision was made jointly by representatives of the client and the agency account management, who were needless to say all men (I being the most junior of them). The decision was also made against the advice of Stanley Resor, the man who in all essentials had created the J. Walter Thompson Company, and who was then coming to the end of his long reign. I presume that in our wisdom, we considered him to be past his best.

I am telling this anecdote to illustrate the way in which this type of research was then treated and used by clients and agencies: it was an interesting but essentially peripheral matter. Decisions about which campaigns to run were made on the basis of different arguments.

This was about the time that television was establishing itself, in the eyes of most clients and agencies, as the most glamorous medium for advertising consumer goods. And it was the arrival of television, with its exciting opportunities but also its massive unknowns, that caused advertising research to be extensively reconsidered by advertisers. This triggered the biggest development in its use, extensive exploration of ideas borrowed from different scientific disciplines, widespread experimentation with different testing techniques, and a still active current of professional controversy about the meaning of the different sorts of research. It has been estimated that by the 1970s, the number of reported research studies was doubling every five to eight years.[3] Today, the literature is vast although variable in quality, very piecemeal, and to an extent contradictory. The progress toward enlightenment has been extremely slow and painful, but few people would deny that some steps have in fact been made.

Reading-and-Noting: Its Fall from Grace

In 1955, in a burgeoning spirit of enquiry, the Advertising Research Foundation embarked on a rigorous validation of recognition and recall research as it was then carried out. A Committee on Printed Advertising Rating Methods (the PARM Committee) was set up to plan and carry out this research. They concentrated on a single issue of *Life* (May 16, 1955), and paralleled the investigations of both Starch and Gallup and Robinson, but using a much larger and more carefully controlled sample.

There were differences between PARM and Starch findings, and between PARM and Gallup and Robinson findings; and a modest amount of debate took place on the reasons for these differences. Suggestions for improvement were made, but nowhere was there a feeling that the scientific basis for these two research methods had been destroyed or even called seriously into question.

However, some years after the PARM investigation had been published (after a period in which there had been surprisingly little serious comment in either academic or industry circles on PARM and what it had brought forth), Darrell B. Lucas, who had been associated with the PARM Committee since 1955, began some fruitful speculation about the implications of the research.[4] When examining recognition scores researched over a two-week period from the publication date of a sample issue, he found that the scores at the end of the two weeks were no lower than at the beginning. In other words, recognition scores did *not* erode over time as memory has always been thought to do (and indeed as Gallup and Robinson recall scores were found to behave). This disturbing finding caused Lucas to try and puzzle out what recognition scores really measured; the more he thought about them, the more he concluded that they could not have much to do with what they purported to measure: whether or not a person had seen that particular insertion before. "Certainly the evidence does not justify the projection of recognition ratings to the actual number of noters or readers per dollar."[5]

On both sides of the Atlantic, much speculation and experimentation then began to take place. This was of two main sorts. First, work was done on factors that were likely to contaminate recognition and recall findings. Second, fundamental exploration took place into the nature of perception, in particular the automatic prescreening processes that appear to be built into the human senses and brain. The concept of selective perception had long been familiar in the study of psychology. This new research was about to demonstrate its relevance to advertising.

The studies of contaminating factors, although they were extensive and fairly comprehensive, are easy to summarize because they generally pointed in a single direction. Experiments eventually isolated at least nineteen factors which could be shown to influence recognition scores.[6] Some of these, as expected, relate to the content of the advertisement itself (size, use of color, pictorial content, attractiveness, meaningfulness, interest level generated, and the product field). Some, also as expected, relate to the medium (position of the advertisement, size of the issue, surrounding material, and interest in the editorial). Some, not as expected, relate to the respondent (interest in the product, product usership, closeness to brand purchase, demographic characteristics, and response "set" of the individual). Some, also not as expected, relate to the research itself (the training of the interviewers, the length of the interview, the research procedure).

The fundamental assumption of the Starch technique is that the scores reflect partly the creative content of the advertisement and partly the particular medium in which the advertisement appears. The fact that exogenous factors relating to the respondent and the interview also have a strong influence on recognition scores means that these scores cannot be taken at their face value. Moreover, detailed improvements in the research technique—a number of which were suggested and tested—do not appear to shake the validity of this broad conclusion, although they may reduce the imperfections marginally.[7]

The investigations into the physical processes of perception provided even more disturbing hard data. The hypothesis set up for investigation was that the eye, in scanning a printed page, picks up impressions in very short time periods, less than a quarter of a second. In these short periods, the hypothesis continues, the eye can see and the subconscious mind can reject some things for being of no interest. If a subject (such as an advertisement in terms of the creative content but also the brand advertised and product field) is registered by the individual's subconscious as interesting, more time is spent on this advertisement, which then enters the individual's memory and is presumably reflected in the recognition and perhaps also in the recall. But if this hypothesis is valid, the recognition and recall scores are not a reflection of whether the individual has seen the particular insertion; they mean that the ad (or brand or product field) is something that caught his or her interest. This information is not irrelevant, but it is not what recognition and recall are supposed to be about.

This may appear to be a complex concept, but it proved remarkably easy to test by the use of an apparatus designed by the Institute of Market Psychology in Mannheim, Germany. A similar machine had been used in the United States in 1940, in the psychology department of Purdue University, and some interesting findings had been published in fall 1941, which (not surprisingly in view of the timing) failed to trigger any academic debate.[8] The European system is known as the direct eye movement observation system (DEMOS); its experimental and validation work was carried out in London by the British Market Research Bureau from 1966 to 1968.

Each person who was to be interviewed was asked to spend time in a waiting room. Here, he or she saw a (prepublication) copy of a newspaper or magazine on a lectern. Since there was nothing else to do, the respondent would begin to read. As this happened his or her eye movements were, without the subject being aware of it, filmed with continuous individual exposures of onequarter of a second so as to establish exactly what pages and portions of pages were looked at, and for how long.[9] The people were then interviewed to establish normal reading and noting scores, which were compared with the precise, scientific DEMOS measurement to confirm (or otherwise) the reading-and-noting findings.

The main validation study can be summarized in a single uncomplicated statistical table.

	Magazine Study: Average for All Advertisements in "Woman's Own"	Newspaper Study: Average for all Advertisements in "Daily Mirror"
Looked at and claimed	8%	6%
Not looked at and claimed	5	1
Looked at and not claimed	35	35
Not looked at and not claimed	52	57

In the magazine study, the average percentage of respondents who claimed to have looked at the advertisements was 13 percent (although only 8 percent of the 13 percent actually did so), while the actual number who looked at the advertisement was 43 percent. The ratio of claim to reality was therefore 13:43 or the equivalent of 100:330, a gross underreporting of 230 percent!

This startling finding dramatically confirms the hypothesis of selective perception, a phenomenon that has of course been known instinctively by advertising practitioners since the days of unregulated advertising for proprietary medicines a century ago. The tiny advertisement with a headline such as "Painful Hemorrhoids" would indeed be noticed by the small but vulnerable target group of sufferers from this distressing condition. But for the majority of readers, the advertisement would of course be easily and simply screened out. The advertiser could safely employ small spaces, which were the only size he could afford in view of the relatively small size of the target audience.

Recognition scores may indeed measure something, but that something has little to do with whether a specific advertisement has been seen in a particular issue of a publication. Recall scores are perhaps a purer measure than recognition since they are more concerned with whether or not a person can recall an advertisement with his or her conscious mind (leaving open the question of whether selective perception might have taken place). But recall measures, like recognition, are by no means free of contaminating factors (as I shall examine in detail in connection with twenty-four-hour recall of television commercials). Remember that all research—and advertising research in particular—is like a minefield. Things that seem firm are often not what they appear, so actions based on them can have unexpected and dangerous consequences. I shall try to chart a course through this minefield.

The Twentieth-Century Philosophers' Stone

When I referred at the beginning of this chapter to the popularity of recall testing, I was thinking about its use not with print but rather with television advertising. Here, the most prevalent variety takes the form of twenty-four-hour recall or DART (day-after-recall-test). Most large advertisers use it. The leading research organization in the field, Burke Marketing Services, has its headquarters appropriately enough in Cincinnati, location of Procter and Gamble, originally its most important client (which also happens to be the biggest advertiser in the United States.)

The DART technique is simple. A television commercial is screened once. The next day (within twenty-four hours of the television exposure) a sample of people is contacted by telephone, asked whether they viewed the television show at about the time the commercial was on the air, and asked to recall verbal and visual elements of the advertisement's contents. The aim is to contact a sample of about two-hundred people who saw the television program. (This takes time for shows with small audiences, a fact which distorts the findings to a significant degree.)[10] The recall scores are then compared with a substantial battery of normative data in similar product fields, and the findings, which are delivered promptly, are crisp, businesslike and eminently actionable.

It will however be no surprise to readers that experimental work has uncovered a substantial number of contaminating factors that influence the recall levels, so that (as with press advertising) what is measured is a good deal more complex than recall of the advertising insertion under scrutiny. The issue is examined most succinctly in a paper by Shirley Young, director of research services for Grey Advertising in New York.[11] Examining ten examples of test and retest of the same commercial, she demonstrates recall levels in the second test to be significantly different from the first in half the cases. (This is typical of investigations of the technique.) Differences in recall levels have been attributed to a miscellaneous collection of exogenous factors, such as differences between test cities, whether the program is liked, brand usage, time of the program, the ad's position in the program, whether the entire program is viewed, various demographics of the respondents, and when within the twenty-four-hour period the interview takes place (reflecting the impact of fading memory).

Sonia Yuspeh, who formerly directed all research and planning in J. Walter Thompson, New York, has published convincing evidence to demonstrate that significant differences in recall scores take place as a result of different program environments. In thirty-six tests (six of each of six different commercials), different programs affected the outcome significantly in fourteen cases.[12]

The literature suggests even more fundamental problems concerned with recall testing. For instance, there is evidence that the *type of claim* will influence the level of recall. Young states unambiguously that recall testing discriminates in favor of explicit copy, "which communicates concrete, product-related benefits," and against implicit copy, "which communicates less tangible or more psychological benefits."[13] It is obvious that in most circumstances, with increases in a brand's store of added values, implicit copy will become relatively more important as it takes on some of the prominence that was held by explicit copy during a brand's introduction.

There is another point of great significance indeed. A powerful body of evidence has established that there is no simple and direct connection between factual recall on the one hand, and preference and buying behavior on the other. The point was first established by Jack B. Haskins in a seminal paper published in 1964, which was based on a total of twenty-eight empirical studies. His conclusion has been much republished: "[R]ecall and retention measures seem, at best, irrelevant to the ultimate effects desired, the changing of attitudes and behavior."[14] Much further evidence has been collected during the intervening two decades, but Haskins's central conclusion has never been seriously disputed.

Rather late in the day, practitioners, disturbed by the weaknesses in the connection between factual recall and attitudes and behavior, have encouraged syndicated research companies to offer "persuasion" measures as a supplement to recall scores. In most cases, the persuasion is evaluated in the highly unrealistic surroundings of theater tests, and simplified scores are adduced to attempt to describe complex attitudinal currents. As with so many ready-made research mechanisms, I fear that they represent nothing more than another step along the path to the philosophers' stone, the mythical device to create boundless wealth. I have first-hand knowledge that one very large advertiser has been collecting "persuasion" scores from day-after-recall tests for ten years, and is presumably attempting to relate the scores from the thousands of commercials tested to the latter's effectiveness in the marketplace. The fact that such scores are not yet used in this company as part of its decision-making process means that we can draw the reasonable inference that there is to date no proven connection between a persuasion score and a commercial's selling power.

The question that immediately suggests itself is why ready-made research techniques, in particular recall testing, are so widely and apparently uncritically employed by many demonstrably successful manufacturing companies as a quality control over their advertising. Perhaps these advertisers have learned special and sensitive ways of interpreting such scores. Perhaps they are attracted by the very simplicity of the findings, a refreshing change in an increasingly complicated world. Perhaps they do not ask themselves what the scores really mean, but accept them in blind faith as prompts to action: go or no-go.

I am inclined to accept the last of these hypotheses, because it has not been unknown in the past for sophisticated advertisers to express unthinking, albeit temporary faith in philosophers' stones. (The name of Schwerin comes immediately to mind.) But in order to examine these hypotheses more seriously, we should take a look at advertising research in broader terms than recall alone. We can do this most sensibly if we include in our discussion some notions of how advertising actually works in the real world. We are going to look in fact at some of the more visible mechanisms of the small apparatus at the center of the large machine described in chapter 1.

"Learn–Feel–Do" and "Learn–Do–Feel"

In the process of developing advertising ideas, making them into advertisements, and then exposing these advertisements experimentally before the expenditure of vast screentime appropriations, advertising research has two roles to play. First, it has a mainly diagnostic and generative role, which takes place before finished advertisements are prepared. Second, it has a quality-control role, which takes place mainly after the advertisements have been finished, and normally as a result of experimental exposure.

In its diagnostic role, the best and most widespread type of advertising research is qualitative, employing groups or small numbers of individual members of a defined target audience. The research is intended to help generate thought, to act as a sounding board for tentative ideas, to assess interest and clarity of communication. The numbers are rarely grossed up; indeed the research requires careful interpretation and is normally used in the main to help creative people in agencies. The sorts of questions the research attempts to provide answers to include "Is something wrong with this idea?", "Why is it wrong?", and "Is this alternative a way of getting it right?"

On the other hand, in its quality-control role, advertising research is primarily a tool for brand management to ensure that the finished advertising as it is about to be widely exposed meets certain criteria, particularly (if possible) in comparison with the advertising for competitive brands.

To simplify the distinction between roles, let me say that the creative, diagnostic research tends to be untidy, subtle, and sometimes implicit. Its purpose is to guide judgment. Quality-control research, in view of its primary function as a management tool, is tidy, ordered, simplified, and standardized. Shirley Young is particularly perceptive in her discussion of this point: "No other type of research, whether product testing, package testing, penetration studies, or strategy research, suffers from the burden of having to provide uniform techniques and simplistic scores to determine a course of action."[15] It would be unkind although not entirely untrue to regard this use of research not so much as a guide to judgment but more as a means of providing standards for managerial action.

If there is a realistic role for advertising research in this quality-control function (something I do not necessarily dispute), then it is undesirable to be inflexible about our systems. We should rather give some thought to the problems that the systems can help solve. This can only be done by analyzing and planning how our advertising is going to work in the marketplace. If the advertising is going to work by influencing consumers' mental processes *A, B,* and *C,* then we can find some research techniques to help us evaluate its effect on *A, B,* and *C.* In such circumstances, it makes more sense to tailor the research to the problem, and not just say, "Here is a research technique. Let's run the commercial through it."

Advertising can only work if it is received, comprehended, and responded to in some way. Response, on which we shall now focus, is partly a matter of psychology. It concerns learning, attitudes, and more importantly, behavior. In consumer goods marketing, behavior generally means buying, either for the first time, more frequently than before, or as frequently as before.

Learning, attitudes, and behavior are all influenced in some way by advertising, but to understand how advertising works, we need to know the order of events, so that we can employ research to help us progress from stage to stage. Here there is no shortage of opinions. As usual what is lacking is empirical validation.

The earliest theory was based on a simple chain of causality described by Charles Ramond as "learn–feel–do."[16] In this theory, people receive factual knowledge about a brand. As a result, their attitudes toward the brand change and they develop a preference for it. Then they buy it. The phase "hierarchy of effects" has been coined to describe the sequence;[17] it has also been entitled the "learning hierarchy."[18] The theory is an old one, the germ of which can be found in Starch's writings in the 1920s.[19] Over the years it has been presented in at least sixteen different forms.[20]

The theory has however been constantly disputed for a variety of reasons, the most serious being:

1. There is substantial evidence that communication also works in the reverse direction. Behavior influences attitudes, as people strive to reduce cognitive dissonance.[21] Indeed, probably the greatest single influence on attitudes to a brand is people's use of it. Behavior also influences learning, as a result of selective perception. In particular, users of a brand are normally those most conscious of the advertising for it.

2. The theory concentrates exclusively on change (increase in learning, improvement in attitudes, first purchase) and gives no attention to stationary patterns of consumer behavior connected with repeat purchasing. As we saw in chapter 5, such stationary patterns are so common as to be the normal situation with real markets.

3. It fails to enlighten us about certain well-established phenomena in the real world, such as the high failure rate of new brands, and the continued existence of minor brands with small market shares and advertising budgets.[22] If change is so simple and sequential, why does it not happen more often?

Perhaps most seriously, there have been only limited attempts to validate it empirically, with results falling far short of conclusive.[23] In the opinion of Michael Ray, who has been responsible for almost all the empirical work in this complex field, the learning hierarchy may possibly operate in cases in which "the audience is *involved* in the topic of the campaign and when there are *clear differences* between alternatives."[24] My own instinctive feeling is that this hierarchy is more likely to operate with print than with television advertising, and especially with direct response, which, when it works at all, does so as a complete stimulus (because a direct response advertisement works on its own on a one exposure basis); it must therefore embrace change of knowledge and attitudes.

A more subtle and pregnant theory than the learning hierarchy is the "low-involvement hierarchy" first propounded in the mid-1960s by Herbert E. Krugman. This has been described by Ramond as "learn–do–feel."[25] The notion hinges on the concept of low involvement, as it applies to people's relationships to products, brands, and media: relationships that might be described as a lack of emotional commitment because of the essential triviality of the purchase decision. Low involvement is something that, "while perhaps more common in response to commercial subject matter, is by no means limited to it."[26]

The theory was developed from Krugman's subjective impressions of the impact of television communication, and also from a somewhat questionable extrapolation of ancient and well-known investigations by the German experimental psychologist Ebbinghaus. But although Krugman's starting point seems far remote from a strong empirically based theory of advertising communication, the theory as it has been developed has an undeniable elegance and plausibility. The core of the argument is that in television advertising, there is a lack of consumer involvement in either brand or medium, and as a consequence, "perceptual defense may be absent . . . persuasion as such, i.e. overcoming a resistant attitude, is not involved at all," and commercials are only received and responded to as simple descriptions of brand attributes.

Decisions about buying are made simply as a result of consumers being subjected to "shifting [of] the relative salience of attributes." This hierarchy proceeds therefore by changing awareness and knowledge of brands, which in turn leads directly to a relatively casual purchase decision, which in turn leads to more knowledge and the development of attitudes stemming from brand use—a chain (in the words of the psychologist) of cognition—conation—affect. "With low involvement one might look for gradual shifts in perceptual structure, aided by repetition, activated by behavioral-choice situations, and *followed* at some time by attitude change."[27]

This theory is distinctly better than the learning hierarchy in two ways. First (and most important), it is compatible with the well-known fact that even if attitudes toward brands influence people's purchase of them, people's experience of brands (following purchase) has an equally important if not more important influence on attitudes. In other words, the interaction between attitudes and behavior is two-way.

The second advantage of the Krugman theory is that it has at least some empirical basis, albeit a rather flimsy one. From experiments in an artificial environment carried out by Michael Ray and his colleagues among a reasonably large sample of respondents, using purchase-intention and not direct behavioral measures, "it is clear that the 'Low Involvement' hierarchy occurs somewhat more often than the 'Learning' one. . . . In all, the involvement variable seems to explain hierarchy effects more clearly than does any other single mediating variable."[28]

Krugman himself carried out a limited program of experimental work, with the use of a piece of apparatus that calls for the most heroic assumptions to make it approximate even remotely to a publication that might be read by any human being, namely "a fourteen-page hard-cover portfolio that contains seven stop watches within the back cover of the portfolio. A complex of unseen pulleys permits the opening and closing of seven of the pages to be precisely timed."[29] There seems from these curious experiments to be evidence of a higher level of involvement with editorial copy than with advertising copy, a difference in involvement between different advertised products (higher for instance with airlines than with margarine), and a seemingly higher level of involvement in magazines than in television with high-involvement products (but not much difference with low-involvement products). These points are all general confirmation of Krugman's theory.

An extension of Krugman's hypothesis is the notion that the two hemispheres of the brain store different impressions and carry out different mental functions. The right hemisphere is supposedly concerned with pictorial impressions. The change in the salience of attributes (without the emotions being committed) which is characteristic of low-involvement learning as described by Krugman, is essentially a right-brain function. On the other hand, verbal processes including reading and speaking are supposedly the function of the left brain; high involvement is concerned with the left brain. (The distinction between these two discrete areas of activity is not irrelevant to the question of recall testing.)

Whether these two types of mental process have different physical *loci* has not been established with absolute certainty, although perhaps this aspect of the problem is not of material importance. But at least one practical attempt has been made (by Sidney Weinstein, and colleagues Valentine Appel and Curt Weinstein) to establish levels of brain wave activity for magazine and television advertising. Their work provides at least directional evidence that magazine advertising generates more brain wave activity than television advertising; that magazine advertising tends to generate more left-brain activity; and that *the more brain wave activity, the higher the brand recall.*[31] (I am quite unable to resist the richly comic image of these three researchers, clipboards in hand, solemnly observing a group of bewildered housewives with wires attached to their heads as they read *TV Guide*.)

In contrast to the learning hierarchy, which (if it operates at all) works with an involved consumer and clear differences between brands, the low-involvement hierarchy works with uninvolved consumers and where there are few obvious differences between the brand alternatives. But what of the cases where the functional differences between brands are of less importance than those based on *added values* which (as we saw in chapter 2) were built by time and advertising? In these cases, which almost certainly represent the majority of brands in real marketplaces, the low-involvement hierarchy does not tell the whole story. But it does lead to a modification of the concept which has, I believe, widespread validity, and which has been developed and explored with considerable intellectual rigor by Andrew Ehrenberg.[32] This hypothesis is the notion of trial and reinforcement, embracing the idea of advertising addressed to existing users of a brand and aimed at reinforcing their preference for it, so that it will remain at least in its present position in their repertoires, and perhaps be upgraded from minor to major brand (in exceptional cases from major to sole brand). The reader who has followed the argument in this book will realize that this notion of trial and reinforcement is entirely compatible with everything I have said, and in particular with the primary role of advertising in providing nonfunctional added values.

As the theory might have been described by Ramond, it is "do—feel—do," or an interaction of the conative and affective processes among existing users of a brand. A word borrowed from natural science, *resonance*, is an evocative way of expressing this continuous interaction of behavior and feelings. In Krugman's terms, this process might encompass the use of advertising to increase the degree of consumer involvement in a brand.

This theory is the only one of those considered so far that explains the way advertising operates as a contribution to the maintenance of essentially stationary patterns of consumer behavior. Krugman's original low-involvement hierarchy (I have scrutinized his writings carefully with this point in mind, and have found repeated emphasis on *changing* patterns of learning, behavior, and attitudes) explains only a minority of cases: new brands, sharply growing brands, and sharply declining brands. It is Ehrenberg's extension of the theory that explains the rest.

The Limited Circumstances when Recall Testing Can Be Useful

The purpose of attempting to analyze people's mental and behavioral responses to advertising is that the increased understanding will, it is hoped, lead to increased efficiency in advertising planning. In particular, if indeed three types of process (cognitive, conative, and affective) are at work, then separate types of research can be carried out to isolate the contribution of advertising to each of these processes. This point (which is by no means obvious until someone makes it, at which point we all react "of course!") was to the best of my knowledge first put forth and illustrated in a short paper by William R. Swinyard and Charles H. Patti based on a real life case.[33] Their paper explains clearly and simply why three different techniques provided different results when they were used to research a single series of commercials. The three techniques were measuring different things; judgment on the relative importance of learning, doing, and feeling in the particular marketing situation was needed to choose the most *relevant* research technique to apply to the commercials. Bearing this important point in mind, let us consider the three processes and the appropriate research techniques to help us understand how a particular advertising situation is likely to influence our choice of which to use.

It is not difficult for the advertising generalist—let alone the research specialist—to understand that in monitoring the "learning" process, recall testing should in theory be useful, despite such formidable difficulties as measurement. In monitoring the "doing" process, there are measures of purchase intention and more reliable measures of actual marketplace buying. In monitoring the "feeling" process, there are a number of ways of evaluating, once or repeatedly, people's attitudes to brands, including particular as well as general attitudes and the strength of all these attitudes relative to other brands. The reader will note that of these three processes, recall testing is concerned only with learning. The relevance of recall testing to a particular campaign depends therefore on the importance of learning in the role that has been (or should be) established for this campaign.

Let us now return to those hypotheses for how advertising works. Let us also make the reasonable assumption that the advertising for some brands works in one way; in a second way for other brands; and in a third way for still other brands. Note the suggestion here that the determining factor for the way in which advertising will work in particular cases is the state of the *brand* and the role of advertising for that brand at that particular time. So, to particular examples.

1. *"Learn–Feel–Do" (The Learning Hierarchy)*

The theoretical framework of this hypothesis makes a seemingly good case for using research in a hierarchical format involving:

recall testing to evaluate learning,

attitudinal and persuasion measures to evaluate feelings,

purchase-intention or actual purchase measures to evaluate behavior.

Much research has been carried out using this framework without any noticeable increase in the efficiency with which manufacturers have been able to launch successful new brands. The system has not worked on many occasions because it suffers from two faults.

First, individual manufacturers have not evaluated with sufficient care whether advertising in their particular cases is going to be working in the way in which the learning hierarchy postulates. As suggested, it seems only to work in exceptional cases in the real world, where involvement and functional discriminators between brands are both relatively high. Second, although the learning hierarchy may work in isolated circumstances, and factual learning about a campaign (or about a brand) may be a desirable quality as a foundation to an argument directed at improving attitudes as well as building preference and eventually purchasing, there is no direct link between factual knowledge on the one hand, and attitudes and behavior on the other. This conclusion has been established as a result of considerable empirical study and is one of the few things we know about factual recall with virtually complete certainty.

We can however conclude that in those relatively few cases in which advertising works by means of the learning hierarchy, recall testing may be of some value. There is however a simpler and more reliable testing mechanism available for direct response advertisements (which I suspect may be the most important examples of the learning hierarchy at work), the sort of testing that direct response practitioners have used for a hundred years. They simply expose the advertisement a couple of times and count the coupons! This is a far more complete and reliable mechanism than recall testing, and in many cases also a cheaper one.

2. *"Learn–Do–Feel" (The Low-Involvement Hierarchy)*

As Krugman's various writings imply, the theory of a low-involvement hierarchy is relevant to the vast majority of packaged goods *in their introductory phase* (before a body of regular users has been built, a period that can vary from six months to two years). As I have discussed in the context of the learning hierarchy, there is a seemingly good case for monitoring recall (at least of a brand's functional characteristics) on the assumption that recall is a basic first ingredient for a working campaign. If for no other reason than to establish brand identity in oligopolistic markets, a manufacturer of a new brand will anyway insist that potential customers be taught *precisely* and vividly that it fights cavities or dandruff, is easy to apply, or tastes of strawberries; or that the pack is large; or that the product is liquid or whatever. The reader will note that I have concentrated on facts about the brand. It is not so easy to make a case for communicating campaign slogans or claims, although Rosser Reeves, a distinguished advertising man and former chairman of Ted Bates, published a best-selling book making just such a case,[34] one which I am convinced is essentially fallacious.[35] Reeves was a powerful thinker and dialectician, but he seems to have strived to propose a general theory for how advertising works with no exceptions. My own inductive approach is quite different, and by its nature admits of exceptions.

But if we are going to use recall testing as part of a research program for a new brand of packaged goods, we shall need to be conscious of all the qualifications in interpreting the data.

In the first instance, we must remember the many measurement problems described earlier in this chapter. There is no certain way to avoid the various factors contaminating the data, but one useful although expensive procedure is to average out their effects by taking multiple measurements, for instance by checking twenty-four-hour recall in a number of different cities and in more than one television show of the same type in each city. There is evidence from Yuspeh's study that this avoids many of the eccentricities of individual recall scores.[36]

A second point is that we should judge carefully whether one *type of claim* will influence the level of recall. As already mentioned, research has provided at least directional evidence that mental activity concerned with verbal processes (the supposedly left-brain variety) generates higher recall levels than activity concerned with pictorial impressions. This is essentially my earlier point that recall testing discriminates in favor of explicit copy and against implicit copy.

A third point is that we should never lose sight of the proven lack of connection between advertisement recall and attitudes and behavior. The communication of factual points is only the beginning of what is required for effective advertising. Much more is needed for an effect. In particular an advertisement must evoke some type of emotional response from the target consumer.

It is possible, by using qualitative techniques, to find how well an advertisement communicates, how well it reflects consumer perceptions of a brand, and how well consumers empathize with it. But these things can be accomplished less well by the use of standardized persuasion measures, which are in effect little more than an extension of recall measures. In any event, the essence of the low-involvement hierarchy is the *absence* of hard persuasion (overcoming a resistant attitude) in the initial purchase process. I consequently find it difficult to understand the value of measuring the ability of a commercial to persuade directly in this way.

A delightfully fresh perspective on the measurement of advertising attention value and its ability to persuade is provided by a well-known paper by Leo Bogart and his colleagues (which will be considered in fuller detail in chapter 9).[37] Their evidence confirms all the other research: "[T]here is almost no relationship between an ad's sales performance—when compared with other ads—and its comparative readership performance, as measured either by recognition or recall."[38] But the researchers also published most interesting data on the abilities of eighty-three advertising decision makers in leading advertising centers in the United States to judge the effectiveness of particular advertisements. This investigation demonstrated that the experts have a good general ability to judge before the event an advertisement's attention-value, but that is about all. "The experts did very well in predicting readership performances, their record in predicting attitude change was mixed, and they could not predict which ads would sell more of the brand." It would not be stretching the case too far to deduce from these findings that recall studies are not only inadequate, they are also unnecessary.

3. "Do–Feel–Do" (The Reinforcement Hypothesis)

"Do–feel–do" is the way in which advertising probably works in most cases in the real world. The hypothesis embraces behavior and feelings exclusively, so factual learning and, as a result, recall testing as a way of measuring consumer knowledge should normally play no part in the process.

There is one minor exception. When a brand is restaged with some dramatic change in its formula, packaging, or advertising claims, it is important to measure once and for all how well the consumer recognizes these changes. In one case I witnessed at an advertising agency, a brand in a weak fourth place (5-percent volume share) in a highly competitive market was restaged with a dramatic change of campaign. It was important for the manufacturer and agency to know that the advertised brand attributes had been communicated quickly, so as to know when the campaign should be taken to its next stage. But advertising changes as radical as those used for this brand's re-launch are unusual, and in this case they were only implemented because of the brand's weak position, which had indeed gotten worse immediately before the restage.

The normal research procedure for ongoing brands in stationary markets and with established campaigns is to monitor campaign effects by means of tracking studies, a process of continuous monitoring. The reader should note that in this we move from measuring the effect of a single advertisement exposure to monitoring the effects on a brand of a total advertising campaign (together with other marketing variables). These studies are common and are often extremely useful. But there can also be problems.

Tracking Studies

Tracking studies are of two main types: those measuring consumer knowledge of advertising and those measuring knowledge of the functional properties and image attributes of brands (which is of course a measurement with strong affective overtones). Of the former, the commonest type is proven advertising recall. It has been widely practiced by Leo Burnett in the United Kingdom, where the data have been extensively analyzed, and generalizable patterns described and published.[39] The word *adstock* is used to describe the measure of advertising recall at the end of a period, representing the effect on recall of the advertising during that period, plus the decayed effect of advertising from previous periods. The term *half-life* is used to describe how long it takes to reduce the *adstock* by half without extra advertising to "top it up." The rate of decay can be measured and modelled. When a newly exposed campaign arrests (or increases) this decay, its effect can be isolated and quantified in terms of its ability to augment (or attenuate) the adstock.

The procedure is plausible; the use of continuous measurement probably eliminates the effect of contaminations in the data. Nevertheless, in the circumstances in which the measure is used as a surrogate for the behavioral effect of a campaign, its users cannot refute the argument that there is no identifiable relationship between recall and sales. Indeed, in the cases in which increases in advertising awareness have been related statistically to increases in sales, the direction of causality has not been established. It can be strongly argued that the progression actually goes from sales to recall, rather than the other way round, since the strongest influence on awareness of (and attitudes to) a brand is normally whether the consumer uses it or not.[40]

A greatly more useful type of tracking study is the continuous monitoring of image attributes. Such studies often reveal subtle relationships which are capable of providing unusual insights. In one real case I saw of a premium-priced brand, the main desired response to the brand was value for money. The advertising did not mention value for money specifically, but was concerned with related brand values, not just physical features. Homemakers were aware of the premium price; when we discovered through continuous image measurement that they were beginning to believe increasingly that the brand offered both the explicit attributes and also good value for money (a point they had to work out for themselves), we knew that the campaign was working in terms of buyer psychology. We also had confirming evidence of effectiveness from econometric studies isolating the results of the advertising from the other marketing variables.

Not many studies of this sort have been published because of the proprietary nature of the data. But I am aware of at least two reliable ones published in simplified form: those dealing with Listerine in Canada[41] and Andrex bathroom tissue in the United Kingdom.[42]

In these published studies (and in the many proprietary ones that I have worked with over the years) the interacting variables are changes in buyers' beliefs in specific image attitudes of the brand and their purchasing of it. Such changes tend to be quite small in the short term, so that mutations may be a better way of describing them.

As with the continuous tracking of advertising awareness, it is unclear from this research whether the mutation in attitude precedes the change in behavior or vice versa. But since the essence of the reinforcement hypothesis is mutual interaction or resonance between the variables, the exact order of events is not materially important here.[43]

There have been some academic investigations of the relationship between attitude measures and sales, but these do not add much to what has been learned by manufacturers from a long-term study of their brands.[44] One of these studies, after examining a number of cases with the use of a fairly complex mathematical model, concluded "The findings have consistently demonstrated that the affective dimension is significantly more effective (sic) in explaining variance in market share than the cognitive or usage dimensions."[45] In other words, this work tended to support the direction of operation from attitude to behavior, rather than the mutual interaction. If this research provides a true picture of the direction of causality, it reinforces strongly the operational validity of tracking studies of image attributes.

The Argument in Brief—And a Footnote on Aggregated Data

Even when we give recall testing the benefit of every doubt, the most serious uncertainties remain. It is not easy to accept uncritically a measure contaminated with such methodological distortions. Nor is it easy to appreciate the relevance of a measure that applies only to reasonably exceptional advertising circumstances. At its best, recall testing is only reliable if used in conjunction with other measures because of the proven lack of connection between recall, and attitudes and sales. There is even sketchy evidence that recall testing is hardly necessary if a campaign is scrutinized by experienced judges of advertising.

Recall tests remain nevertheless the most widespread type of advertising research. They are a standard operating procedure of many successful companies, whose very success robs academic criticism of much of its plausibility, at least in the eyes of people unacquainted at first hand with large, successful companies. But some of us believe that no company is so successful that it can ignore scrutiny of *all* its operating procedures; there might be some surprises.

The facts described in this chapter show clearly that recall testing is only relevant to a minority of advertising situations. There are three such situations. First there are cases where the learning hierarchy applies (although in many of these, direct response may be a simpler and more reliable testing system). Second, there is the introductory phase of a new brand, a period of six months to two years, when the brand is building its body of regular and occasional users. Third is the rare occasion when an ongoing brand reaches a situation requiring radically new advertising that puts special emphasis on functional benefits. This is generally when the brand is losing occasional users, and the role of the advertising is to encourage them to reappraise the brand by reconsidering its salient physical attributes. It follows from these points that recall testing should only be used for the examination of factual, product-related advertising claims.

There are also strong indications that recall testing should not be employed in isolation. In particular, it should be used in conjunction with the generally more reliable and sensitive mechanism of continuous image measurement. In most advertising situations (for ongoing brands sold to existing regular and occasional users), image measurement should be the basic tool for advertising research.

There is great emphasis on multiple measurement in the 1982 PACT ("Positioning Advertising Copy Testing") recommendation (or "Consensus Credo") of twenty-one leading advertising agencies in the United States.[46] This document makes a number of sensible general recommendations concerning advertising research, although surprisingly it does not comment on individual techniques such as recall testing.

It is also necessary to use a large data base for recall testing. For twenty-four-hour recall, a number of cities and more than one television program in each city should be employed. The greater the number of recall readings that are averaged, the more the possibility of eliminating the factors contaminating individual measures. But naturally the cost goes up in direct proportion.

It is also important to use the data *comparatively,* not absolutely. Norms for product categories provided by the major twenty-four-hour recall services are reasonably useful, although care is needed when we compare recall of specific commercials with these norms.

Even Starch, with all its imperfections, can be enlightening if used on a broadly aggregated basis, in comparison with norms. For instance, one measure from among many that could have been chosen—an examination of the following findings from 250 tests of magazine color page advertisements—indicates clearly the superiority of advertisements containing recipes over those not containing recipes.[47] The large data base averages out the effects of many of the statistical contaminations discussed in this chapter. What matters is the *comparative* interpretation here.

	Median "noted" ratings		Median "read most" ratings	
	Rating	Index	Rating	Index
All 250 ads	51.7%	100	13.4%	100
Ads containing recipes	57.5	111	21.3	159
Ads without recipes but showing end results	51.4	99	11.4	85
Ads without recipes and without end results	40.6	77	7.4	54

The precise meaning of this table is *not* that in representative cases 57.5 percent of people noticed before and therefore recognize now an advertisement with a recipe, as opposed 40.6 percent of people who noticed before and therefore recognize now an advertisement without a recipe or end results. Nevertheless, I have no doubt that the data are an unambiguous indication not only that food advertisements containing recipes are more valuable than food advertisements without them, but that the ratio of preference for recipes compared to no recipes is at least of the order of the "noted" ratings (and maybe even the "read most" ratings.) By this process of using aggregated data comparatively, we have avoided precise explanations of what the Starch data mean, and have focused attention on what matters in this analysis: the relative values of food advertisements that contain recipes and those that do not. Is it not true here that the Starch information is being used similarly to how a catalyst is used in a chemical process: as a means of making other things happen (in this case a comparison of advertising techniques) without itself entering directly into what is happening? It would not be a bad objective for us to use advertising research universally in this particular way.

Notes

1. For example, a research report I recently received from a major university in the Midwest included an analysis of responses from a sample of ninety-four individuals. These responses were percentaged to one decimal place, which created an entirely spurious impression of accuracy within narrow limits.

2. The turnover of Burke Marketing Services was over $66 million in 1984, according to *Advertising Age,* May 23, 1985: 17.

Among a sample of thirty-seven of the largest users of televison advertising, twenty-six were found to be users of day-after-recall in 1980. Barbara Coe and James MacLachlan, "How Major TV Advertisers Evaluate Commercials," *Journal of Advertising Research* (December 1980): 51–54. From my many discussions with manufacturers and advertising agencies, I believe that the technique is still used extremely widely, although in the mid-1980s, it is most commonly used in conjunction with other types of advertising research.

3. Charles Ramond, *Advertising Research: The State of the Art* (New York: Association of National Advertisers, 1976), p. 2.

4. Darrell B. Lucas, "The ABCs of ARF's PARM," *Journal of Marketing* (July 1960): 9–20. Although Lucas was the first investigator to publish his thoughts on this subject, he was not the first to examine it. See also Valentine Appel and Milton L. Blum, "Ad Recognition and Respondent Set," *Journal of Advertising Research* (June 1961): 13–21.

5. Lucas, "The ABCs of ARF's PARM," 16.

6. W.A. Twyman, *The Measurement of Page and Advertisement Exposure—A Review of Progress of the ARC* (London: Agencies Research Consortium, 1972).

7. D. Morgan Neu, "Measuring Advertisement Recognition," *Journal of Advertising Research* (December 1961): 17–22; Lyman E. Ostlund, "Advertising Copy Testing: A Review of Current Practices, Problems and Prospects" in *Current Issues and Research in Advertising,* ed. J. Leigh and C. Martin, Jr. (Ann Arbor: University of Michigan, 1977), p. 99.

8. J.S. Karslake, "The Purdue Eye-Camera: A Practical Apparatus for Studying the Attention Value of Advertisements," *Journal of Applied Psychology* 24 (1940): 417–40; J.J. McNamara, "A New Method of Testing Effectiveness through Eye Movement Photographs," *The Psychological Record* (Bloomington, Indiana, September 1941): 399–460.

The importance of these pioneer studies is discussed by David R. Aitchison, "Some Thoughts on the Readership of Advertisements," *Admap World Advertising Workshop* (1970).

9. The experimental work preceding the validation is discussed in Twyman, *The Measurement of Page and Advertisement Exposure—A Review of Progress of the ARC,* pp. 22–25. See also Robert Fletcher and Bill Mabey, "Reading and Noting Revived!," *Admap* (December 1971): 422–28.

10. Art Shulman, "On-Air Recall by Time of Day," *Journal of Advertising Research* (February 1972): 21–23.

11. Shirley Young, "Copy Testing without Magic Numbers," *Journal of Advertising Research* (February 1972): 3–12.

12. Sonia Yuspeh, "The Medium versus the Message: The Effects of Program Environment on the Performance of Commercials" in *Tenth Attitude Research Conference,* Hilton Head, S.C. (American Marketing Association, 1979).

13. Young, "Copy Testing without Magic Numbers," 6.

14. Jack B. Haskins, "Factual Recall as a Measure of Advertising Effectiveness," *Journal of Advertising Research* (March 1964): 2–8.

15. Young, "Copy Testing without Magic Numbers," 3.

16. Ramond, *Advertising Research: The State of the Art,* pp. 14–22.

17. Kristian S. Palda, "The Hypothesis of a Hierarchy of Effects: A Partial Evaluation," *Journal of Marketing Research* (February 1966): 13–24.

18. Michael L. Ray, Alan G. Sawyer, Michael L. Rothschild, Roger M. Heeler, Edward C. Strong, and Jerome B. Reed, "Marketing Communication and the Hierarchy of Effects" in *New Models for Mass Communication Research,* ed. Peter Clarke (Beverly Hills, Calif.: Sage, 1973), p. 151.

19. Daniel Starch, *Principles of Advertising* (Chicago and New York: A.W. Shaw, 1923), pp. 159–60.

20. Ramond, *Advertising Research: The State of the Art,* p. 15.

21. This notion was introduced by Leon Festinger, "Cognitive Dissonance," *Scientific American* (October 1962): 93–102.

22. These arguments are developed by Andrew Ehrenberg in "Repetitive Advertising and the Consumer," *Journal of Advertising Research* (April 1974): 25–33.

23. Henry Assael and George S. Day, "Attitudes and Awareness as Predictors of Market Share," *Journal of Advertising Research* (December 1968): 3–10; Terrence O'Brien, "Stages of Consumer Decision Making," *Journal of Marketing Research* (August 1971): 283–89. Ray *et al.,* "Marketing Communication and the Hierarchy of Effects," chap. 5. pp. 147–76.

24. Ray *et al.,* "Marketing Communication and the Hierarchy of Effects," p. 151.

25. Ramond, *Advertising Research: The State of the Art,* p. 18.

26. Herbert E. Krugman, "The Impact of Television Advertising: Learning without Involvement," *Public Opinion Quarterly* 29 (1965): 350–56.

27. *Ibid.,* 355.

28. Ray *et al.,* "Marketing Communication and the Hierarchy of Effects," pp. 158–64.

29. Herbert E. Krugman, "The Measurement of Advertising Involvement," *Public Opinion Quarterly* (Winter 1966–67): 586, footnote.

30. *Ibid.,* 587.

31. Sidney Weinstein, Valentine Appel, and Curt Weinstein, "Brain Activity Responses to Magazine and Television Advertising," *Journal of Advertising Research* (June 1980): 57–63.

32. Ehrenberg, "Repetitive Advertising and the Consumer."

33. William R. Swinyard and Charles H. Patti, "The Communications Hierarchy

Framework for Evaluating Copytesting Techniques," *Journal of Advertising* (Summer 1979): 29–35.

34. Rosser Reeves, *Reality in Advertising*. In a nutshell, his theory is predicated on the notion that knowledge of advertising claims determines brand purchase. This ignores, among other things, the reverse influence: as is widely known, users of a brand pay more attention to advertisements for it because of selective perception.

35. This point has been nicely demonstrated by Kim B. Rotzoll in "The Starch and Ted Bates Correlative Measures of Advertising Effectiveness," *Journal of Advertising Research* (March 1964): 22–24.

36. Yuspeh, "The Medium Versus the Message."

37. Leo Bogart, B. Stuart Tolley, and Frank Orenstein, "What One Little Ad Can Do," *Journal of Advertising Research* (August 1970): 3–13.

38. *Ibid.*, 12.

39. *The Leo Burnett Book of Advertising*, ed. Simon Broadbent, (London: Business Books, 1984), pp. 86–98. Stephen Colman and Gordon Brown, "Advertising Tracking Studies and Sales Effects," *Journal of the Market Research Society* 25, no. 2 (1983): 165–83.

40. Ehrenberg, "Repetitive Advertising and the Consumer": 29.

41. Stephen A. Greyser, *Cases in Advertising and Communications Management*, 2d ed., pp. 148–67.

42. Stephen King, *What Is a Brand?* pp. 5–9.

43. See the general discussion on this point in Roy H. Campbell, *Measuring the Sales and Profit Results of Advertising: A Managerial Approach* (New York: Association of National Advertisers, 1969), pp. 61–63.

44. Joel N. Axelrod, "Attitude Measures that Predict Purchase," *Journal of Advertising Research* (March 1968): 3–17.

45. Assael and Day, "Attitudes and Awareness as Predictors of Market Share": 3–10.

46. The Positioning Advertising Copy Testing Agencies, "Positioning Advertising Copy Testing" (January 1982).

47. Data from *Ladies Home Journal* (July 1959).
The Starch readings relate to reading-and-noting figures for 250 four-color page advertisements which appeared in sixteen issues of the *Ladies Home Journal*.

7
Advertising Campaigns—Strategy and the Leap

"Language is worth a thousand pounds a word!"

"I shall dream about a thousand pounds tonight, I know I shall!" thought Alice.

I t is time to pick up again the main line of the argument and in fact to approach the most important part of it. We shall be mainly concerned in this chapter with advertising as it influences a typical established brand. It would not harm us, in view of our recent digression, to start by reviewing how the various forces in the market have influenced such a brand and guided it to its present position.

As a result of more or less effective planning of all the eight major factors determining the success of a brand (as discussed in chapters 3 and 4), our brand has against the odds built a position vis-à-vis other brands, and is on the repertoire of a group of regular and occasional users. Now that the brand is off the ground, this position is maintained largely by two of these factors: the brand's functional performance in comparison with its competitors, and by the added values that have been built in the main by the advertising. Most of this advertising is, as we have seen, now directed at existing users, in order to maintain the brand as first choice for the regulars and to increase the frequency of purchase of occasional buyers. The advertising works in the way suggested by the reinforcement hypothesis to build up, for buyers of the brand, a resonance or mutual interaction and reinforcement of behavior and attitudes.

In the process of repeat buying, inertia (unthinking continuity of behavior) plays a large role and is a major force leading to the sort of stationary conditions described in chapter 5. The total market in which our brand competes is reasonably constant in size. The brand's market share is also reasonably stable. There is no shortage of activity in the market, but much of this is self-cancelling by the very nature of oligopolistic competition, such activity taking place for basically protective reasons. Changes in consumer behavior are quite small; it is the *repetition* of this behavior that has the major long-term effect on sales.

The normal brand is restaged once every three years or so, with restaging commonly involving adjustments to both functional performance and advertising (as the fount of added values). What makes the effect of advertising often quite large is how it influences both the repeat business generated by new consumer trialists and also the extra profit yielded by all marginal sales increases.

For a brand with a 10-percent volume share, a restage would be considered successful if it added a clear one or two percentage points (the equivalent of a 10-percent or 20-percent increase in the brand's sales in a stationary market). Such an increase would partly come from the acquisition of a few infrequent users. (The reader will remember the direct relationship between share growth and penetration growth.) But it will also come—more substantially—from increased purchasing by existing users. It follows that if the restage is successful, it will influence more existing users than new users, and they will be responsible for much the largest quantity of extra sales. There is therefore virtually never any question of addressing restage advertising exclusively to new users rather than existing users of the brand. The latter will remain the group with the greatest sales potential.

We have then an established brand about to be restaged. To be precise about our objectives, we should think not exclusively in volume terms, but also of profit. Let us now look at four ways in which advertising can influence the success of the restage. A restage in the real world would involve an adjustment to more than one of these ways, and would also involve (as we have seen) nonadvertising variables (notably the brand's functional performance and how this is displayed on the packaging).

Of the four advertising variables, one is concerned with the budget; two are concerned with the media in which this budget is deployed; and one is concerned with the campaign itself. Of the four factors, three are quantitative; one is qualitative.

1. The advertising budget can be changed. It can be increased, with the intention of increasing sales, and this depends on the advertising elasticity of the brand as discussed in chapter 4. In theory of course, the advertising budget can also be decreased, with the intention of increasing not sales but profits, which also depends on the advertising elasticity of the brand and on its advertising:sales ratio. But with a restage, there are psychological reasons why a budget will not be reduced, so that the pressure variable will always be pressure increase.

2. The media can be changed. Completely fresh media can be used and/or the individual media vehicles (television dayparts, print magazines, and so on) can be changed.

3. The media can be differently phased. Advertising can take place at dif-

ferent times of the year and/or it can be compressed into shorter periods or extended into longer ones.
4. The campaign can be changed.

During normal restages, a modest budgetary increase (say, 10 percent above any normal increase reflecting media inflation) is commonplace. This is done as much as anything else as an act of faith to all concerned (not least the sales force and retail trade) that the manufacturer is taking the restage seriously.

The problem with increases of a much greater magnitude than this is that they must demonstrate their effectiveness dramatically in order to be justified financially, at least in the short term. The funds to cover the cost of the extra advertising pressure must come not from the increased volume of sales, but from the increased volume of net profit generated by those sales (which represents of course only a fraction of the total revenue). The reader can easily explore the financial implications of, say, a 50-percent uplift in the advertising budget for brands that yield the manufacturer different levels of net return. For a brand with an advertising:sales ratio of 5 percent and that makes a 10-percent profit, a 50-percent advertising uplift would need a sales increase of at least 25 percent to justify it. If the profit is only 5 percent, the sales increase has to be at least 50 percent.

From my own experience of ongoing brands in reasonably stationary market conditions, increases of 25 percent or 50 percent are normally not realistic objectives for tests of increased pressure and nothing else. Indeed, it has been estimated that 95 percent of pressure tests actually fail.[1] This is more complex to evaluate empirically than it appears at first glance. Published cases naturally deal mainly with the more dramatic or at least unambiguous successes, but even here sales increases of a substantial order are rare indeed. The most favorable of the published cases of which I am aware, which is for a brand of cold remedy, shows a higher offtake (measured in market share) of approximately 40 percent in regions of high advertising compared with regions of low advertising. (The maximum advertising uplift was 50 percent). But the overall 40-percent increase attributable to the advertising includes a number of months of low-season sales, so that the increases if measured in absolute terms could have been of a lower magnitude.[2]

Two other published cases are a good deal less dramatic. In one, which was presented at the 1973 Advertising Research Foundation Conference, a doubling of advertising expenditure yielded a volume sales uplift of approximately 20 percent.[3] In the other, a complex media and pressure test for the launch of the AT&T Princess telephone, one group of areas received three times the pressure of advertising that other areas did, with substantially indeterminate results when measured in sales. There was a difference in advertising recall, and readers of chapter 6 will note that here is yet another case in which measured recall response bore no resemblance to measured sales response.[4]

My skepticism about the viability of pressure testing is based on the assumption that there is no differential rate of profit at the two levels of sales, with and without extra advertising pressure. If however the extra advertising is funded by an increase in the retail price of the brand, the possibilities of profitable increases in advertising of course become much greater.

The two factors relating to media do not stand up very well on their own. A change of medium is, as often as not in the real world, really a change of campaign, and so is best judged when we look at the influence of the creative, or qualitative variable. It is rare indeed for agencies to decide on the media strategy and then write a campaign for the selected medium. With real brands, the campaign decision and media decision are made together. This does not mean that there is not a great deal of discussion in agencies about the media implications of proposed campaign changes, but the very fact that a fruitful new creative idea is expressed in a particular medium is normally the strongest argument for using that medium.[5]

The second factor relating to media is the question of phasing, the most important aspect of which is a comparison of "flighting" (concentration of weight) and "drip feeding" (dispersion of weight). It is however a subject normally related to reductions in budget weight for an ongoing brand, rather than a restage strategy, a point to be picked up in chapters 8 and 9.

I should however emphasize that all that has been talked about so far is quantities, what I impolitely described in chapter 4 as brute force. Deploying these quantities with the help of econometric tools can on occasion be a fruitful endeavor. Profits in the competitive capitalist system are made essentially at the margin, and small adjustments of input variables can yield disproportionate results. But if luck favors our brand and there is a positive result, this is something controllable, to an extent predictable, and probably fairly small. In the search for an increase of a different order of magnitude, a jump rather than a modest progression, we must look to the last of the four variables concerned with advertising, the one to which the rest of this chapter is devoted. We must get near to the small apparatus at the center of my large machine, and devote ourselves at last to a study of how it works.

The Qualitative Variable

This section is devoted to five distilled case studies. Four come from the British market. This is simply a reflection of my professional experience rather than any lack of appropriate American material. I simply prefer to discuss cases of which I have first-hand knowledge.

How are we to evaluate the contribution of advertising in comparison with contributions made by other marketing variables? It is commonly believed that the influence of advertising cannot in any precise scientific way be disentangled from these other variables.[6] This view is however disputed by those who have had experience of field experiments, and in particular by those who have found ways of fitting mathematical models to certain market conditions.[7] These analyses can be very convincing. When they simply cannot be carried out for lack of appropriate data, it is often possible to provide serviceable surrogates, some of which will be used in this chapter.

Advertising always has two types of effect, and the relative weight attached to each of these can vary considerably. But since both effects stem from the one source—advertising—it may not always matter that we cannot separate the effects of the two with scientific rigor.

The two effects are:

1. *The direct effect.* This is advertising's ability to induce people to buy a brand once (the short-term direct effect), and also the repeat purchase which results from this sale (the long-term direct effect).
2. *The indirect effect.* This is the influence of advertising on certain other marketing variables, notably advertising's ability to inject adrenaline into the sales force and the retail trade, leading in particular to better display at point of sale.

In frozen food (a product field in which I was engaged for four years) the prime determinant of sales is the stock and display of a brand in the freezer compartment of the supermarket (an area of fixed size, which makes any increase in the display of one brand automatically at the expense of others). This product field also has a very short retail pipeline, with changes in consumer offtake being reflected in ex-factory sales within a period as short as a week. My routine evaluation of store displays and ex-factory sales over the years made me virtually certain that advertising operates with frozen food almost exclusively in an indirect way: by influencing the sales force and the retail trade. This did not mean that the advertising with which I was concerned was not working. On the contrary, it was working well, but it did so almost entirely by influencing people *other than* consumers.

In many cases in which advertising is evaluated, the main decision about whether to increase, continue as before, reduce, or stop a campaign is made on the basis of a number of reasonably simple measures. These must include consumer sales and generally also some continuous measurement of consumers' attitudes to brands.

Of our five case studies, two are evaluated by means of rigorous mathematical analysis. The other three employ simpler ways of examining the data, but in most cases use *multiple* measures that tend to be self-confirming. The reader should be in a position to weigh all these types of evidence. In my judgment, they are all convincing.

But first, a qualification. Readers will not get from this chapter or indeed from this book a set of rules to enable them to write successful advertisements. The quality of advertising campaigns depends essentially on the quality of the people who write them. Some people possess and some people do not possess the ability to discern a special route (sometimes a most unexpected one) to solve a creative problem. It follows from this that rules cannot be devised, because rules lead to predictable solutions.

Next, an amplification. In the writing of advertisements, three separate procedures are involved: the strategy, the leap, and the craft skills. These are all equally important. They are quite different from one another. And they are relatively easy to describe.

First is the Strategy. At least three factors should be included in writing a strategy: a description of the target group; the brand's attributes which are to be emphasized; and the main role of the advertising. All agencies and many clients have their own ways of drawing these up, and the ground covered is always fairly similar. This process is essentially analytical and judgmental—what a perceptive analyst Edward de Bono calls "vertical," meaning straight and logically compelling.[8] In developing a strategy, we follow a route of "high probability." The facts move us along sequentially in a single direction. When different and equally talented people face the same facts, no matter how convoluted the problem, they all tend to end up with approximately the same strategic solution: presumably because they have gone through the same mental steps, as likely as not a result of the fact that they have all been educated in the same way.[9] In my observation, good strategic thinking is one of the (smaller) benefits of the traditional academic disciplines taught at respectable universities.

Second, the Leap. The leap, the discovery of the campaign idea, is a type of intellectual process quite different from formulating a strategy, requiring almost invariably a different type of mind from the one that has been so fastidiously groomed by the processes of formal education. Formal education simply is not a great deal of help in copywriting. Analytical skills are not of much use. The essence of the process is the ability to discover directions that are sometimes totally unexpected and/or to generate ideas that strike an intensely personal chord with the audience, which will therefore evoke emotional as well as rational responses. Some people can write advertisements and some people cannot. At first glance, it seems that the skills are innate and cannot be acquired, but my experience makes me think again; experiments I have regularly carried out with students have on occasion yielded the most surprising results. Readers will have guessed that the leap is at the very heart of my small apparatus, and they can rest assured that I shall be coming back to it later in this chapter.

Third, the Craft Skills. These are the relatively simple and easily described techniques for making effective use of a thirty-second television film, a color page advertisement, a billboard, and so on. Unlike the process of making the creative leap, rules *can* be drawn up about craft skills. An extensive literature describes many of these principles, which have been hallowed by time and experience. The best and most intellectually accessible work dealing with these issues is David Ogilvy's first and best book, *Confessions of an Advertising Man.*[10] Most professionals in the advertising business at least pay lip service to his ideas, but it is staggering to observe the number of advertisements, particularly those in print media, whose authors give no evidence at all that they believe in the simplest craft rules.[11]

I believe that there are five major factors involved in the development of campaigns. But instead of describing them in platitudes, I am going to illustrate them by means of five case studies.

In most of these five cases, as in most advertising situations, all five factors operate. I have however chosen each case to highlight one factor in particular.

Five Case Studies

Horlicks

Horlicks is an old established English branded beverage, a comforting bedtime drink. It is a powder mixed with hot milk to make a sweet, heavy liquid with a singular taste, which devotees often acquire at an early age. In English folklore it is incomparably good for relaxation and restful sleep. Perhaps unexpectedly, it has always been sensitive to advertising, and was built before 1939 by a classic campaign written by J. Walter Thompson in the form of a strip cartoon, the first major British brand to be advertised in this way. The strips featured a "slice of life," a technique which re-emerged on the television screen thirty years later. The stories were always about people whose sleep was not relaxed enough, and how they found themselves in trouble at work or in their personal lives until a friend told them about Horlicks. A memorable phrase associated with this early campaign was "night starvation," and how Horlicks provides reserves to compensate for the energy that is lost even in sleep. "Night starvation" is a phrase which has entered the English vocabulary.

In time the manufacturer, a long-standing family concern, was absorbed by the large, diversified, aggressive Beecham organization, but this did not impair the continued progress of Horlicks. Horlicks had by this time begun to use television advertising successfully. At the beginning of our story (1970–71), the brand was supported by television advertising devoted to restful sleep, which from evidence from qualitative research appealed strongly to *heavy users,* of which the brand has a large body.

Horlicks has a number of competitors: brands such as Bournvita and Ovaltine, which are also mixed with milk but which contain different ingredients. They are not drunk exclusively to promote sleep and relaxation, and are sold more for their taste and for what they contain. They are also not as strong as Horlicks in the marketplace. Of the light users of Horlicks, some do and some do not drink these competitors. (Those who do not are of course light users of the product field as a whole.)

The important marketing decision made around 1970 was to take a hard look at these light users as a likely means of boosting total consumption. It emerged from qualitative research that these people did not feel the need to drink Horlicks to enable them to sleep better, but they felt that Horlicks was good for general relaxation. The current television campaign therefore successfully appealed to existing heavy users (the people who used Horlicks to promote sleep), but *not* to light users, who believed but perhaps needed reminding that Horlicks is excellent for relaxation.

The strategic direction suggested by this research was toward a campaign concentrated on relaxation. A television film appropriately entitled "Relax" was exposed in one television area starting in January 1973. The danger with such a strategy of course was that the commercial would not work as well as a sleep-directed campaign to heavy users who, with Horlicks (as with nearly all brands) account for the greater proportion of tonnage sales. A "Sleep" commercial was therefore run in all parts of the country except in the relatively self-contained area where "Relax" was under test.

The evaluation of the sales effect of "Relax" was carried out by an econometric model. The system developed by Beecham, the area marketing test evaluation system (AMTES) is based on an extensive historical analysis of sales of a brand in an area, to isolate the many special influences of the area, including the ways in which there may have been a differential response to factors influencing the country as a whole. Superimposed on any special area trends (measured in terms of the area's sales as a percentage of national sales), additional variables are fed into the model to represent all the other factors thought to affect sales. This is of course a judgmental as well as a mathematical process, but Beecham has learned how to use the model in real situations, and it has for some years been of good predictive value. Derek Bloom, the executive then most associated with the AMTES model, is a respected analyst, and it is his published findings that have provided the data for this particular case.[12]

With the Horlicks test, the model produced projections for the course of 1973 demonstrating for the test area the normal ups and downs that would have been expected as a result of past trends and the particular idiosyncrasies of this area, *excluding* the effect of any new campaign. In other words, the model predicted sales in the test area on the assumption that it would receive the same advertising as the rest of the country.

Assuming that this trend line in the area represents a fair approximation of what might have been, then the *actual* sales in the area would give a reasonable estimate of the relative effect of the "Relax" film, especially since two special factors operated to give weight to the findings. First, Horlicks has always been a relatively advertising-intensive brand. Advertising is not and never has been a peripheral activity as far as it is concerned, so that a significant advertising effect would be expected. Second, Horlicks is a stronger brand than its competitors, so that the influence of retaliation can be discounted.

The result of the test was clear and quite dramatic. The relative sales uplift achieved by the "Relax" commercial was a best estimate of 20 percent for a period of a year, with some weakening at the end. Taking the most conservative estimate projected at the 95-percent confidence limit, "the increase could not have been less than 11% cumulatively over sixteen months."[13] When the commercial was subsequently exposed nationally, the best estimate of uplift was 14 percent for the whole of the first sixteen months of national exposure.

The reader will note the particular strategic analysis which preceded this successful test. Subsequent qualitative research indicated a favorable effect of the campaign against heavy users as well as against the specially targeted group of light users. But it should not need emphasizing that this impressive sales success would never have taken place unless the target group had been *explicitly analyzed in terms of brand usage,* unless the light users had been specifically isolated, and unless the subsequent campaign had been directed sharply at what was known about the attitudes of these people. This is the prime lesson of this case.

California Avocados

Californian avocados account for the lion's share, normally between 60 percent and 80 percent of the total United States market. Therefore the California industry quite rightly sees its main task as stimulating total consumption of avocados, rather than increasing its already dominant share of the market. Publicity is carried out with this goal in mind, although the timing of the campaigns is such that an extra emphasis can be given to California by concentrating efforts on when there is a seasonal shortage of avocados grown in other places.[14]

As with most primary products, there is a secular tendency for production to increase, encouraged by the long-term improvement in the producer price. In the five seasons 1970–75, total production was 128 percent above the five seasons 1950–55. But supplies will not keep in store from year to year, so the season's crop will therefore all be sold or thrown away. The role of advertising, as is invariably the case with agricultural products, is therefore mostly concerned with the producer price. Before the beginning of major advertising and promotional efforts, the producer price per bearing acre had in fact slipped by 30 percent on average during the five crop years 1955–60, compared with 1950–55. What the advertising aimed to do therefore was not to sell more avocados in the short-term, but to stimulate demand in order to sell what avocados were available at the highest possible price for the farmer.

The size of the crop is determined by the season's weather. On occasion bountiful seasons have led to dramatic price collapses. As a result of one such collapse, in 1959–60, the California Avocado Advisory Board was set up, to use advertising and sales promotion to increase consumer demand. The Board directed its efforts toward both regular and occasional users, making the assumption that when prices are high, irregular users drop out of the market and have to be won back with great effort.

A striking feature of the avocado market is the low level of consumption. According to consumer data collected in 1968–69, even the heaviest users then bought avocados only six times a year. The proportion of households buying avocados at all was also low (23 percent), but it was judged, probably correctly, that it is an easier task to persuade the homemakers who already buy this delicious fruit to buy more of it than before, than it is to persuade people who had not bought it at all in the past to overcome their unfamiliarity. The level of penetration and usage means that the advertising and promotional campaign was able to influence primary demand—overall basic demand for avocados. This is an unusual effect, for in the vast majority of markets, advertising only influences market shares, and has no effect at all on primary demand.

The campaign was funded by means of a maximum levy of 6.5 percent of the value of the avocado crop. This is an exceptionally high rate of contribution compared with my own experience of commodity advertising campaigns. This maximum was never spent, but the more normal going rate of under 5 percent was still rather a high figure.

The annual budget varied during the early 1970s between $900,000 and $2,700,000 (depending on the value of the crop). Rather less than half of this total was spent on advertising in a normal year, although cooperative programs with manufacturers of branded foods often augmented this significantly. Rather more than half the original budget (before the inclusion of cooperative funds) was spent on promotions, publicity, and public relations.

There is no doubt at all that the whole effort was led by the advertising, including the cooperative campaigns, while much of the supporting program, such as the production of recipe booklets, was directly related to the advertising.

The advertising is an example of the relatively rare type of campaign that provides a consumer service. Anyone who has experience of food advertising and how homemakers respond to it will be struck by the style and implicit understanding of the needs of the homemaker that it displays. The main medium was magazines, where advertisements consistently and with considerable skill exploited the appetite appeal and versatility of avocados, in order to encourage more frequent use. The cooperative advertising was entirely consistent with this strategic emphasis on usage. With considerable imagination, the board and its agency Erwin Wasey (now Wasey–Campbell Ewald) explored unorthodox routes to additonal usage, for instance cosmetic use (avocado face masks) and houseplant growing (from the avocado stone). The reader can take the campaigns as model examples of a correct strategic direction; a creative execution which involves the consumer (sometimes with unexpected turns); and an impeccable standard of craft skill.

The results of the total effort appear to be unequivocal. First, the improvement in the producer price (measured in dollars per bearing acre) was remarkable. As we have seen, this price had fallen by 30 percent, from the average of the five seasons 1950–55 ($588) to the average for 1955–60 ($413). It was the end of the 1959–60 season that the advertising and sales promotion campaign began. Thereafter, the average price rose. For 1960–65 it was $529; for 1965–70, $928; and for 19706–75, $1,756. These increases took place against an overall rising trend in avocado production. Even taking account of the increasing sophistication of the average household cuisine, increasing population, increasing incomes, and inflation, these rises are impressive. They were moreover virtually continuous from year to year.

Consumer data indicate a faster rise in consumption than in penetration, (48 percent as opposed to 13 percent for the season 1973–74 compared with six years before). This is entirely in line with the advertising strategy. The very fact of repeat purchase means that the major volume of consumption for a brand or commodity is going to come from this source. The clear lesson of this case is that advertising that encourages such consumption is often far and away the most effective.

Dettol

Dettol is a well-established, premium-price antiseptic and disinfectant brand marketed by the large, diversified British manufacturing group Reckitt and Colman. It is a liquid in a bottle of distinctive design, has a very characteristic smell, and offers the unique feature of turning water cloudy when a few drops are added. It is widely familiar to British families, has a remarkable 70-percent household penetration, and is in complete retail distribution.

The earlier success of the brand had been built on personal use as an antiseptic to prevent infection from wounds and insect bites. But this use cannot account for large volumes of consumption. Dettol is also used as a more general household disinfectant and germ-killer, for instance for wiping bathroom surfaces and cleaning after pets (uses that can dispose of large amounts of the product). But for these uses, Dettol's market share is small, because store brand disinfectants can be bought for half (sometimes only a third) of Dettol's price. Such was the situation in the mid-1970s.

It was at this time that sales began slipping seriously as a result of inflation, reduced advertising investments, and production problems. The advertising agency, D'Arcy, MacManus and Masius (now D'Arcy Masius Benton & Bowles), in reviewing alternative advertising approaches, was tempted to change the content of the advertising campaign to encourage people to use Dettol more as a disinfectant, but this was clearly a questionable step unless the influence of Dettol's premium price could be isolated and evaluated.

The agency therefore began a program of econometric work to examine all the factors likely to influence demand for the brand. Nielsen data (both national and regional) provided a total of 150 observations. Statistically significant relationships were established between Dettol sales and four variables: real personal disposable income; Dettol's price in real terms; seasonality, with more sales in the summer months; and advertising, with both short-term and long-term effects (the latter reflecting repeat purchase) The relative weight of each of these four factors was established, and the agency estimated that 90 percent of the brand's sales could be accounted for by them. The econometric model constructed for the brand was projected forward to 1978—a brave and sometimes dangerous thing to do (insofar as one's belief in mathematical models is concerned!)—but the actual sales performance followed this projection with a most remarkable accuracy. This is especially noteworthy because the model, reflecting a change in the campaign, forecast an *increase* in offtake.

One of the findings of this investigation was that the price elasticity of demand (-0.44) was a good deal less pronounced than the income elasticity ($+2.26$), which meant that the sales reduction in the mid-1970s had been more due to a lack of buoyancy in personal incomes because of general economic conditions than it had been to Dettol's premium price. In any event, the decision was made to change the content of the campaign in 1978 to a story based on Dettol as a disinfectant. The campaign employed television commercials and magazine advertisements featuring children in a way that was highly involving to the homemaker. The media expenditure was not increased, which meant that in real terms it declined, because of inflation in media rates.

The effect of the campaign was monitored by large-scale "usage and attitude" enquiries in January 1978 and January 1980. As a result of this research, it was apparent that homemakers were both buying and using Dettol more often than before; and that it was being employed increasingly for the uses featured in the advertising (for instance, bathroom surfaces and kitchen garbage pails). The traditional uses of Dettol (such as on cuts and stings) had also modestly increased, possibly as a secondary effect of the advertising for a related brand, Dettol Cream. And overall there has been improvements in the image of Dettol as a disinfectant. As the capstone of success, the upturn in sales ex-factory in 1978 over 1977 was 20 percent. This higher sales level was maintained in 1979.

This is more than a demonstration of market analysis of a high order. The case represents a courageous switch in the content of the campaign, against the argument for caution suggested by the premium price of the brand. The whole story demonstrates in a striking way that what really matters with campaigns is their central message. There is not always a trade-off between content and form, but when there is, it is the content that is decisively important.[15]

Campari

Campari is a pink bitter aperitif of Italian origin made, like so many proprietary drinks, from a secret formula. It is sold in most countries of the world, but drinkers take some time to get used to the taste and an even longer time to get to like it.

Our story begins in Britain in 1975. During the previous fifteen years, the advertising, which had made an important contribution to establishing the brand, had taken the form of a long series of skillfully written press advertisements which had built added values of sophistication and elitism. As a natural consequence of this style of advertising, Campari was drunk mainly by older upper-income people. Sales had grown satisfactorily from the brand's small beginnings, but by the mid-1970s the growth of Campari (as with many other alcoholic drinks) was slowing, partly as a result of depressed economic conditions. The only drinks that were growing against the total market trend were those appealing to younger people, which Campari did not.

The solution to Campari's problems came from both a product change and an advertising change. The client and the agency, J. Walter Thompson, had discussed the product change: the fact that many drinkers were mixing the brand differently than before. A concentrate, Campari is mixed traditionally with unflavored soda water, ice, and a slice of orange. This makes it a long, sparkling, cool, but still bitter drink. The change taking place in the market was that Campari was being used with sweeter mixers: with lemon

soda and with orange juice, both of which provided a long drink of quite a
different nature from the traditional Campari and soda water. These mixtures
were generally more appealing to the young.

The new advertising campaign, starting in late spring 1976, capitalized
on this change in the mixers, but the campaign provided an impetus for the
brand far beyond what the new mixer idea could have provided on its own.
(The proof of this statement is that there was a strong movement to the new
mixers before 1976, when the sales were relatively stagnant.) The new campaign was conceived for television. The budget was virtually unchanged at a
fairly low level of about $500,000 deployed mainly over the high-selling sum-
mer season.

The campaign itself deserves close scrutiny. Four films were made between 1976 and 1980, each featuring an encounter between a young woman
and a man. They are both drinking Campari: he with the traditional unflavored soda, she with one of the new sweeter mixers. He is surprised at her
choice of mixer, but in a line or two of dialogue which leaves much unsaid,
she gets the better of the encounter. The idea appears extremely simple, but
there are overtones which add a peculiar distinctiveness. The woman is elegant and beautiful, but when she speaks she does so in a sharply working-
class accent, a fact immediately apparent to everyone who has ever lived in
Britain, where consciousness of such matters is still strong. The man is obviously upper class by his way of speaking, but he is foppish and rather weak,
what the British describe as "wet." It is obvious why the woman seems to
win through; she has the more substantial personality. In the situation, then,
there are a number of dissonances or conflicts: between the woman and the
man, between her social class and the man's social class, and especially and
strikingly between her upper-class appearance and her working-class voice.[16]

Such overtones make the commercials a joy to watch. The last of Campari's four commercials is an "oddball" in which the girl appears with a Hum-
phrey Bogart lookalike in a brilliant pastiche of *Casablanca*. There is no
doubt whatsoever that in all four films there is communication between the
advertiser and the viewer, that the advertiser makes a step toward the viewer,
and also that the viewer makes a step toward the advertiser. This is the real
meaning of involvement: communication as a two-way process. At a more
subtle level still, the game that the commercials are playing with the bizarre
British class system echoes a flirtation on the part of the upper-class young
with working-class symbols during the 1970s, a phenomenon connected with
the popularity of working-class musicians (which many parents of children
in private fee-paying schools in England at the time can confirm from their
own direct observation).[17] The best advertising copywriters are often those
whose antennae are sensitive to nuances and hints of this sort.

Little need be said about the success of the campaign, which was immediate and prolonged, with 1980 sales volume 62 percent above 1976, against

all industry trends. Information on usage and attitudes confirmed that Campari became progressively a drink for the younger person, achieved significantly higher levels of awareness and trial, and was drunk increasingly with the new, sweeter mixers. The young woman in the commercial also became the heroine of her own television series, scripted by Terence Howard, the copywriter who had written the Campari commercials.[18]

The point about this case on which the reader is invited to dwell is the nature of the advertising communication, especially the involvement of the viewer. How is it that in a 30-second commercial, so many subtle signals and such entertaining communications can be compressed? How is it that the client and the agency expressed the mixer strategy in a way so unlike how that same strategy would have been expressed by any other client and agency? The Campari campaign is the very opposite of the pedestrian and the obvious. The strategy of the campaign is not especially original; it completely dictated the *direction* of the creative leap. The height of this leap was determined however by the person who wrote the sixty magic words which comprise all that can be fitted into any 30-second commercial. When I said in chapter 1 that if we establish within narrow limits what the contribution of advertising can be, and that this contribution can often be shown to be very large indeed, it is this striking type of creative contribution I had in mind. It is also in this sense that Lewis Carroll is generally right in saying that language is worth a thousand pounds a word.

Oxo

Oxo is an important and in some ways typically British brand: a compressed meat cube (originally beef, but different flavored cubes were subsequently introduced), which when added to stews and casseroles gives them body and flavor, and which can also be drunk on its own mixed with boiling water to make a savory hot drink on a cold day. First sold in 1910, the brand was well attuned to the British cuisine, which tends to be dull and unadventurous, because Oxo is able to provide strength and character to many bland and generally undistinguished dishes. (I can say all this without seeming impolite because I am myself British.) It also helps homemakers to make the most of the poorer cuts of meat, so that—not surprisingly—Oxo made its greatest progress during the two world wars, when food supplies were short for nearly all Britishers.

By the 1950s however, full employment and the postwar boom had begun to mean rising standards of living in Britain and a degree of affluence for large numbers of people who had never known it before. At this point, Oxo started to lose its relevance, although it was still widely used, with an almost 60-percent household penetration and a substantial volume of tonnage sales accounted for by people who used it every day.

In 1958, a major restaging took place. The manufacturer refused to accept counsels of despair that the brand was in the decline phase of an inevitable life cycle. The cubes were repackaged. A newly appointed advertising agency developed a radical new campaign. The advertising budget was modestly increased. These three factors were used as the trigger for an increased selling effort by a strengthened sales force. The brand eventually responded well.[19]

The central figure in the advertising campaign was a lady called Katie, who became one of the most striking figures in the history of British television advertising. Katie was a young homemaker, wife of Philip, an up-and-coming business executive. Each commercial told a simple story about the life of the young couple and in particular about the food they ate. Oxo was shown to play a modest but nonetheless real and ubiquitous role in all their meat cookery. The selling was neither strident nor implausible; Katie's life and her ways of using Oxo were presented in a friendly, low-key, natural way; and the many television commercials were made with a high degree of craft skill.

Geared mainly for existing users, the strategy of the campaign was perfectly clear. With the brand's long association with making the most of austerity, Oxo needed some type of image improvement to make it relevant to more affluent times. Moreover, because it was such an old brand, it also needed to be associated with younger people. Katie and Philip were skillfully selected as aspirational figures, a little higher in social class and a little younger in age than the normal user of Oxo, but not so different that the users could not aspire to be like Katie. There was a constant emphasis on usage in the commercials, with a wide variety of recipe ideas, including some employing the new Oxo flavors. And in every case Katie was rewarded by the gratitude of her husband and eventually her son (once the latter arrived on the scene and became old enough to enjoy his mother's Oxo dishes).

Katie was launched in 1958. Before her appearance, the brand had made virtually no progress since the end of the war in 1945. In fact, volume sales had slipped by almost 10 percent in the ten years before the Katie campaign. The campaign itself had a interesting early history. Sales did not respond at all for more than a year, during which time the patience and resolve of both client and agency must have been exceptional. But sales did eventually pick up, continuing to improve for about seventeen years. Five years after the introduction of Katie, volume sales were a third higher than before; and although the repackaging and the sales force activity contributed to this success, there was never any doubt about the main cause of this remarkable reversal in the brand's fortunes.

This was clearly a favorable situation for the client and agency to find themselves in, but one not devoid of problems. In particular, there arose the difficulty of maintaining the sales impetus. There was also the problem of finding a replacement if for some unexpected reason Katie's effectiveness declined.

The point of this case study is to demonstrate that both the client and J. Walter Thompson made conscious efforts to find a replacement for Katie during the long years when she was riding the crest of the wave. This did not imply that there was any boredom with Katie on the part of the client and agency. They were interested, quite rightly, exclusively in the *effects* of the campaign; but they were at the same time resolved to have an alternative ready and waiting for use if Katie should begin to falter.

This required time, effort, and resources. The procedure was to develop and expose an alternative campaign in a single self-contained television area, and in this area monitor not just the sales of the brand, but also a battery of brand and user attributes, so that if there were clear success (or failure), there would be diagnostic clues to suggest why. One such test campaign was exposed for three years, during which time the campaign concept was fine-tuned as a result of ad hoc qualitative research and a continuous measurement of its effectiveness.[20] But in the event, this campaign, like the others, was not judged a viable alternative to Katie.

The result of all this conscientious and largely (but not entirely) wasted effort was that when the Katie campaign did eventually run out of steam, client and agency were prepared. The eventual advertising life of our heroine was seventeen years, during which time variety and interest had been maintained by the progress of Philip's career (including a lengthy sojourn in the United States, which provided the opportunity for a spectacular series of commercials made on location). But eventually a weakening of the user imagery, accompanied by a marginal decline in the frequency of use of the brand, was detected just before these factors began to have a significant effect on ex-factory sales.

The impetus of the brand was maintained by a change of campaign away from Katie. But for a further period, Katie continued to be exposed and closely monitored in a single small television area, where a continued weakening confirmed the wisdom of the decision to change the campaign nationally.

One of the most perceptive comments about this justly celebrated campaign was that the agency made only one major mistake. They provided Katie with a son instead of a daughter. A daughter might of course have been able to learn to cook when she grew up, thus providing that interest and rejuvenation necessary to carry both the campaign and the brand forward.

The Argument in Brief

The five cases just described are pregnant with lessons for advertisers, so much so that the specific message of each case requires some amplification. The main lessons of the five cases have been concentrated under five headings, called rules 1 to 5.

*Rule 1:   Use Data about Consumer Usage of the Brand
to Describe the Target Group in the Advertising Strategy.*

The reader will remember from chapter 5 that the main route to increased sales of a brand is increased penetration. But increased penetration is in the first instance going to come from somewhere. The first strategic question which should *always* be asked is "Where is our business going to come from?"

It is possible that the source of potential business could lie completely outside the field of obvious direct competition. A well-known example is Parker Pens, which were traditionally considered to be gifts, and to compete therefore with things like cigarette lighters and silk scarves and only to a limited degree with other pens.[21] But with the majority of repeat-purchase packaged goods, the range of competition is generally more narrowly defined.

The key is always to regard the competition from the consumer's point of view. The new business for our brand might come from nonusers of the product field, because it is undeveloped or perhaps because the competition is ill-defined (as with California avocados). Or it might come from nonusers of our brand who use specific named competitors; or from minor users, who are light users of our brand but heavier users of specific named competitors; or from major users, who are heavy users of our brand, and whose consumption should be maintained and sometimes increased. [22] On this strategic decision as to the source of sales hangs the whole thrust of the advertising strategy, including which brand benefits should be emphasized in the campaign. The secret of the Horlicks success stemmed from the decision to concentrate on the light users of the brand.

Targeting in terms of brand usage is the most useful way of isolating the people to whom we are addressing our advertising. But this is rarely discussed in the marketing and advertising literature, where there is normally a considerable amount of otiose generalization about demographic target groups. In drawing up an advertising strategy, demographics are of very little value—save in the single matter of media planning and buying; and demographic data are only valuable here because media research is analyzed demographically. The reason why demographic target groups are of so little use is that for directly competing brands (especially those within a functional segment, where such a thing exists in a market), demographic usage patterns are normally so close that the large majority of users of one brand are similar to the large majority of users of other brands, and any differences are merely in the importance of minor groups (in other words, differences of emphasis at the margin). Also, as we have seen in chapter 5, users of competing brands are often the same people.

Demographic analysis is simply not sensitive enough to provide any operational discriminators, a point that can easily be checked by studying the standardized data published by Simmons or Mediamark. Moreover, the various demographic categories *describe* usage patterns, but they do not *explain* much about them. The usage of different brands is influenced—in some cases determined—by life styles and attitudes, and these might indeed differ between demographic groups. But to understand brands, we should look into the life styles, and not simply at the demographic descriptions of those people who have them.

This brings us to the fashionable practice of defining target groups in psychographic terms—a genuine step beyond demographic targeting. However, although psychographics occasionally provide real insights into the differences between brands as these are perceived by consumers, there are three problems with this tool of analysis. First, it is extremely imprecise since it is difficult to measure the various attributes sensitively and uniformly. Standardized "image battery" questions are often shallow and unsubtle. Second, the psychographic characteristics of directly competing brands are often extremely similar to one another, and do not provide what we are looking for, which is a point of real difference. (Think of Coca-Cola and Pepsi-Cola, where there are enormous psychographic similarities and few differences.) Third, when there *are* differences between brands, they often directly reflect previous advertising, and are therefore of little help to us in developing a new campaign. This point comes clearly through when we ask consumers to describe advertised brands in human terms. What emerges is a reflection of the previous advertising and little else.

An interesting footnote to this whole matter is provided by the popular technique of naming competitors in a brand's advertising. Opinion is by no means undivided about its general effectiveness and desirability.[23] But in the cases in which it has been effective, I suggest that its success stems from the explicit definition of where it is hoped that sales will come from: in every case from the specific named competitors featured in the advertisements.

Rule 2: Use Advertising to Expand Volume Usage of a Brand.

In dozens of product fields, from sticky tape to mustard (and in our examples Dettol and Oxo), one brand can be found in two-thirds or more of all homes. Sometimes a pack has been forgotten in a cupboard for months, and only by encouraging repeated use in quantity can these supplies be used up and more packs bought, thus pulling the brand through the distributional pipeline.

One way to boost sales is by consciously increasing inventories in the home. I have known two cases in which major improvements took place in the sales of different brands of soft drink by the simple expedient of introducing larger size bottles. This strategy worked by stimulating interest in the brand, because once these bottles were opened, the contents were rapidly drunk and presumably appreciated, and the bottles quickly replaced. Although the California avocados case was concerned with a commodity rather than a brand, precisely the same principles apply, although unpaid publicity (to encourage use, for instance via the dissemination of recipes) is normally more difficult to obtain for brands than for unbranded commodities.

Rule 3: The Most Important Thing about a Campaign Is Its Content and Not Its Form.

This is substantially although not entirely a matter of the advertising strategy.

The problem here is to define what comprises content and what comprises form. The distinction was clear enough in the Dettol example, but in many cases, distinctions tend to be hazier. The difficulties are highlighted by attempts to use research to distinguish between the two. I refer particularly to the controversy surrounding proposition testing.

The most extreme view in this controversy is taken by Stephen King, who argues that proposition testing is simply not a viable procedure.[24] Despite its impeccable logic, however, King's work is light in empirical support. One of the major problems concerns the manner in which the propositions—the central advertising arguments—are to be tested. King takes the line that if these are written as sentences, then the procedure is valueless, because the communication of a finished advertisement would be quite different; and if they are embodied in finished advertisements, then what is being tested is advertisements (in King's view a legitimate procedure) and not propositions (a much less legitimate one).

Unfortunately for this case, Mark Lovell and Jack Potter's experiment testing the same proposition as words and as schematic advertisements yielded substantially identical conclusions,[25] although this does not make proposition testing any less complex to plan or less difficult to interpret. But their point is that there *are* occasions when it is possible to test verbal propositions, and these are when the propositions are based on what Shirley Young calls "concrete, product-related benefits." The technique does not work where the propositions concern "less tangible or more psychological benefits."[26] David Ogilvy's often quoted example of a test of ten propositions for Helena Rubinstein Deep Cleanser is concerned with the former type of product-related claim; and this is clearly an example that worked in practice and contributed to building a brand.[27]

Whether or not proposition testing is a valid and legitimate procedure (the implication of Lovell and Potter's point is that it becomes less valid as a brand develops and as its added values become more important), what matters most is *the content of the campaign,* whether it is concerned mainly with the brand's functional performance, with its added values, or with both these

these things. This is the criterion that should be used when any advertisement is written; when a television commercial is shot and edited; and when a press advertisement is illustrated. An advertisement is not essentially a piece of entertainment, still less a design or a purely artistic expression. It is an argument. This does not mean that it is always an argument employing rational persuasion; sensory and emotional stimuli are often as effective or more effective than appeals to the reason. But an advertisement is a means of affecting a person's response to a brand, and in doing this, it is the substance or the concept of the advertisement that bears the burden of the task.

Rule 4: For Successful Advertising Communication, the Receiver of a Message Must Take a Step toward Its Sender.

The content of an advertisement cannot be hammered like a nail into a person's head. He or she can only too easily avoid this unpleasant process by screening out the advertisement by not noticing it. If an advertisement is to communicate effectively, the receiver must at least half want it to, and be prepared to take a step toward the sender. It follows that effective advertising is rarely hectoring or even loudly explicit. On the contrary it tends to be good mannered. If there are cases in which the homemaker is thought to have been successfully browbeaten into acquiescence by breathless hard-selling, I would argue that subtler and more involving methods might have worked better.

Effective advertising is often (albeit incidentally) entertaining. Entertainment is a specific article of faith of one at the most creative, successful, and interesting British agencies, Collett, Dickinson and Pearce. Unpublished British data suggest that if this entertainment involves mental participation from the audience, it is likely to be more effective.[28] Such advertising is often humorous. The possibilities of humor depend of course on the brand advertised, but the weight of evidence concerning its use suggests that although humor is not of ubiquitous value, it often both attracts attention and generates warm feelings on the part of the audience.[29]

Effective advertising is often emotionally involving. It is frequently attuned to the homemaker's life and day-to-day problems. There is evidence that identification strongly improves the chance of persuasion.[30]

More often than not, a successful campaign has a strong element of the unorthodox or the unexpected, a quality that good advertising shares with much worthwhile literature. The core of Koestler's theory about the creative process is the notion of "bisociative fusion," or the coming together of thoughts from completely unconnected sources—a powerful expression of the value of the unexpected.[31]

A prime example of the unexpected in literature is the writing of Lewis Carroll, which is yet close enough to real life that we can recognize people and situations in our own experience that have striking resemblances to people and situations encountered by Alice. The vividness of such resemblance is related to the relative *incompleteness* of Lewis Carroll's communication; the reader has to fill in some of the gaps.[32] Similarly, it has been suggested that incompleteness may strengthen an advertisement's power to communicate.[33] A close study of *Alice's Adventure in Wonderland* and *Through the Looking Glass* is, in my sober opinion, a better stimulus for the copywriter than study of any other book, in particular any technical text.

These points are not meant to be rigid dictates. The reader should look upon them in the same way that a physician looks at symptoms: as external manifestations of an underlying condition. Creative people should address themselves to the underlying condition, what David Ogilvy calls the "Big Idea." One point that they all have in common is that the advertisers who run advertisements with these sorts of qualities are not egotistical; they are not more concerned with their brands than with their consumers. As an axiomatic rule, consumers are less interested in a brand *per se* than in what that brand can do for them. Demonstrating the latter is the way in which potential customers can be coaxed into making that fragile and uncertain first step toward what the advertiser is trying to bring about. But once the consumers have made that step, the advertisement will almost invariably be effective.

A more controversial point relates to the importance given to the advertiser's brand name. I believe it to be a distinct advantage if this does not appear too early or too prominently in an advertisement. It is much more important to make sure consumers become interested in the bait on the hook which will induce them to pay attention; this bait is the most delicate and important part of every piece of advertising communication. But the reader is perhaps wondering about the supposed "glancer" (and the television equivalent) to whom "brand registration" will be lost if the brand name does not appear early and prominently. However, as I said in chapter 6, getting glances is not really the problem; the problem is to prevent the reader or viewer from immediately and unconsciously screening the message out, a process that immediately eliminates four out of five of all advertisements. I cannot help feeling that early and bold brand names will actually encourage this screening.

Successful campaigns are normally unique in their product field. Uniqueness is not however something that should be striven for (except in the sense that advertising stereotypes such as the "slice of life" should be fastidiously eschewed unless executed with exceptional skill). The uniqueness of a campaign, like the profit earned by a business enterprise, is less an actionable objective than a reward for excellence in doing a job. But how many businesspeople regard profit in this sense? I would be surprised if there were many. How many advertisers and agencies regard creative work in such a way? I would be equally surprised if there were many.

*Rule 5:   Campaigns Can Have a Long Life, But They
Can Lose Steam, Which Can Have a Dangerous Result
Unless There Has Been Serious Contingency Planning.*

There is no absolute rule dictating that a campaign should not continue forever. Yet long-lived campaigns are rare indeed. The Lux Beauty Soap campaign featuring movie stars (which effectively built the brand into the largest selling bar soap in the world, a position it still holds) has had an active life of nearly sixty years, and shows no sign of flagging. This must surely be a world record. Katie, with a life of seventeen years, supposedly holds the longevity record for British television advertising.

I believe that generally clients and agencies grow bored with campaigns before the public does. As a general rule (one offering considerable economies in creative effort, and also in the time and strain involved in management evaluation and decision making), I recommend that clients and agencies adopt the position that a campaign should run indefinitely until there is early evidence of its faltering. Such evidence should of course be looked for in a continuous evaluation of usage and attitude measures, to enable problems to be detected before they work themselves through into ex-factory sales, when it could be too late to avoid measurable loss of business.

This type of long-range thinking follows our examination of the Oxo case. But the other lessons of this case—the need for an unrelenting search for alternatives—is also an essential policy for the custodians of major brands, who in a competitive world have so much to lose by neglecting this type of difficult, exhaustive, expensive, and generally disheartening contingency planning.

Notes

1. Callaghan OHerlihy, "How to Test the Sales Effects of Advertising," *Admap* (January 1980): 32–35.

The relatively low advertising elasticity for the average brand also demonstrates the difficulty of achieving large sales increases from changes in advertising pressure. See chapter 4.

2. Roy H. Campbell, *Measuring the Sales and Profit Results of Advertising: A Managerial Approach,* pp. 102–105.

3. *Effective Frequency: The Relationship between Frequency and Advertising Effectiveness* Ed. Michael Naples (New York: Association of National Advertisers, 1979), pp. 107–108.

4. Stephen A. Greyser, *Cases in Advertising and Communications Management,* 2d ed., pp. 473–87.

5. This view, which some people might regard as unorthodox, is argued in more detail in John Philip Jones, "Media Cartography," *Admap* (February 1977).

6. See, among others, J.A.C. Brown, *Techniques of Persuasion* (Harmondsworth, Middlesex, United Kingdom: Penguin Books, 1963), p. 185.

7. Campbell, *Measuring the Sales and Profit Results of Advertising: A Managerial Approach,* pp. 19–72.

8. Edward de Bono, *Lateral Thinking* (New York: Harper Colophon Books, 1973), pp. 39–45.

9. I have tested this hypothesis over many years of teaching marketing and advertising students both in professional life and in a university.

10. David Ogilvy, *Confessions of an Advertising Man.*

11. Thomas C. Amico, a Syracuse University honors student whose work I supervised, prepared a careful albeit small-scale examination of the extent to which these well-established craft rules are ignored in advertisements in major American magazines. This as yet unpublished investigation demonstrated that out of a sample of 223 advertisements, 89 percent broke at least one of the rules, and 45 percent broke at least three of them. David Ogilvy has commented favorably on it in a private letter.

12. Derek Bloom, Andrea Jay, and Tony Twyman, "The Validity of Advertising Pre-tests," *Journal of Advertising Research* (April 1977): 7–16.

13. *Ibid.,* 11.

14. Greyser, *Cases in Advertising and Communications Management,* pp. 23–61.

15. Angus Thomas, Andrew Roberts, Gerard Smith and Mia Ospovat, in "Dettol: A Case History" in *Advertising Works: Papers from the I.P.A. Advertising Effectiveness Awards* (London: Holt, Rinehart and Winston, 1981), pp. 59–77.

16. Referring to pairs of antagonists in literature, Koestler writes: "[E]ach pair is locked in an everlasting duel in which we act as seconds for both. In each of these conflicts two self-contained frames of reference, two sets of values, two universes of discourse collide. All great works of literature contain variations and combinations, overt or implied, of such archetypal conflicts inherent in the condition of man, which first occur in the symbols of mythology, and are restated in the particular idiom of each culture and period." Arthur Koestler, *The Act of Creation* (New York: Macmillan, 1964), p. 351.

17. The point has been perceptively argued by Piers Paul Read, "Delusions of Equality," *The Observer,* London, June 13, 1982. See also a thoughtful but rather chilling essay, Jeffrey Richards, "The Hooligan Culture, Violence and the Ethic of the Undermass," *Encounter* (November 1985): 15–23.

18. Frances Foster, "An Evaluation of the Effectiveness of the Current Campari Campaign" in *Advertising Works: Papers from the I.P.A. Advertising Effectiveness Awards,* pp. 117–24.

19. Stephen King, *Developing New Brands* (London: Pitman, 1973), p. 3.

20. R.T.J. Tuck and Jill Firth, "Can Research Join in the Creative Process?" *Proceedings of ESOMAR Seminar* (Lisbon, Portugal, November 1973): pp. 149–72.

21. In view of Parker's poor performance in the marketplace, this definition of its competition has been much debated. See *Advertising Age,* July 26, 1982.

22. The July 1985 decision to reintroduce the original flavor of Coca-Cola in the United States, after its brief but disastrous replacement with a new flavor, is a timely and topical reminder not only of the importance of the existing users of a brand

(all of whom liked the original Coke flavor), but also of the pressures of oligopolistic competition which led to the ill-advised change.

23. J.J. Boddewyn and Katherin Marton, *Comparison Advertising: A Worldwide Study* (New York: International Advertising Association, Hastings House, 1978), pp. 75–101.

24. Stephen King, "How Useful is Proposition Testing?" *Advertising Quarterly* (Winter 1965–66): 24–34.

25. Mark Lovell and Jack Potter, *Assessing the Effectiveness of Advertising* (London: Business Books, 1975), pp. 49–62.

26. Shirley Young, "Copy Testing without Magic Numbers," *Journal of Advertising Research* (February 1972): 3–12.

27. Ogilvy, *Confessions of an Advertising Man*, p. 94.

28. These and related points are discussed by Timothy Joyce, "What Do We Know About How Advertising Works?" in *How Advertising Works* (London: J. Walter Thompson, 1974), pp. 3–31.

29. Brian Sternthal and C. Samuel Craig, "Humor in Advertising," *Journal of Marketing* (October 1973): 12–18; Arthur Koestler, *The Act of Creation*. Koestler's difficult but fascinating book explores the relationship between humor, tragedy, and intellectual synthesis.

30. Joyce, "What Do We Know About How Advertising Works?" pp. 24–25.

31. Koestler, *The Act of Creation*, pp. 35–38.

32. The reader is encouraged to study Koestler's concept of "infolding," *ibid.*, pp. 337–40. One phrase in this discussion sticks vividly in the mind: "[E]conomy demands that the stepping-stones of the narrative should be spaced wide enough apart to require a significant effort from the reader."

Koestler also quotes a remarkable passage from Sir Joshua Reynolds writing about the work of Gainsborough:

> I have often imagined that this unfinished manner contributed even to that striking resemblance for which his portraits are so remarkable. Though this opinion may be considered as fanciful, yet I think a plausible reason may be given, why such a mode of painting should have such an effect. It is presupposed that in this undetermined manner there is the general effect; enough to remind the spectator of the original; the imagination supplies the rest, and perhaps more satisfactory to himself, if not more exactly, than the artist, with all his care, could possibly have done. (p. 398).

33. Joyce, "What Do We Know About How Advertising Works?" p. 25.

8
Advertising Pressure: "A Diminishing Rate of Yield"

First, however, she waited for a few minutes to see if she was going to shrink any further: she felt a little nervous about this; "for it might end, you know," said Alice to herself, "in my going out altogether, like a candle."

I n chapter 7, we were in the domain of the artist. We must now forsake this realm for the world of the artisan. Nevertheless, we should not lose our appreciation of the cardinal importance of the creative content of advertising campaigns as we return to the more mundane matter of advertising weight. The relationship between absolute amounts of advertising and sales was examined in chapter 4, which demonstrated how these two variables are interrelated. This chapter examines another important relationship: the short-term effect on sales of incremental advertising pressure. This is its immediate effect within the purchase interval, which with most packaged goods is a period of one to three weeks. The influence of incremental pressure is here a matter of real financial importance to a brand. We are going to examine whether progressive amounts of advertising yield an increasing, constant, or diminishing return in sales.[1] As we shall discover, it will not be possible to arrive at a single conclusion applicable to all conditions, but the variations in the patterns offer the possibility of generalization.

The normal and most useful way of describing the principles of increasing and diminishing returns is with simple geometry, employing a two-dimensional diagram with advertising measured on the horizontal axis and sales on the vertical. Two alternative opinions on the ways in which advertising might work are expressed in the following figures. The opinion of most analysts (at least those who search for general theories and universal uniform patterns) is that the diagram on the left provides a simplified description of the continuous diminishing returns which they believe to apply everywhere in the real world. The diagram on the right demonstrates a theoretical alternative: returns might progressively increase at lower levels of advertising pressure and then change to progressive decreases.

The curve on the left is known as the concave-downward function. The reader will see that its shape demonstrates that equal marginal increments on

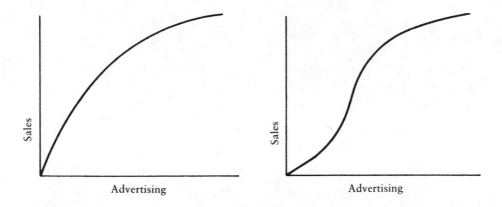

the horizontal axis (representing progressive "doses" of advertising) are associated with *decreasing* marginal increments on the vertical axis (representing sales stimulated by these doses). The curve on the right is for obvious reasons knows as the S-shaped function. In this, at low levels of advertising (up to the bend in the S), equal marginal increments of advertising on the horizontal axis are associated with *increasing* marginal increments of sales on the vertical. Then, at the bend of the S, the curve changes to the shape of the concave-downward function, representing a change to progressive diminishing returns. The place where the slope of the curve changes is known as the inflection point. In this chapter we shall try to find out whether such points exist with any real brands and—if they do—where on the curve they occur.

Although the S-shaped function is the simplest description of how returns first increase and then diminish in response to pressure, it is not the only way to describe a response pattern that changes at some point. For instance, if the first advertising exposure has no effect on offtake, the curve will be shaped

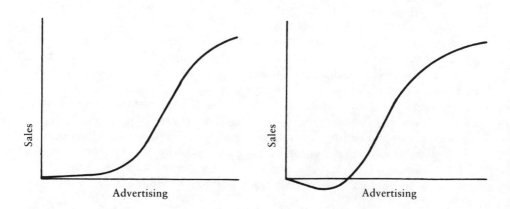

like that on the left of the pair at the bottom of the previous page. If the first exposure has a *negative* effect, the curve will resemble that on the right. Both these configurations are relevant to the cases described in chapter 9. The apparently unorthodox shape of the curve on the right provides a good description of case 16. Note that the relationship is extremely short-term, tracking increases in doses of advertising, and their immediate direct effect on marginal sales in the marketplace.

Note also that it is nowhere suggested that increasing returns are anything but limited and temporary. It is therefore quite wrong to state that there is a widespread belief in professional circles that advertising is a general world of increasing returns: "Advertising practitioners quite generally believe that increasing returns exist, at least in some cases. And the advertising trade press has been virtually unanimous in backing the idea of increasing returns."[2] It would be nearer the truth to say that people who market and advertise repeat-purchase packaged goods have in many cases reason to believe that increasing returns operate at the lower levels of advertising pressure; but that at high levels of pressure, there is universal belief that returns progressively diminish. The surest evidence for the truth of the latter part of this statement is that there is always a ceiling to advertising expenditures. If increasing returns were ever thought to operate indefinitely, there would be no limit to advertising appropriations, and manufacturers would find ways of raising money in order to advertise more, in the certain expectation that this continuously increasing investment would have a continuously increasing payoff.

As justification for my statement that at low pressure, increments of advertising yield increasing returns, we shall examine case by case. Inflection points on specific advertising response functions are difficult to find, because they represent often subtle changes, which come into effect at different levels of pressure with different brands. We shall certainly not be able to find them if we take a macro approach since it is simply not good enough to make crude blanket generalizations such as the following reference to a total of 107 European brands: "Since semilogarithmic (in the advertising variable) and double-log regressions invariably performed better than linear forms, this is evidence that the shape of the advertising response curve is concave-downwards."[3] Before such a generalization would be acceptable, we would need to be convinced both of the general applicability of the mathematical model and that the observations provided a satisfactory coverage of both low and high advertising pressure (in other words, that they covered more than the greatest upward length of the curve, which of course shows diminishing returns in both the concave-downward and S-shaped configurations).

But even if we confine ourselves to the study of individual cases, problems abound. There are four main types of problems to keep in mind as we progress through our analysis.

In the first place, although there is no shortage of examples, these examples are patchy and employ different ways of examining advertising. There are, for instance, at least three ways of evaluating the progression of returns, from:

> Increased exposure of the *same* advertisement in the *same* medium,
>
> Increased exposure of *different* advertisements in the *same* medium,
>
> Increased exposure of *different* advertisements in *different* media.

In most published cases, no attempt has been made to distinguish between these three variations, although it has been suggested (admittedly on the basis of recall data, which are very imperfect), that the progression of returns from increased exposure of the same advertisement in the same medium can be quite different from the progression of returns from different advertisements in the same medium.[4] In the majority of published cases, pressure is examined crudely, using dollar appropriations as the weight variable, with the actual advertising presumably encompassing increased exposure of different advertisements in different media.

In these cases, there is no attempt to distinguish between advertising appearance and commercial appearance. For the simple reason that in a sizeable minority of circumstances a different creative treatment can have a massive influence on advertising effectiveness (as detailed in chapter 7), the fact that the published cases ignore the creative content of campaigns is a formidable complication: one the reader of these cases should never overlook. The major exception is the case of direct response, where good data are available of the purer variety—from progressive exposure of the same advertisement in the same medium.

My second point is that little attempt has been made to measure in any uniform way the advertising increments whose results are being evaluated. In some cases the data are measured in "opportunities to see" (potential exposures), in other cases in expenditure per capita, and in yet other cases in absolute expenditures. If we want to search for an inflection point and define where it occurs in specific cases, it is essential to have some sort of uniform measurement of pressure, so that the point's location can be compared case by case. In the following cases, I have therefore attempted wherever possible a uniform measurement, opportunities to see: a more precise term than "frequency." The conventional way of estimating opportunities to see for a particular advertising schedule is by dividing the total gross rating points (GRP) by the net reach of the schedule, measured (insofar as this can be done) in terms of the demographically defined target audience. One problem with this measure is the implicit confusion it causes between vehicle exposure and advertisement exposure.[5] Nevertheless, of all the imperfect measures available, advertising practitioners believe this to be the least imperfect. It is in any event vastly superior to measures based on recall.

Following directly from this, my third point also concerns measurement. In a number of cases, advertising effects have been evaluated not by sales but by certain intermediate measures, such as recall and intention to purchase. Although it means reducing the range of the empirical data under consideration, I am rejecting these intermediate measures, partly because they are too unrefined to detect the small changes in which we are interested, but mainly because of my general skepticism of recall as a measure of anything. The only criterion sensitive and precise enough to support robust conclusions is behavior. I shall therefore confine myself to sales measurements. I am not alone in accepting this discipline. "There is now adequate published evidence to *prove* that the links between ad recall, brand recall, image change, intention to buy and actual sales are simply not direct enough to be used instead of sales."[6]

The fourth problem with our evaluation of cases is that the type of analysis is in many instances obscure, as frequently is the interpretation of conclusions. Econometricians, with all the enthusiasm engendered by their novel and frequently arcane skills, are rarely diffident about either their analyses or their subsequent policy recommendations, but the businesspeople who have to make decisions based on such recommendations—decisions affecting the health of their brands in the short and probably also the long term—are not uncommonly faced with contradictory interpretations of the *same* data by different experts. Such experts tend often not to help their own case by their attitude toward their clients, which has been described as a "combination of confident recommendations for action with an almost total opacity to questioning."[7] There is often also a real problem with their ability to express their thoughts in writing in a way that is intellectually accessible to nonspecialists.

If the reader thinks that I exaggerate, he or she is recommended to read some of the more sulphurous published exchanges between econometricians.[8] These are in any case more entertaining reading than most contributions to this debate, which are often turgid and obscure. If we are to glimpse the sometimes original and fruitful thoughts waiting to be uncovered, we are all too often forced to penetrate a smokescreen of obfuscation and jargon. It is also salutary to remember that econometric models are always a matter of judgment as well as observed fact, so a change in assumptions can cause a radical change in conclusions. This will be apparent from the Lydia Pinkham case, which we shall shortly examine.

The reader may however be forgiven for asking, in view of the intractable complexity of the data and the seemingly contradictory nature of some of the conclusions, whether the search for truth is worth the effort. What does it matter whether or not any real brands have an S-shaped response function with the inflection point low down the curve? The answer is that it *does* matter. Not only is it of theoretical importance in helping us to understand better how advertising works; it is also of great operational importance in the planning of advertising.

The main practical point about diminishing returns is that, within the levels of advertising pressure at which they operate, it is a wasteful procedure to expose advertising of a high intensity: the scheduling of advertising in "bursts," "flights," or "pulses", as it is technically described. Within these operating limits, it is more productive to disperse advertising expenditure, either over time (by "drip feeding" within each medium), or over more media, or over more geographic areas. This is because with dispersion instead of concentration of pressure, the marginal dose of advertising will be on a lower (that is, more efficient) part of the curve. Since pressure is thereby reduced, money is made available to cover more time periods, media, and/or geographic regions than could be done with a concentrated schedule.

The debate is therefore about the value of advertising dispersion (suggested by a belief in diminishing returns) as opposed to concentration (suggested by a belief in increasing returns). As discussed, it is universally agreed that diminishing returns set in when we pass a threshold level of advertising pressure, and this argues strongly that media schedules should be more dispersed as budgets are increased. In my judgment there should in fact be more dispersion than at present in the majority of schedules, although the Americans are not as great offenders as the British in this regard.[9]

The importance of establishing the existence (or otherwise) of an S-shaped curve, and the location of the inflection point in particular cases, is that these will tell us the approximate minimum level of pressure to accept. They will tell us how low we should go to optimize the returns from our advertising. The goal of our investigation is therefore the extremely practical matter of providing the *limits for the dispersion* of advertising budgets. It is hardly possible to think of a matter more directly relevant to the day-to-day work of the advertising media planner.

This chapter is then substantially concerned with inflection points. A useful way of beginning our enquiry is by looking at a type of advertising in which they most certainly do not exist: a category which, according to an overwhelming body of evidence, yields diminishing returns from the very first insertion: continuously falling returns from the *same* advertisement in the *same* medium. I am referring to direct response, an important and rapidly growing category of advertising, and one whose results are so precise and immediate, and complications and contaminating factors so few, that observers are quick to learn a great deal of specific, practical information of priceless value in the marketplace. One of the most astonishing unknowns about advertising is whether the lessons from the byways of direct response apply equally to the broader highways of advertising for repeat-purchase goods.

An Illustration of the Concave-Downward Response Function

Case 1. Examples of Direct Response

There is plentiful (and not seriously disputable) evidence that with direct response, diminishing returns set in with the first insertion and progress thereafter at a continuous and often more or less uniform rate.

Evidence of diminishing returns was first published in 1912 by mail order practitioner W.A. Shryer in an attempt to examine the validity or otherwise of the arguments used by magazine space salespeople that advertising operates cumulatively, as water drips on a rock, making it finally split open.[10] (This is rather a curious analogy for such a supposedly powerful force as advertising. Water would have to do a great deal of dripping to split most rocks.) Shryer published a range of precise statistics, including the response rates of repeat exposure of the same advertisement in each of seventeen magazines and newspapers. In every case the productivity of the second exposure was a good deal lower than that of the first, as measured by the increased cost per order, the normal way of evaluating mail order responses. It would be apparent from these findings that the drops of water would hardly dampen the surface of the rock before they petered out, let alone split it asunder, and we can only conclude that the magazine salespeople were persuaded by this evidence to abandon their platitudinous and inaccurate analogy.

Many other practitioners have confirmed the general application of these findings, the measurements including both mail orders and coupon enquiries.[11] The only important gap in the data is the absence of study of decay of response to insertions beyond the second or third insertion. This lack of information has an obvious cause. People who run direct response advertising cut off their repeated use of an advertisement in one medium for the very reason that its returns diminish so steeply; and they consequently disperse their media expenditure over sometimes vast media lists. This is evident from any study of direct response media schedules; its general validity has been confirmed by Julian Simon, who has made extensive studies of diminishing returns from advertising in the United States, with the general conclusion that they operate with virtually all advertising and in virtually all circumstances.[12] I shall refer to much of his work in this chapter, but the reader is warned that I differ from him in important respects.

To fill the gap just mentioned, data are available relating to the repeated exposure of the same advertisement in the same medium a total of seven times. The information covered four separate British national newspapers. The progression of decay was continuous in every case, the cost per reply of the seventh advertisement in each newspaper moving inexorably to the levels measured in the fourth column in the following table.[13]

Publication	Number of Insertions	Time Period (Weeks)	Cost of Reply for Seventh Advertisement. Index, First Advertisement = 100
(Daily) *A*	7	30	540
(Daily) *B*	7	30	410
(Daily) *C*	7	27	360
(Sunday) *D*	7	32	440

It is unusual (to say the least) that the client and agency were prepared to accept this rate of diminishing returns when they were selling real merchandise for a profit. But the findings provide us with confirmation that the fall-off in response shows no diminution with repetition. This information confirms strongly Simon's claim that diminishing returns operate universally with direct response advertising. But of course it says nothing about whether there are substantive differences between other sorts of advertising and direct response.

The product being sold was a collectible item costing about $10, a low price for such merchandise, but a high price if the product had been in the repeat-purchase packaged goods category. The fall-off in my example, and indeed with all direct response, is connected with the progressive mopping up of the best prospects. By the time the last insertions were appearing, which yielded respectively 4 percent, 4 percent, 5 percent, and 5 percent of the number of orders generated by the first advertisement in each of the four newspapers, the business was probably coming substantially from small numbers of new readers who bought their copies at the newsstand and who had not read the issues with the earlier advertisements.[14]

The relevance of the lessons of direct response to other types of advertising will be debated in chapter 10. In the meantime, we should turn our attention to products that are not sold by direct response (mainly fast moving consumer goods). There are important differences between many of these and direct response goods in the way in which their sales respond to incremental advertising pressure.

Advertising Cases Demonstrating Different Response Functions

There are thirteen cases which make instructive reading. First, they provide details of the different degrees of advertising pressure applied. Second, they give reasonably specific as well as trend data on offtake. Third, they provide sales and not exclusively cognitive and/or affective measures. Chapter 9 contains four additional cases examining the response function from a slightly different point of view.

I have wherever possible employed opportunities to see as the best comparative measure of advertising pressure. I have also attempted a clear interpretation of the resultant offtake, taking account of the possible imperfections of any mathematical models used in the analyses. In some cases the practical implications of diminishing returns have been applied to a "dripfeed" schedule, and implications of increasing returns to a schedule of concentrated bursts, with the results of the two compared. But even in these seemingly simple cases, interpretation is by no means unambiguous, as we shall see with the Andrex case (13).

The cases fall into three groups.

1. Four reasonably well-documented examples show increasing returns at lower levels of pressure.

2. Three good examples present diminishing returns at higher levels of pressure.

3. Six other cases vary in many ways, not least in the adequacy of their data, in showing diminishing returns at intermediate levels of pressure.

Increasing Returns at Lower Levels of Pressure

Case 2. Five Lever Brothers Brands

In a well-known published study, five unnamed Lever Brothers brands were examined by Ambar G. Rao and Peter B. Miller. [15] They employed a distributed lag model for fifteen sales regions based on bimonthly input data over 1971 and 1972. The variables included in the model were network television, spot television, print advertising, price and nonprice promotions, the brand's market share in each area, and its share of premium-price brands. The model's predictions (based on the aggregate of the constituent elements) were shown to fit reasonably well when tested against actual Nielsen readings in individual areas.

When the marginal effect of advertising was isolated, it was found that "the relationship of sales to advertising expenditure is approximated by a family of S-shaped curves."[16] The evidence appears to be quite consistent.

I do however share some of Julian Simon and Johan Arndt's impatience with the fact that (presumably for reasons of confidentiality) the published data have been severely restricted.[17] In fact the main measures have been veiled, although this has not affected the ratios between them. The problem with such concealment is that it prevents any precise examination of the actual location of the inflection points. The only generalizations that can be made about these data are:

1. The inflection point appears to vary significantly between brands. With two brands whose curves are published in Rao and Miller's article, the inflection point of one appears at about twice the advertising pressure of the other.

2. For at least three-quarters of the diagrams published in Rao and Miller's article, the observations on which the curves are based are *below* the point of inflection, which indicates that at the normal level of opportunities to see for these ongoing brands, the advertising was operating within the range of increasing marginal returns. The analysis showed that it was possible for Lever Brothers to fine-tune their appropriations to nearer the inflection point of the curve, but bearing in mind the wide limits of the model's accuracy, this would have been a tricky procedure.

One factor unquestionably operating in the markets for these brands, if they resemble most brands marketed by Lever Brothers, is the intense nature of the competition. This theme will recur in more than one of the cases in this chapter and the next.

Case 3.   Unnamed Brand

In this simple case with few complications, television was exclusively employed.[18] Two scheduling patterns were transmitted by cable to different households over a three-month period. Household purchases of the brand were monitored, so that the two media schedules could be compared. One scheduling pattern was continuous at quite a high level (about 100 Gross Rating Points per week); the other was a similar schedule in total expenditure, but with pressure concentrated into two week flights, each of about 200 GRPs per week, and with two-week gaps.

At the beginning, purchases in the home receiving the flighted schedule were fortuitously at a slightly higher level than in the homes with the continuous schedule, and ended up at a level 3 percent *above* what they had been at the beginning. Purchases in the homes that received the continuous advertising ended up 12 percent *below* the level at the beginning of the test. One interesting feature of the pattern of sales is that, although there were a number of erratic variations between purchases in the two samples, the superiority of the flighted schedule was only demonstrated in the weeks after the end of the test. This suggests that the penetration of the brand had been increased more by the flighted than by the continuous schedule; and that repeat purchase had maintained or augmented this superiority.

A schedule concentrated into two week "flights" of four-hundred GRPs, (or about an average of five opportunities to see with a net reach of approximately 80 percent) was, despite its gaps, more productive than a continuous advertising pattern. Since total expenditures on the two schedules were the same, the marginal productivity of the flighted schedule must have been greater.

Data from this test did not indicate what would have happened at higher levels of advertising pressure, so we can only conclude that the response curve shows increasing returns up to about five opportunities to see within a two-week period, and that the inflection point might have been there or maybe higher.

One important characteristic of the brand in this case also is the nature of the competition. The brand had in fact fairly recently suffered from competitive pressure from a new entrant into the market. The flighted schedule helped the brand recover its competitive position.

Case 4. *Eight Liquor Brands*

This was a study of purchasing habits and attitudes of readers of *Time* and *Sports Illustrated* in two Midwestern regions during the eleven months ending in September 1980.[19] Each respondent's opportunity to see (OTS) advertisements for eight brands of liquor was established by recording the home deliveries of the particular magazines, and relating these to the advertisements appearing in them. The total sample was 16,500 respondents.

The most important conclusion from this substantial investigation relates the brand of liquor bought to the respondents' opportunities to see advertisements for that brand.

Number of OTS for the Brand During Previous Four Weeks	*Users Buying the Brand*
None	11.1%
One	12.3
Two	12.6
Four	18.9

The sample for this survey was too large to allow such conclusions to be statistically insignificant. It can be seen that, despite the discontinuity in the number of opportunities to see, the improved performance of four opportunities over two (6.3 percentage points) is so much greater than that for two opportunities over one (0.3 percentage points), that for these eight brands, the part of the curve below a pressure level of four opportunities to see in four weeks must be the lower part of an S-shaped configuration. Again the effects of higher pressure are not monitored, so that the inflection point could be at this pressure of four opportunities in four weeks, or possibly higher.

Again, this was an examination of a competitive market.

Case 5. Teflon

This study recounts Du Pont's experience of reintroducing cookware coated with Teflon nonstick coating, following an earlier introduction of coated cookware of an inferior quality.[20] The reader will note that this case, unlike the others reviewed so far, is concerned not with packaged goods, but with a relatively low-price consumer durable.

Market experiments took place continuously. As it turned out, this procedure provided data to help us establish the presence and location of an inflection point in the response curve.

The first test, carried out in fall 1962 and the first three months of 1963, covered thirteen cities. The 1962 advertising was at three levels—high (ten TV spots per week) in four cities; low (five TV spots per week) in five cities; and zero in four cities. In 1963, the cities were switched and similar (although rather lower) levels of advertising pressure were applied. The experiment was appropriately balanced, and purchases of cookware were monitored by telephone interviews with one thousand housewives in each of the thirteen cities, purchase levels being related to advertising pressure in each separate locality.[21]

The topline conclusions were as follows:

Advertising Patterns Associated with Purchase Levels	Purchases of Cookware Units per 1,000 Households
Zero/low in 1962, high in 1963	282
High in 1962, high in 1963	255
Zero/low in 1962, zero/low in 1963	299
High in 1962, zero/low in 1963	205

These are in some ways curious findings, but the extra effect of the higher marginal dose of advertising in early 1963 seems fairly clear. This was a situation in which marginal increases in pressure called forth marginally increased sales.

It is difficult to estimate what the relative advertising pressures of the different schedules represented in real frequency. The high pressure during the first three months of 1963 represented the considerable total of about ninety daytime exposures. What this would mean in terms of average opportunities to see is anybody's guess; mine would be in the five to ten range. But it became clear from further experiments that the inflection point was higher than this.

Subsequent testing of additional advertising pressure yielded further increasing returns. And as a result, Du Pont's national advertising and sales had by 1965 been pitched at a significantly higher level than ever before. Even further levels of pressure were then tested in different markets, until the expected diminishing returns set in: "extremely high levels of advertising did not move enough additional cookware to pay for the advertising costs in the shortrun period."[22]

This case, like the Lever Brothers one, seems to suggest an S-shaped curve with quite a long sweep of increasing returns. Otherwise, there are few resemblances between the two. Teflon cookware is a durable, and the amount of competition is strictly limited. The rather special findings of prolonged increasing returns may however be connected with the previous unsuccessful launch of Teflon with all the problems caused by inferior product quality. Advertising and word-of-mouth communication about the much more effective and durable coating that had at last come onto the market could gradually have persuaded the skeptics, causing the advertising to have an unusually slow-burning and perhaps cumulative effect. This in turn may have caused the exceptional pattern of sales we have noted here.

Diminishing Returns at Higher Levels of Pressure

Case 6. U.S. Department of Agriculture

This case was a relatively simple examination of the effect of different levels of advertising and promotional expenditure on the sales of liquid milk, these expenditures being measured on a per capita basis. When they were lifted from 2 cents to 17 cents, sales responded by a 4.5-percent lift; when expenditures moved upward from 17 cents to 32 cents, the increase in sales was an additional 1.4 percentage points.[23]

These data demonstrate clearly a diminishing rate of marginal return. However, since the first increase in pressure was 750 percent above the base, and the second increase was 1,500 percent above the base, my clear conclusion is that this was a test solely embracing the region at the top of the advertising response curve. It says nothing about whether the configuration was concave-downward or S-shaped at more normal operating levels of advertising pressure.

The reader will also note that the product in this test, milk, is something for which there is no direct competition.

Case 7.   Camels, Lucky Strike, Chesterfield, and Other Cigarettes

This is one of the most rigorous analyses of the relationship between sales and advertising expenditures in an exceptionally advertising-intensive market.[24] It covered data from the earliest days of these brands (Camels being first sold in 1913) to 1960. Telser fitted regressions to the variables and established both a short-term and lagged relationship between sales and advertising, concluding that "the levels of advertising were high enough to place the companies at the point where there were diminishing returns to advertising."[25]

The competition between brands was conducted almost entirely by advertising in the 1920s and 1930s. Only in the postwar years did product changes become a significant competitive strategy. In 1938, the advertising expenditure on Camels alone totalled well over $15 million, a massive investment by the standards of the time.

It seems to me that this celebrated case study merely serves to confirm the diminishing returns configuration at the upper reach of the curve. Like the milk case, it says nothing about its shape at the lower levels. The operating levels of pressure in this market are (or were) toward the top of the curve, as a result of the force of an extreme type of oligopolistic competition in which product differences were considered less important competitive weapons than advertising expenditure. Telser confirmed explicitly that the cigarette manufacturers had succeeded generally in moving up their advertising expenditures outside any possible range of increasing returns, with Camels in particular supplying consumers "with more advertising than they want."[26]

Case 8.   A British Multiple Retailer

This case concerns an advertising pressure experiment in thirty-two stores (in different localities), members of a retail chain selling relatively expensive consumer durables.[27] The medium was local newspapers; there were four levels of pressure, the lowest being zero advertising. The advertising was exposed for six months, running weekly in the local press. This is on the face of it a high rate of strike, although the paper describing the test (a subtly important example of the inadequacy of the published data) does not clarify the form taken by lower advertising pressure: fewer insertions over the six months and/or smaller spaces. (The latter is implied by the description of the frequency of the campaign just quoted. The records unfortunately no longer exist.)

This sort of schedule implies a high number of opportunities to see: as many opportunities as insertions, because there is no internal duplication between the local newspapers used in such a schedule. For products purchased as infrequently as those sold by this chain of shops, such a level of advertising pressure is intense.[28]

It is therefore not really a surprise that the response function of the advertising seems to demonstrate a pattern of diminishing returns. But even in this, the concave-downward configuration is clearly marked only for the smaller shops comprising half the panel. The shape of the response is apparently linear for the larger shops comprising the other half.

This case seems to be yet another in which diminishing returns are present only in the upper reaches of frequency. It provides no enlightenment about the existence of either diminishing or increasing returns at the lower levels.

Diminishing Returns at Intermediate Levels of Pressure

Case 9.   Chicken Sara Lee

This case was a matched experiment to compare different weights of newspaper advertising to support the launch of a new food brand.[29] The test market (Fort Wayne, Indiana) was divided into districts, which were subjected to different advertising pressures. A total of about six thousand personal interviews explored housewives' awareness, attitudes, and purchases. This analysis will be confined to the last of these measures.

The experiment yielded interesting conclusions, although it is difficult to make absolutely firm generalizations because of the very small number of people found to be purchasers of the brand. The advertising exposures were approximately equal to opportunities to see, because only one newspaper was used for the campaign.[30]

Consecutive Advertising Exposures Associated with Purchase	*Purchasers in Each Group*	*Percentage Increase in Purchasers*
Zero	0.53%	
Four in four weeks	1.45	+174%
Eight in eight weeks	2.06	+ 42
Twenty in twenty weeks	1.84	− 12

If the growth in the number of purchasers had followed a straight-line trend reflecting the advertising frequency, the purchasing level of the people who had received eight opportunities to see would have been twice that for those who had received four, but in fact it grew by only 44 percent. The purchasing level for twenty OTS would have been two-and-a-half times that for eight, but in fact it actually decreased slightly (a piece of erratic behavior presumably associated with the very small number of purchasers).

The diminishing rate of yield is therefore evident, although the tiny data base encourages some skepticism of its complete validity.

The reader will note that this brand was a new introduction, so that the majority of sales were (presumably) to first-time buyers. Also, the advertising was in print media and not on television.

Case 10.   Two Proprietary Drugs

This is an important early study of family purchases of two competitive proprietary drugs, monitored (via a panel of about 1,800 families) during the first half of 1943.[31] A model was constructed covering a number of demographic variables, family purchasers of the brands, and advertising exposure (monitored by recording the magazines containing advertisements for the two brands that entered the home).

Roberts himself expressed reservations about the assumptions made by his model. He nevertheless concluded that for one of the two brands, the experiment showed evidence of diminishing returns, which he illustrates diagrammatically in his article. "*If the assumptions enumerated are not too restrictive* (Roberts's emphasis), this curve represents a very rough productivity curve for the effect of advertising on total revenue."[32]

Given a grain of faith, Roberts's conclusion seems acceptable, although the reader will be conscious of the qualifications the author makes about his analytical methods. An inspection of the actual curve shows the greatest flattening (the most extreme diminishing returns) only at the highest levels of advertising pressure: from about ten exposures upward.

The reader will note that this is another example in which the advertising was exposed in print and not audiovisual media.

Case 11.   A New Brand of Food

This case described a six-month experiment in the launch of a new brand of food in four test markets. Three levels of price and two levels of television advertising were examined, the higher level representing 70 percent more household impressions that the lower.[33]

The attempt made to interrelate the effects of price and advertising pressure makes this an interesting study. But Eskin admits that his mathematical model needed adjustment to isolate the effect of advertising on sales, because of contamination between the variables. This procedure naturally causes doubts to arise. After adjustment, the figures show that sales associated with the higher advertising were, progressively for each of the six months of the test, 43 percent, 48 percent, 48 percent, 27 percent, 17 percent, and 19 percent *above* the sales associated with the lower advertising level. What these figures indicated is by no means crystal clear, but diminishing returns to increased pressure is one inference that can be drawn. The point could however be equally well made that the figures show that the campaign was itself running out of steam and only attracting diminishing numbers of new users (the case being concerned, of course, with a new brand launch). We are then left, if not in the dark, at least in the evening shadows.

Case 12. *Lydia Pinkham Vegetable Compound*

This, one of the most exhaustive and widely discussed examples of econometric analysis, concerned an examination of sales and advertising expenditures over a fifty-two-year period for Lydia Pinkham's Vegetable Compound, a patent medicine for menstrual and other exclusively female disorders.[34] Advertising was thought to have been the main influence on sales of the brand. This in turn meant that it was possible to reduce the number of variables over and beyond advertising which needed to be included in the mathematical models (although an extensive range of models was eventually developed by Palda and other analysts, which in turn triggered widespread technical discussion of their strengths and weaknesses).

The investigations in the main concern the extent of the carryover effect of advertising. The different models produced very large differences indeed in their estimates of this extent. But an early conclusion of Palda that advertising volume seems to explain sales volume when the former is expressed logarithmically led him to conclude that his analysis provided evidence of diminishing returns to advertising pressure.

As part of the controversy surrounding this case, it was demonstrated that Palda, by his use of annual observations, produced estimates of the duration of the effect of advertising on sales seventeen times as large as estimates derived from the use of monthly data. The unexpected extent of the variation in the findings caused by seemingly small changes in the inputs has in fact led to much skepticism. "The conclusions gleaned in most cases could probably have been accepted as valid descriptions of the industry patterns if the authors had used alternative traditional sources of information, e.g. trade talk, interviews with key executives, policy documents within the key firms, etc. Drawing these conclusions inferentially from the observations of behavior reduced to data sets is potentially more error prone."[35]

Leaving on one side the treacherous nature of the "processed" data, one special characteristic of the Lydia Pinkham advertising must be borne in mind. The campaign followed the classic pattern of early proprietary medicine advertising, which normally employed small press spaces with a headline boldly featuring the medical symptoms and problems that Lydia Pinkham Vegetable Compound was formulated to treat. Such advertising is widely thought to work through the process of selective perception. It registers and is noticed by the minority of people who at any one time suffer from the medical conditions the brand is made for; such people are therefore in the market for it. The small size of the spaces does not prevent the advertisements from being noticed; and of course this very smallness means that they can affordably be exposed at high frequency. The Lydia Pinkham campaign was then essentially a campaign of relatively high pressure, certainly higher than people have judged it to have been from Lydia Pinkham's relative insignificance as a brand. The likelihood of diminishing returns is therefore not really unexpected.

Case 13.   Andrex Toilet Tissue

This happens to be one case with which I have first-hand experience.[36] A remarkable brand, in the mid-1970s Andrex had a 30-percent market share and large volume indeed (the seventh largest brand in unit terms audited by A.C. Nielsen in Great Britain). It is almost a stereotype of what a successful brand should be, with its combination of excellent functional performance and added values built by an emotionally involving and absolutely consistent advertising campaign, exposed at a reasonably high rate over a period of more than twenty years.[37]

Since the early 1970s, the advertising response function for Andrex had been analyzed through various econometric techniques, although a great deal of controversy had attended the conclusions. It was eventually decided to put the matter to the test, and expose in certain television areas a continuous schedule of approximately one hundred GRPs per month, and in other areas the same weight of advertising, but compressed into flights. The reader will understand from the form of this test that what was being examined was the hypothesis of diminishing returns (tested in the drip-feed areas), versus the hypothesis of increasing returns (tested in the flighted areas).

The explanation of what actually happened has been simplified in Branton's article for reasons of brevity. Readers of this book will also note that (because of the confidentiality of the data) none of the actual diagrams disclose the real market observations, but are instead confined to smoothed curves. "The results were analyzed after a six month period and established beyond reasonable doubt that the convex response curve (i.e. the concave-downward function) was the best fit."[38] The controversy in the interpretation was concerned with the length of the period over which the observations were analyzed, a point mentioned but not commented on in much detail in Branton's paper. Some interpreters suggested that nothing at all had happened as a result of the test, but this in turn probably goes rather far.

If we take Branton's analysis as broadly correct, we are left with the possibility that diminishing returns set in for this brand at somewhere above the
100 GRP level (say at an average of two or three opportunities to see). This
represents probably the lowest level at which diminishing returns may operate in any of the fourteen examples in this chapter. But there is one factor
that *does* make Andrex an unusual brand: the lack of important advertised
competitors in the market, a point explicitly mentioned by Branton in the
conclusion to his article.[39]

Case 14. Budweiser Beer

This well-documented published case was characterized by a long series of
econometric experiments in test markets.[40]

What the researchers aimed to do was to track the sales response to reductions in advertising pressure in a number of controlled sales regions (of
course segregating the influence of contaminating variables). Advertising reductions are normally aimed at increasing *profit*; it is not logical to expect
them to achieve a sales increase unless they are accompanied by a fundamental change in one of the other variables, such as the campaign copy or the
advertising media. But the astonishing conclusion of the long series of Budweiser experiments was that a reduction in advertising actually increased
sales, making the advertising response function bend down like an inverted
U, a bizarre configuration. This is a highly exaggerated form of diminishing
returns, the normal expression being the progressive flattening of the concave-downward curve, which nevertheless continues to rise, but at a diminishing rate.

The analysts' explanation was that this response function is an expression of supersaturation of certain demographically defined target groups.
This is, to say the least, a questionable notion. From what we know about
the actual weight of the Budweiser media schedules against the consumer, it
is quite easy to calculate how little actual exposure is made by even the largest
and most persuasive advertising campaigns (a mean potential exposure measurable *in minutes per year*.) This point is developed in Allaire's comment on
the first of the papers by Ackoff and Emshoff.[41]

Whatever the reason for this remarkable phenomenon of reduced advertising increasing sales, the conclusions made by Ackoff and Emshoff (which
covered more than pressure reduction alone) were embodied in astonishingly
effective policy recommendations. "During this period (1962–68) sales of
Budweiser increased from approximately 7.5 million to 14.5 million barrels
and its market share increased from 8.14 to 12.94 percent . . . and advertising
expenditures were reduced from $1.89 to $0.80 per barrel, a 58 percent
reduction."[42]

Looking at this seven-year period as a whole, I would be inclined to attribute Budweiser's extraordinary performance to three factors. First is the operation of advertising scale economies. Budweiser had been on a powerful rising trend since 1957, one continuing more or less to this day. The brand must therefore offer the consumer a highly (and increasingly) attractive combination of functional performance and added values. As I have demonstrated, large brands with this characteristic can often be supported by advertising investments well below the norm for the product field.

The second factor is a media change implemented in 1964, following an econometric evaluation of outdoor advertising's contribution, or lack of contribution, to sales. This medium was dropped from the Budweiser schedule, saving approximatelly $3.5 million from the brand's advertising budget. On the assumption that this medium was indeed ineffective for the Budweiser campaign, the residual advertising for Budweiser actually *increased* in 1964.

Budweiser Estimated Advertising Budget ($ Millions)

	Media Other than Outdoor	Outdoor	Total
1963	20.5	3.5	24.0
1964	23.5	—	23.5

The third factor is, frankly, an unknown. The literature describing the case gives no details of creative changes in the campaign, changes in expenditure below the line, changes in consumer price, or indeed any other alterations in the mix. Any of these factors could have influenced sales significantly. Indeed there is a strong hint that price may have had a bearing on the results.[43]

Economies of Scale and the Advertising Response Function

This entire chapter has been concerned with short-term relationships. The argument has described how increases in advertising pressure generate an immediate sales response. Certain cases, however (notably Budweiser), touched on matters of longer-term importance, in particular scale economies accruing to larger brands. Between the short and the long term there can sometimes be a puzzling contradiction.

On the one hand, the advertising response function, which examines a brand from a short-term point of view (in a usually stationary market situation) demonstrates either increasing or diminishing returns at low levels of advertising, while at high levels of advertising pressure it invariably shows diminishing returns. On the other hand, we have seen brands grow (in our analyses in chapters 4 and 5) to the upper levels of market share, in which there are clear economies of scale operating, connected in behavioral terms with the penetration supercharge: the tendency of a large brand to have a higher frequency of purchase and repurchase than a small brand. These trends manifest themselves in an ability of larger brands to be successfully supported at a relatively low advertising volume. In chapters 4 and 5, the analyses were of brands considered from a long-term point of view.

On the one hand we have what seems to be a strong underlying tendency to short-term diminishing returns, and on the other a strong underlying tendency to long-term economies of scale for certain brands. Increasing returns and scale economies are different concepts, but in certain circumstances they can be related: the latter can contribute to the former. How can we explain this apparent contradiction between short-term diminishing returns and what looks dangerously like long-term increasing returns?

The most plausible explanation is that the scale economies associated with successful brands apply to *all aspects* of those brands, stemming as they do from their functional and nonfunctional values, and also from such things as distributional ubiquity and high usage, factors leading eventually to the penetration supercharge.

An unquestionably elegant demonstration of this phenomenon appears in Simon and Arndt's analysis of Lambin's review of 107 European brands and his findings that larger brands have advertising economies. Lambin noted: "For large brands, the inverse relationship between the advertising–sales ratio and market share."[44] The reader will appreciate that this is virtually the same point I have been making about the scale economies of larger brands, although Lambin uses the advertising–sales ratio measurement while I have used the brand's contribution to the total advertising level in a market.

When Simon and Arndt came to consider this widespread phenomenon, they rightly concentrated on the *overall* scale economies associated with the larger brands: "It is reasonable and likely that firm E has a much more extensive distribution network and a larger sales force than firm A. That would explain *both* why firm E has a higher response function *and* why it advertises more in total than does firm A. And, depending on the particular slopes of the functions, the advertising–sales ratio could well be lower for the larger firm for this reason alone."[45]

Although Simon and Arndt are thinking in terms of the firm rather than the brand, they have clearly grasped the essential point; and their diagrammatic expression of this point explains the position of the larger brand with its scale economies. (I have only shown the configuration at the top of the

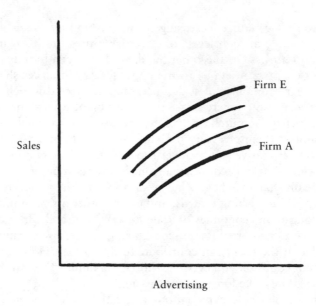

curves, thus avoiding a continuation of the discussion about whether this configuration is concave-downward or S-shaped at the lower levels of advertising pressure.)

The authors show the possibility of a *family* of advertising response curves. Here the position of the large firm with scale economies (firm *E*) would of course be *higher* than that of the small one without the scale economies (firm *A*). From this analysis, it is obvious why a given incremental dose of advertising has a greater effect for firm *E*. The position of the two curves relative to one another is not a reflection of the advertising alone, but of the relative strengths of the firms overall, to which advertising has naturally made and continues to make a contribution. This point in its own way encapsulates my main message in this book.

The Argument in Brief

This chapter has examined the response of sales to increases in advertising pressure. In the category of direct response advertising, there is overwhelming evidence that the pattern of response is represented by the concave-downward function which describes progressively diminishing returns from all increments of advertising, starting with the first.

The chapter examined fourteen cases mainly describing repeat-purchase packaged goods. Thirteen cases were grouped into three different response patterns. Four cases showed the S-shaped response configuration, describing increasing followed by diminishing returns. Three cases showed diminishing returns to high pressure. With these, the curve could have been either concave-downward or S-shaped for most of its length; the data are not full enough to tell us which. Six cases showed diminishing returns (as with direct response advertising).

Fragile clues point to possible reasons for the different types of response function. One such clue is the possibility that the S-shaped configuration describes repeat-purchase packaged goods, because of the competitive nature of the markets in which they operate, with more competition tentatively suggesting a high inflection point on the curve. Low competition could be associated with a concave-downward response pattern. This and other signals will be examined in chapters 9 and 10.

Notes

1. The concept of diminishing returns comes from classical economics and is concerned with the diminishing productivity of agriculture and extractive industry (a reflection of the falling fertility of the soil and the higher cost of bringing minerals out of deeper mines). The concept has over the years been applied broadly to other matters than economics, and is entirely apposite to advertising. In the chapter title, "A diminishing rate of yield" is a quotation from Alfred Marshall, *Principles of Economics* (New York: Macmillan, 1961), p. 167.

2. Julian L. Simon, *Issues in the Economics of Advertising* (Urbana, Il: University of Illinois Press, 1970), p. 7.

3. J.J. Lambin, *Advertising, Competition and Market Conduct in Oligopoly over Time* (New York: American Elsevier, 1976), p. 95.

4. Simon, *Issues in the Economics of Advertising*, p. 18.

5. Jack Z. Sissors, "Confusions about Effective Frequency," *Journal of Advertising Research* (December 1982): 33–37.

6. Callaghan OHerlihy, "How to Test the Sales Effects of Advertising": 32–35.

7. Tom Corlett, "Anyone for Econometrics?" *Admap* (August 1978).

8. See for instance:

Corlett, "Anyone for Econometrics?"

Callaghan OHerlihy, "Why Econometrics Can Make Advertising and Marketing Scientific," *Admap* (October 1978): 472–80.

Richard W. Pollay, "Lydiametrics: Applications of Econometrics to the History of Advertising," *Journal of Advertising History* (January 1979): 3–18.

9. OHerlihy, "Why Econometrics Can Make Advertising and Marketing Scientific": 472.

10. W.A. Shryer, *Analytical Advertising* (Detroit: Business Service Corporation, 1912) as described in Simon, *Issues in the Economics of Advertising*, pp. 11–14.

11. Simon, *Issues in the Economics of Advertising*, chap. 1.

12. *Ibid.*, 22.

13. John Philip Jones, "Universal Diminishing Returns—True or False?" *International Journal of Advertising* 3, no. 1 (1984): 27–41.

14. These figures are crude percentages of the actual number of replies. The sizes and costs of the spaces varied to some degree during the campaign. Figures of cost per reply in the table in this chapter take account of the different space costs.

15. Ambar G. Rao and Peter B. Miller, "Advertising/Sales Response Functions," *Journal of Advertising Research* (April 1975): 7–15.

16. *Ibid.*, 12.

17. Julian L. Simon and Johan Arndt, "The Shape of the Advertising Response Function," *Journal of Advertising Research* (August 1980): 22.

18. *Effective Frequency: The Relationship between Frequency and Advertising Effectiveness*, appendix B, case 4.

19. Time Inc. in association with Joseph E. Seagram and Sons, Inc., *A Study of the Effectiveness of Advertising Frequency in Magazines* (New York: Time Inc., 1982).

20. Malcolm A. McNiven, "Choosing the Most Profitable Level of Advertising: A Case Study" in *How Much to Spend for Advertising? Methods for Determining Advertising Expenditure Levels*, ed. Malcolm A. McNiven (New York: Association of National Advertisers, 1969), chap. 7.

21. James C. Becknell, Jr., and Robert W. McIsaac, "Test Marketing Cookware coated with 'Teflon,'" *Journal of Advertising Research* (September 1963): 2–8.

22. McNiven, "Choosing the Most Profitable Level of Advertising: A Case Study": p. 93.

23. Wendel E. Clement, Peter L. Henderson, and Cleveland P. Eley, *The Effect of Different Levels of Promotional Expenditures on Sales of Fluid Milk* (Washington: U.S. Dept. of Agriculture, Economic Research Service, 1965).

There is a small arithmetical error in Julian Simon's presentation of the data from this report. See Simon, *Issues in the Economics of Advertising*, p. 10.

24. Lester G. Telser, "Advertising and Cigarettes," *Journal of Political Economy* (October 1962): 471–99.

25. *Ibid.*, 498.

26. Ibid., 499.

27. Peter Doyle and Ian Fenwick, "Planning and Estimation of Advertising," *Journal of Marketing Research* (February 1975): 1–6.

28. In a letter to me dated March 8, 1983, Professor Doyle confirmed that the advertiser in question "became one of the highest spenders among U.K. retailers."

29. John B. Stewart, *Repetitive Advertising in Newspapers: A Study of Two New Products* (Cambridge, Mass.: Harvard University, 1964).

30. The data in this table come from *ibid.*, p. 269. A more complex extrapolation of Stewart's figures (which I cannot reconcile with the originals) appears in Simon, *Issues in the Economics of Advertising*, pp. 20–21.

31. Harry V. Roberts, "The Measurement of Advertising Results," *Journal of Business* (July 1947): 131–45.

32. *Ibid.*, 142.

33. Gerald J. Eskin, "A Case for Test Market Experiments," *Journal of Advertising Research* (April 1975): 27–33.

34. Kristian Palda, "The Measurement of Cumulative Advertising Effects," *Journal of Business* (April 1965): 162–79.

35. Pollay, "Lydiametrics: Applications of Econometrics to the History of Advertising": 13.

36. J.J. Branton, "The Bowater-Scott Approach to Media Phasing," *Admap* (January 1978): 24–26. (At the time this paper was published, I was the account director on Andrex in the London office of J. Walter Thompson. Jim Branton, then marketing general manager of the Bowater-Scott Corporation, was my client.)

37. Details of this campaign and of the early history of the brand are given in Stephen King, *What is a Brand?* (London: J. Walter Thompson, 1970), pp. 5–9.

38. Branton, "The Bowater-Scott Approach to Media Phasing": 26.

39. *Ibid.,* 26.

40. Russell L. Ackoff and James R. Emshoff, "Advertising Research at Anheuser-Busch (1963–68 and 1968–74)," *Sloane Management Review* (Winter 1975): 1–15 and (Spring 1976): 1–15, 91–98.

41. Ackoff and Emshoff, "Advertising Research at Anheuser-Busch," Spring 1976; Comment by Yvon Allaire and rejoinder by Ackoff and Emshoff.

42. Ackoff and Emshoff, "Advertising Research at Anheuser-Busch" (Winter 1975): 10–12.

43. *Ibid.,* 6.

44. Lambin, *Advertising, Competition and Market Conduct in Oligopoly over Time,* pp. 127–32.

45. Simon and Arndt, "The Shape of the Advertising Response Function," 21–22.

9

Advertising Pressure: What Two Little Ads Can Do

The Carpenter said nothing but
"Cut us another slice.
I wish you were not quite so deaf—
I've had to ask you twice!"

One of the most intrinsically interesting fields of advertising is that for proprietary drugs. Part of the interest stems from its long history, and part from the well-established and generally successful techniques that have been applied. As the reader will remember from the discussion of Lydia Pinkham in chapter 8, the classic format for this advertising is small spaces with bold headlines to attract attention to the medical condition, whose sufferers will often notice the advertisements unconsciously, using selective perception, and respond accordingly.

I have personal experience of only two proprietary medicine advertisers (each however with a portfolio of brands); both of these were during my early years in the advertising agency business. One client made both proprietary and "ethical" brands (brands advertised only to doctors) for the treatment of muscular rheumatism; one of its proprietaries was both large in size and typically advertising-intensive, measured by its ratio of advertising expenditure to sales. The media policy for this brand was unusual: the main campaign employed large spaces (full and half pages) in Britain's leading national newspapers, with exhaustively long copy which included testimonials and complicated scientific explanations, all written in an impeccably editorial style. The insertions ran intermittently, even haphazardly; the spaces were in fact bought by the client himself as a result of personal forays among the newspaper proprietors in Fleet Street, where with ready money he would snap up bargains offered by those advertisement directors who had spaces to fill in a hurry and were reluctantly prepared to cut their rates to find a buyer. In this, the client was pointing the way to the type of opportunistic media buying that was to become normal for advertising agencies twenty years later.

The client, a successful and rather remarkable man, operated more by instinct than calculation, and was perhaps so successful simply because of his unorthodox methods. Because his advertising was working in a basically unplanned way, with reliance on the impact of individual advertisements rather than on frequency of insertion, his sales inevitably had to be responding to individual exposures. This pattern of media buying was quite unlike any other advertising with which I had been involved at the time; and I was not too inexperienced to realize that this was an example of advertising working in a highly unorthodox way, in comparison with most of the other brands handled by the agency, which had conventional high-frequency advertising schedules. This experience also caused me to speculate about whether impact could have as great an effect as frequency (or perhaps even a greater effect), a speculation to which this chapter will be substantially devoted.[1]

The instincts of many advertising practitioners tend to lead them toward policies of concentration in most normal conditions. I indeed saw this trend when my pharmaceutical client was in the heyday of his success. This basic instinct to concentrate has been abetted by psychological theory and much research into the rapid decay of human memory, the relevance of which to advertising deserves to be seriously questioned, quite apart from the formidable difficulties of measurement.[2] On the other hand, the few opponents of extreme concentration, despite the evidence that can be marshalled of the universal application of diminishing returns at the higher levels of advertising pressure, have tended to take a similarly emotional line about the folly of any concentration at all; here they appear to be unable to see that if advertising yields diminishing returns at high pressure, this does not automatically mean that it yields them at *all* levels, including levels of low pressure.

As suggested in chapter 8, this debate has always lacked any consistent empirical examination of inflection points for specific brands. Fortunately however there has been a parallel, equally heated but generally more fruitful professional debate on a somewhat different issue: the *minimum* levels of frequency to which brands can be expected to respond. This has been an essentially pragmatic affair, involved with how well sales can be maintained and expanded at the lower real advertising expenditures made necessary by the pressures of media inflation on more or less fixed budgets. American advertisers have entirely justifiably been so worried by this matter that, in order to stimulate thought and discussion, their professional organization, the Association of National Advertisers (ANA), in 1979 published *Effective Frequency* (edited by Michael Naples, formerly of Lever Brothers and more recently president of the Advertising Research Foundation), an important book which collected and commented on the best published and unpublished contributions to this debate over the previous twenty years and more.[3]

If readers will think of the implications of this study of effective frequency, they are likely to agree that it has a significant bearing on the debate about increasing or diminishing returns. But the examination looks at the matter from a slightly different viewpoint from that in chapter 8. There, our evaluation of increasing or diminishing returns was carried out by looking at a brand's response curve as a whole, even (in a number of examples) exclusively at the upper reaches of this curve. The evaluation of effective frequency, on the other hand, is concerned with the lower parts of the curve. This is appropriate for a practical debate concerned with the best deployment of finite and possibly diminishing resources; it is about one, two, or three opportunities to see in a limited period, certainly not about ten or more opportunities, the effects of which are explored in the upper parts of the response curve—a place which would overstretch the media budgets of most ongoing brands.

The debate about effective frequency is concerned essentially with whether one single advertising exposure can have an immediate effect. If it does have such an effect, and if the second has less, then clearly diminishing returns are operating. But on the other hand, if the second exposure has more effect than the first, then the response curve must have the S-shaped configuration describing increasing returns at low pressure. If the first advertising exposure does not have an effect but the second one does, then (a fortiori), the curve must be S-shaped. Here is the heart of the effective frequency debate and the concern of this chapter.

If this all sounds dishearteningly theoretical, the reader may be surprised to discover that there is quite an amount of good data to flesh out these theoretical bones. This chapter looks at the question of increasing or diminishing returns from the low-pressure end of the response curve, and examines the eminently practical matter of the best operational policies for building advertising schedules, in particular the minimum weights that can be deployed.

I shall be examining data published in the ANA's *Effective Frequency* and other sources. As usual, I am concerned with behavioral facts rather than cognitive and affective changes. *Effective Frequency* includes sections dealing with both sales and nonsales data. Generally speaking, those that employ sales measures argue the case for lower levels of frequency, while those that employ nonsales measures tend to argue for higher levels. However, this present chapter, like chapter 8, is exclusively concerned with sales.

Four Further Case Studies

We will now look at four new case studies. Comparisons will be made with the fourteen cases in chapter 8.

Here we shall specifically be searching for whether the first advertising exposure achieves a sales response, and how the size of this response compares with those from subsequent exposures. In certain cases, the first exposure will be shown to generate a response; in other cases it will not. The interesting part of our discussion will concern reasons why a single exposure works in some cases and not in others. This difference has great operational importance. For example, if a policy of extreme media dispersion is applied to a brand for which it can be proven that advertising does not work on a one-exposure basis, then such an advertiser is in grave danger of reducing the effectiveness of (or even wasting) his entire advertising budget.

Case 15. *Twenty-Four Brands of Packaged Goods*

This suggestive but slightly defective case attracted considerable attention when it was first published.[4] But the fact that it is not included in *Effective Frequency* is presumably because it is statistically not very robust; also it is untypical of repeat-purchase packaged goods cases in the important respect that it concerns press and not television advertising.

The case involves a June 1968 test in six cities covering twenty-four high-volume brands of packaged goods and seven durables. Quarter-page advertisements were placed in the morning newspaper delivered to a sample of selected homes in each town, thus providing each home with an opportunity to see the advertisement. A total of 2,438 home interviews was carried out with the homemakers in these residences the next day (an average of thirty hours after the delivery of the paper). This was time enough to read the paper and do normal shopping, where the advertisements tested were theoretically able to influence the brand choice.

Each homemaker was exposed to advertisements for more than one brand, but the sample was carefully balanced, and each subsample had a matched control. As a result, each advertisement was evaluated by six hundred personal interviews (one hundred in each city.)

The interviews included questions to measure brand purchase, plans to buy, likelihood of buying, and various aspects of recall and recognition of the advertising. Because of my usual reluctance to look at nonbehavioral measures, I shall be concentrating on the brand purchasing. And since for the durables covered in the test, brand purchase was virtually nonexistent, the findings I will quote are confined exclusively to the twenty-four brands of packaged goods. The test then was of the immediate effect of a single advertisement exposure for each of a representative range of packaged goods against a reasonably large and balanced sample of consumers.

Although the sample was of a good size and durables were excluded from the measurement of purchasing, the numbers of homemakers buying the brands under test were (not entirely unexpectedly) rather small. This is a salutary reminder that even for major brands in important product fields, only a minority of homemakers are in the market on any one day. In the test, the smallness in the numbers of purchasers indeed affected the statistical significance of the conclusions, as we shall shortly discover.

"Taking the aggregate of all the ads and brands under study, we found that in comparison with the control group [who had not been exposed to the advertisements] the test group showed 14% more purchases of the advertised brand." This could have taken place by chance only about three times in twenty. This is unfortunately a weaker level of significance than the normal one chance in twenty which is in general considered necessary for firm conclusions from market research data. An additional interesting finding is that the test group showed 18 percent *fewer* plans to buy the test brand the next day (again at a lower-than-normal level of statistical probability). This drew the inference from the researchers that "the ads worked to trigger faster buying action on the part of women who were otherwise vaguely 'in the market'."[5]

This test seems to provide imperfect although strong directional evidence that a single newspaper advertisement exposure for a brand of repeat-purchase packaged goods is capable of generating immediate sales, but that the effect of such an increase is obscured by the likelihood of the sales being transferred from the next day. Thus, within the purchase cycle of the brand (which could be a two-week period or more), the effect of the single exposure is likely to be hidden. The bringing forward of purchases however suggests diminishing returns.

There is not much more to be said about this interesting but rather frustrating case beyond noting the entirely expected lack of correlation between sales of the brand and both recognition and recall of the advertising (a point discussed in chapter 6).

Case 16. Nine Complete Packaged Goods Product Fields

This is one of the few longitudinal examinations of the effects of advertising that can be looked upon as a model of how such studies should be carried out.[6] Only two variables were examined: opportunities to see advertising and brand offtake. Although econometric techniques were not used, McDonald was scrupulous to avoid the contamination of other variables. Fieldwork took place in the United Kingdom over a three-month period in 1966. The paper describing the findings (which had been used in the intervening years by J. Walter Thompson, who had commissioned the research) was read publicly at the Conference of the European Society of Opinion and Marketing Research in 1970, and published in the United Kingdom. The paper has been reprinted and extensively referred to in the literature by both practitioners and academics, although it has been accorded a rather more favorable reception by the former than the latter.[7] The study was considered so important by the Association of National Advertisers that it was reprinted in its entirety in an appendix to *Effective Frequency;* it also prompted considerable comment in the text itself.

It was an exhaustive diary study of the purchasing behavior and exposure to advertising of a representative sample of 255 housewives in the London area. The housewives wrote daily in their diaries the details of all their purchases in nine product fields; and listed the issues they had seen of thirty-two different newspapers and magazines plus details of all viewing of commercial television. The media measure of opportunities to see was chosen in preference to recall, because it is generally considered in professional circles to be the best of the measures of advertising exposure (which are all imperfect).

One important aspect of the test was that, by relating purchasing and advertising exposure to each respondent individually and avoiding conclusions from premature aggregations of the data, McDonald managed to eliminate the influences that might have contaminated his data, so that he was able to speak of cause (advertising exposure) and effect (brand purchasing) with certainty. He also based his conclusions on the most uncompromising measure of short-term advertising effect: brand switching. McDonald's care in planning and interpretation have made this piece of research methodologically the most solid of all the cases published anywhere in which the effects of advertising have been measured (with due respect to Simon and Arndt).[8]

The period in which purchasing and advertising exposure were related was the purchase interval, which varied between brands and between housewives, but since opportunities to see the advertising were counted from the diaries for every one of the purchase intervals for every product field and for every housewife over the thirteen weeks of the test, the variation in the length of the purchase intervals was taken care of in the tabulation. The reader can readily visualize the vast accumulation of information provided by the three months of data collection, and appreciate the mechanical problems of digesting and evaluating all these facts and distilling them to produce a small number of simple and actionable conclusions. There are three conclusions of real importance.

The first relates to short-term brand switching. As the reader will remember from chapter 5, we are not necessarily talking about permanent changes in brand preference, but the normal rotation of brand choice within the homemaker's repertoire. The purest measure of such brand switching is the number of switches to the brand under examination (brand X) as a percentage of all switches. The test demonstrated that the percentage of switches to X varied with the number of opportunities to see advertisements for X, in the following way.

Number of Opportunities to See Advertisements for X in the Purchase Interval	Percentage of Switches to X out of All Brand Switches
0	50.1%
1	46.8
2	54.0
3	53.3
4 or more	53.7

"The response curve measured in these terms is S-shaped. Two features stand out. When *one* OTS for X is seen, the proportion of switches *to* X falls below the 50 percent mark (lower than when no OTS is seen); and three or more OTS do not appear to have stronger effect than two."[9] The advertising can clearly be seen not to have had a positive effect (in fact rather the opposite) after a single response. The critical level of exposure for it to have an effect was two opportunities to see, and there was no improvement at greater exposure than this.

The second important conclusion from this study relates to the times within the purchase interval when advertising has its greatest demonstrable effect. The evidence is clear that advertising works most dramatically within four days of the purchase; but within this period, the last day of all before purchase is the least valuable.

The third finding relates to continuity of brand purchasing rather than to switching between brands. In view of the general importance of repeat buying in markets, it is a notably important conclusion that the critical level of exposure that leads to increased repetition of purchase is again two opportunities to see the advertising for the brand.

McDonald's data base is so extensive that the test provides a number of additional conclusions. In particular, it explores the largely unopened territory of intermedia comparisons.

But putting aside these and other insights and speculations triggered by McDonald's study, we should return to the central question of whether one advertisement exposure has an immediate effect. The research suggests this does not take place, but the reasons need careful examination. Indeed, McDonald claims that his investigation "does *not* mean that one advertising exposure has no effect. It does suggest, however, that as far as short-term stimulating effect is concerned, one exposure tends to be beaten by two or more occurring at the same time." Amplifying this point in a slightly different context, he says: "When people do see an advertisement for X, in a much higher proportion of cases they also see advertisements in the same intervals for other brands including the other one in the pair" (that is, from which the switch might take place to brand X). "Quite often, therefore, a brand for which two or more OTS are seen 'wins' over a brand for which, *at the same time,* only one OTS is seen."[10]

McDonald is talking essentially about the minimum level of advertising exposure necessary to cut through the "noise" of competitive advertising in a market.[11] This specific aspect of the matter will also be examined in the next case study, but here we shall be substantially concerned with brands which have a *low degree* of advertised competition, with interesting resultant effects on response patterns. And following this study, the shape of responses and in particular what influences that shape—things which at the moment appear rather shadowy—will begin to take a much more deeply etched shape and substantial form.

Case 17.   Five Major Brands

This case was an analysis of the diary-recorded purchases of five major American brands within an Ad Tel split-cable market.[12] The test covered nine months of purchasing beginning in September 1974, together with television viewing data for two-week periods in November 1974 and February and July 1975. There was therefore a satisfactory base period for the measurement of household buying, and a media measurement during relatively short periods of television advertising, which were in turn projected to cover the entire test period.

Unlike McDonald's study, which was confined to an exhaustive examination of the relationship between the two simple variables of purchasing and advertising exposures, the Ad Tel study was based on a series of mathematical models which related probability of purchase to a number of additional variables: number of exposures, share of exposures, growth of exposures, and nonexposure compared with exposure. The data also examined users and nonusers separately over four-week purchasing periods. Users were defined as those who had bought the brand within the previous three months.

The reader will note how much more complex this test was than McDonald's. Buying probabilities for each of the five brands are presented in the form of smoothed curves, with no observations plotted on them. In fact, the regression coefficients are uniformly low, although they are significant because of the large sample sizes.

Four reasonably clear conclusions can be drawn about the response patterns, although Naples's commentary is not too explicit about the immediate effect of the first advertising exposure (something that the curves themselves seem clearly to indicate).

In the first place, the effect of advertising on *users'* probability of buying is much greater than on that of nonusers. This finding is true to a greater or lesser degree for all five brands. As far as nonusers are concerned, there seems to be a general lack of response to advertising for all the brands. Some of the curves suggest growth, but the smoothing is such that it is difficult to make well-supported specific points about either individual brands or general patterns, except to note that where there seems to be any response, this appears to be associated with diminishing returns from the first exposure. The demonstration of greater response by brand users is consonant with virtually everything I have been saying in this book.

The second point is that the levels of response to larger amounts of advertising are higher than those for smaller amounts (certainly for brand users). This differential response jibes with the conclusion reached in chapter 4, in the discussion of the dynamic difference, that in the majority of cases there is a causal relationship between advertising pressure changes and sales changes.

The third conclusion is that, as far as users' purchases are concerned, the first exposure certainly seems to have an effect in the cases of four of the five brands studied. The exception, brand C, has a special characteristic which has probably caused the advertising response to follow a different course (a point to be considered later). For the four brands showing an immediate response, the function appears either to have a pronounced concave-downward configuration, or else a linear one with a slight inclination toward diminishing returns.

The fourth and most important conclusion from the analysis is that with brand C, the effect on users is less pronounced than with any other brand. There is no suggestion of a concave-downward response function unless it is concealed in the smoothing. The curves are in fact apparently linear. It is also a possibility that the smoothing may have concealed a slight tendency to an S-shaped configuration.

The clue to the difference between brand C and the others lies in the actual strength in the market of these brands. They were all reasonably large brands measured in terms of the annual level of advertising expenditure put behind them. (These appropriations date from the mid-1970s, so that in real terms the advertising schedules are heavier than similar dollar appropriations would provide in the 1980s.) But in the case of four of the five brands, they clearly have either few or weak competitors (or both). This is made absolutely clear by the column of figures on the right in the following table, which shows the various brands' shares of total advertising in their markets. These figures indicate those brands' dominance in advertising dollars, and almost certainly their dominance in market share as well.

Brand	Approximate National Advertising Rate	Average Share of Advertising
A	$8,200,000	58%
B	2,100,000	72
C	7,600,000	15
D	5,100,000	61
E	4,700,000	42

relatively small when measured by the scale of the market. The explanation for the difference between the response pattern for C and the other brands must, in Naples's opinion (and mine), be related to C's weaker market position.

C's performance can in fact be explained by McDonald's argument based on the total level of advertising in a market. If the first exposure of C's campaign has a smaller apparent effect than the first exposures of A's, B's, D's, or *E*'s, this is surely because the noise of this exposure is not loud enough to cut through the competition. If we think exclusively of the brand switching situation analyzed by McDonald, the stimulus to switch *to C* is probably negated by the higher number of stimuli to switch to other brands *from C*.

Regarding the other four brands, evidence of effectiveness of the first advertising exposure seems reasonably clear, as does the tendency to diminishing returns starting with this first exposure. And in considering these brands, there is another resemblance which the observant reader may have noted: a similarity in pattern between them and Andrex (case 13 in chapter 8). It will also be apparent to the reader that *in their dominance of competitive markets,* and in the resulting special pattern of advertising response (high initial response followed by diminishing returns), all these brands are *exceptions*. The pattern of normally balanced oligopolistic competition is better exemplified by the brands analyzed in McDonald's study and by brand *C;* and for these, as we have seen, the response pattern was essentially different: S-shaped or linear.

Case 18. A Beverage Brand

This most interesting series of experiments began in 1975, and continued for more than two years.[13] It was based on audited regional tests of advertising variables, which included two creative alternatives and various media patterns employing different television dayparts and radio.

The effects of the various alternatives were incorporated in a mathematical model, which also included among the variables real disposable personal income and the price of the brand in comparison with an index of all consumer food prices. Since the findings of the model led to adjustments in the media strategy for the brand, which in turn caused significant sales gains, the model must have represented a fair approximation of the relative importance of the factors contributing to sales. The change in copy in particular was calculated to account for 39 percent of the total sales variation—yet another confirmation of the great importance of qualitative factors.

The importance of this case lies in its attempt to construct response curves for different media: television for one campaign, and radio for two campaigns. Responses are expressed in the analysis as a family of S-shaped curves, which are presented in some detail, with a clear indication of the inflection points. In fact, the analysis is worked with such precision that it provides a double inflection point: first, a minimum level at which advertising has an effect (the lower threshold) and second, the "true" inflection point, above which advertising begins to yield diminishing returns to incremental pressure. The no-man's land between the two is quite narrow, but it is an area of importance for media planning and buying.

The lower threshold and true inflection points are described in both gross rating points and average frequency (equivalent to the measure of opportunities to see used in this chapter and in chapter 8). The frequency estimates have even been adjusted to provide special figures for viewing by more attentive viewers, but these data must regretfully be ignored in the following table because similar adjustments are not available for the other estimates of opportunities to see in this book, and my intent is to provide as much comparability as possible in the information presented.

This table distills findings of the tests. Levels of opportunity to see are counted over standard four-week periods, not purchasing intervals.

	Minimum OTS for an Effect	Inflection Point Measured in OTS
Television, new campaign	2.7	3.4
Radio, new campaign	5.1	8.0

Notice three striking situations in this table.

First, the rather large differences between the levels for television and radio can be explained by the general characteristics of radio as an advertising medium in comparison with television. This difference mainly stems from the fact that radio receives less audience attention and participation, with the result that it presumably requires more gross ratings to penetrate it.

A second point concerns the location of the inflection point in the television response curve. Remember that the various approximations suggested in chapter 8 put the inflection point above the level of five opportunities to see in the cases analyzed there, although these did vary in their reliability and in the periods covered by the data. But our present figure of 3.4 is at the lower end. It is probable that the level of competition in a market influences the location of the inflection point, with more competition requiring more frequency to cut through competitive advertising noise.

My third conclusion is that there is a close proximity between television's lower threshold of 2.7, and the true inflection point of 3.4 opportunities to see. This means that the amount of leeway for effective media planning and buying is exceedingly constricted. In this particular case, it is hardly worthwhile advertising at all at a frequency lower than 2.7 over the four-week period, and wasteful to advertise at a higher rate than 3.4. In how many cases do media planners in agencies work within such disciplined margins? In my experience the answer is never. The reader is invited to consider what this type of analysis and its logical conclusions might mean to the operating procedures of Madison Avenue. Media planning and buying is a branch of the advertising business that has always combined analytical strategies and opportunistic tactics, with the emphasis varying at different times between the two. The sorts of change that this analysis seems to suggest are necessary, would move the normal operating procedures to a more disciplined extreme than they have ever approached in the past; not only agencies, but also clients and the media would be affected.

A Note on the Practical Implications for Media Planning

The four supplementary cases described in this chapter led on from the discussion begun in chapter 8, but were concerned with one specific issue of considerable practical importance: whether one advertising exposure can have an effect in the marketplace; and, if not, what is the minimum number needed to trigger a sales response. The consensus of the cases that employed television advertising (cases 16, 17, and 18) is that in practical circumstances one exposure will be ineffective, and two (more probably three or four) should be regarded as the effective minimum number within the brand purchase interval. The shape of the response function describing this phenomenon would show zero offtake below the inflection point.

There is little doubt that this notion of a minimum effective frequency has penetrated the advertising industry, and that a minimal exposure level is regarded as a practical objective of media buying in a number of important and influential agencies: an example of an apparently arid theory bringing forth a harvest of fruit.[14]

An important practical aspect of media planning for minimal effectiveness needs to be briefly noted. Media schedules are traditionally analyzed in terms of their net reach and *average* opportunities to see. The best alternative selected from all the schedules evaluated on a routine basis is invariably that which provides the best optimization of these two variables within the confines of a given budget.

The concept of effective frequency means that the examination of frequency by means of averaging the opportunities to see is now inadequate, because this average conceals the percentage of the audience that is exposed to the advertising at a frequency below the effective minimum, and also the percentage exposed wastefully (at a frequency above the inflection point in the curve.)

What is required is an analysis of alternative schedules by the *frequency distribution* of opportunities to see, and a concentration on the coverage provided of those people who are exposed by three or more opportunities (or whatever number is chosen as the effective minimum). This type of analysis will have a strong bearing on the tactics of media buying. For example, it has been demonstrated that, comparing two $800,000 schedules, each of which delivered a net reach of adult males of 78 percent, one schedule (entirely composed of fringe spots) delivered 39 percent of the audience a minimum of five times, while a mixed schedule including some prime time delivered a mere 32 percent.[15]

This introduces the notion of "effective rating points" (the number of ratings needed to ensure that the audience is exposed to the campaign more than a defined minimum and less than a defined maximum number of times). This elegant concept was developed by agency practitioner Al Achenbaum.[16] But, to the best of my knowledge, it has not been incorporated as operational policy by any major agency.

Some Hypothesized General Patterns

The eighteen cases in this and the previous chapter represent the total corpus of usable experience that to my knowledge has been published. While there is no reason to believe that they are grossly untypical of the complete consumer goods field and indeed some of the individual cases are based on a strong empirical foundation, they of course do not represent a sample large enough or carefully enough selected for us to draw statistically robust conclusions for the packaged goods field as a whole. However, here as in many other types of research, small samples can often support strong qualitative inferences. I shall now attempt some impressionistic propositions.

In evaluating what I am about to say, the reader is invited to consult the analysis of British advertising practitioner Stephen King, who has described a device that scales the stages of directness or indirectness by which advertising for various products and brands might work in normal circumstances.[17] King's scaling represents a continuum of roles for advertising which he assesses subjectively. Some readers may dispute details of his order, but the general form of the analysis is simple, sensible, and eminently practical.

Most Direct	Direct action
C	
O	Seek information
N	
T	Relate to own needs/wants/desires
I	
N	Recall satisfactions/re-order/short list
U	
U	Modify attitudes
M	
Most Indirect	Reinforce attitudes

My following five hypotheses are based on this scaling.

1. The concave-downward response function is probably most widespread at the direct end of the continuum.

2. The S-shaped function is most likely to operate at the indirect end.
3. At the indirect end, the point of inflection may be higher, the further the brand is engaged in direct competition based on added values, in particular *the higher the amount* of competitive advertising.
4. Advertising seems to work most indirectly for repeat-purchase packaged goods. In these situations:

    The reinforcement hypothesis can be used most often to explain how the advertising works.
    There is a high level of competitive advertising activity.
    Consumer prices are relatively low and the purchase decision is rarely rational and considered.
    There is a tendency toward parity of good functional performance as product improvements quickly become copied by competitive brands.
    There is a large role for advertising in the building of added values.
    Television carries the main burden of the advertising.
5. The implication of what I am saying here is of course that, since the advertising for repeat-purchase packaged goods (including food) represents such a large category, a sizeable proportion of all advertising is going to yield increasing returns, although in most cases this will be for a very short stretch at the lower levels of advertising pressure.

We cannot prove or deny these hypotheses on the basis of our eighteen cases, but they do offer a strong directional confirmation.

The cases include six (perhaps seven) examples of an S-shaped response configuration (cases 2, 3, 4, 5, 16, 18, and possibly brand C in case 17). With a single exception, these brands are all conventional packaged goods.

The eighteen cases also include twelve examples of a concave-downward response (cases 1, 6, 7, 8, 9, 10, 11, 12, 13, 14, 15, and brands A, B, D, and E in case 17). Certain of these are not complete concave-downward response functions, and only describe the region at the top (high pressure) part of the curve. Of these twelve, only Budweiser (case 14) can be considered a classical repeat-purchase television-oriented, packaged goods case. The others are either:

At the direct end of King's continuum (cases 1 and 8),

Have little competition (cases 6 and 13 and brands A, B, D, and E in case 17),

Were cases of a launch rather than an ongoing brand (cases 9 and 11),

Or were examples of the use of press and not television advertising (cases 7, 10, 12, and 15). Press was the medium also in cases 1, 8, and 9.

The Argument in Brief

This chapter's four cases of advertising response functions described the sales offtake calculated from low frequency schedules. Indeed, three of the cases were originally published to throw light on the explicit possibility of low-frequency scheduling as an answer to rapidly increasing media costs.

Two of the four cases demonstrated an S-shaped response curve, while case 17 (which covered five brands) suggested strongly that the degree of competition is the prime determinant of the shape of the response function, low competition probably being associated with the concave-downward configuration.

The chapter introduced King's continuum illustrating the degrees of directness of effect by which advertising campaigns can be planned and evaluated. This continuum indicates generalizable patterns among the response functions in our eighteen cases.

It was hypothesized that direct response advertising and other advertising at the direct end of the continuum operate with a concave-downward response function. But at the indirect end of the continuum, there is more chance of the S-shaped configuration. Most campaigns at the indirect end are for repeat-purchase packaged goods selling in competitive markets. It was also hypothesized that in markets with a high degree of such competition, there will be a higher inflection point on the S-shaped curve. This represents the increased productivity of the more concentrated advertising, the greater concentration working to break through the competitive advertising in such a product field.

Notes

1. Many readers will recognize that this chapter's title is borrowed. See Leo Bogart, B. Stuart Tolley, and Frank Orenstein, "What One Little Ad Can Do," *Journal of Advertising Research* (August 1970): 3–13.

I hope that Dr. Bogart, Dr. Tolley, and Mr. Orenstein will forgive me not only for appropriating the title of their interesting and important article, but also for changing the number of advertisements in the level of pressure under evaluation from one to two.

2. For examinations of the effects of memory decay, see, among others: Hubert A. Zielske, "The Remembering and Forgetting of Advertising," *Journal of Marketing* (January 1959): 239–43; Hubert A. Zielske and Walter A. Henry, "Remembering and Forgetting Television Ads," *Journal of Advertising Research* (April 1980): 7–13; Lois Underhill, "How Much Frequency is Enough?" *Media and Marketing Decisions* (November 1978): 74–134.

3. *Effective Frequency: The Relationship between Frequency and Advertising Effectiveness.*

4. Bogart, Tolley, and Orenstein, "What One Little Ad Can Do."

5. Ibid., 10.

6. Colin McDonald, "What is the Short-Term Effect of Advertising?" in *Effective Frequency: The Relationship between Frequency and Advertising Effectiveness,* chap. 3 and appendix A.

7. Compare for instance the comments of Herbert E. Krugman, "Memory without Recall, Exposure without Perception," *Journal of Advertising Research* (August 1977): 10, with the majestic dismissal by Julian L. Simon and Johan Arndt, "The Shape of the Advertising Response Function," *Journal of Advertising Research* (August 1980): 17.

8. The only point over which McDonald can be taken to task concerns his slight lack of consistency in describing potential advertising exposure. See Jack Z. Sissors, "Confusions about Effective Frequency," *Journal of Advertising Research* (December 1982): 33–37.

9. McDonald, "What is the Short-Term Effect of Advertising?" p. 97.

10. Ibid., p. 97.

11. In a letter to me dated February 14, 1983, McDonald illustrated another aspect of the relationship between sales and the advertising weight necessary to cut through the competitive advertising. He referred to a "reasonable looking rising curve" which relates a brand's market share to its *share* of advertising OTS. The forces at work here are of course essentially the same as those discussed in chapter 4 when the dynamic difference model was described.

12. *Effective Frequency: The Relationship between Frequency and Advertising Effectiveness,* chap. 5.

13. *Ibid.,* appendix B, case study 3.

14. There is frequent mention of such operational guidelines in the trade press.

An unpublished Master of Science thesis by George Sweda, *The Effective Frequency of Advertising* (Syracuse N.Y.: Syracuse University, 1985) describes interviews with senior executives in a number of leading advertising agencies in the United States. They all subscribed to the notion of a minimum level of effective frequency.

One major American advertising agency has published its belief in the general operation of the S-shaped response function. David Berger, *How Much Advertising is Enough* (Chicago: Foote, Cone and Belding Communications, 1979), pp. 14–18.

15. Howard Kamin, "Advertising Reach and Frequency," *Journal of Advertising Research* (February 1978): 21–25.

16. Michael Naples, "The Relationship between Frequency and Advertising Effectiveness" in *Effective Frequency: An Advertising Research Foundation Key Issues Workshop* (New York: Advertising Research Foundation, 1982), pp. 50–51.

17. Stephen King, "Practical Progress for a Theory of Advertisements," *Admap* (October 1975): 338–43. See also John Philip Jones, "Universal Diminishing Returns—True or False?" *International Journal of Advertising* 3, no. 1 (1984): 27–41; also John Philip Jones, "The Various Roles of Advertising and Their Influence on the Advertising Response Function" in *Proceedings of the 1983 Convention of the American Academy of Advertising* (Lawrence, Kans.: University of Kansas, 1983), pp. 143–47.

10
How Does Advertising Work?

"It takes all the running you can do, to keep in the same place. If you want to get somewhere else, you must run at least twice as fast as that!"

A number of different ideas bearing on how advertising works have been floated in earlier parts of this book. It seems appropriate before going any further to bring these together in this chapter and reflect on how they relate to one another. This chapter is a mere beginning of an answer to the large question posed in its title; and I am presenting a synthesis of ideas in the hope that other people will contribute to the debate. Incidentally, when I refer to advertising working, this means working to generate sales; and although the psychological influences of advertising on consumers sometimes lead to, and virtually always accompany, a behavioral effect, I shall only consider that advertising works if it demonstrably achieves the latter.

Four aspects of the subject will be covered in this chapter. I shall examine them by attempting to answer four apparently simple but in reality rather difficult questions.

1. How can we measure the short-term and long-term effects of advertising?
2. Can advertising work on a single-exposure basis?
3. If the answer to question 2 is yes, why then do we need "two little ads?"
4. How can we explain the influence of share of voice (share of total advertising in a market) on the market share of individual brands?

How Can We Measure the Short-Term and Long-Term Effects of Advertising?

Let us first define short and long term. Two different meanings are relevant to the argument. First, there is a simple temporal division into periods of, say, up to a year and over a year. There is no absolute rule establishing a year as the dividing line, but I use it here since it fits satisfactorily into elements of the argument in other parts of this book. Advertising budgets are normally set for the calendar year, which makes the division a useful one.

Second, there is a special and more complex meaning originating from Alfred Marshall's microeconomic analysis of the firm. The consumer demand schedule in a market is a short-term concept; a shift in this schedule is a long-term effect. The supply schedule of the firm or the industry is a short-term concept; a shift in this schedule is a long-term effect. The long term by this definition could be a year, or more, or less; the period of time is not significant. What is important is the time taken to change the position of either of the two schedules, the curves whose juxtaposition demonstrates how price is theoretically determined.[1]

In terms of the present discussion, the most important change in variables concerns the supply schedule. The time needed for the firm to organize itself differently (for instance by an increased use of capital equipment) following a changed level of demand is a long-term change. The long term therefore encompasses changes in the organization of firms. To extend this point, when we compare different firms in the expectation that some will change in response to competitive pressures, then we are assuming long-term changes.

Short-Term Effect of Advertising

The short-term effect of advertising can be demonstrated in at least three different ways.

First, the normal procedure in firms is to evaluate sales measured by ex-factory shipments, alongside retail audit and/or consumer panel estimates. Other variables are also commonly examined, such as tracking data on brand awareness and image attributes for all brands in the market. The evaluation of the effects of advertising is made on judgment. This procedure is what determines decisions to increase, continue as before, reduce, or cancel advertising campaigns in the cases of at least 80 percent of major national advertisers in the United States. The data collection is relatively simple, and the analyses provide a rough-and-ready but often serviceable surrogate for more precise measures. But they lack the ability to isolate the variables in any controlled scientific way.

Second, there is the construction and application of market models, a process requiring experience, judgment, and substantial data inputs. Some marketplace experimentation is also needed to test and refine the models' predictions. With the use of models describing advertising response functions, it is possible to isolate the *immediate* effect on sales of a single advertisement exposure or a small number of exposures, including the incremental effect of progressive exposures within the purchase interval. Often a virtually instantaneous effect, this was demonstrated by the cases in chapters 8 and 9. The measures are operationally valuable because they help us determine the optimum degree of media concentration in the extreme short term (for example, the weight of television flights within the brand's purchase interval).

Third, modelling can also measure the effect on sales of changes in absolute amounts of advertising pressure within a budgetary period, a period not quite as short as the purchase interval, in most cases a year. This can lead to a computation of the short-term advertising elasticity (as discussed in chapter 4), which can only be calculated from econometric analyses requiring a substantial number of market observations. The operational value of the measure is the help it can give us in determining the optimum advertising budget level over the course of the budgetary period.

Enough cases have been published to demonstrate conclusively that advertising can have a short-term effect. (Such an effect is of course not axiomatic, because some campaigns, appropriation levels, and/or media plans do not work because of endemic weaknesses.) However, for examples of effectiveness, the reader will remember the five cases described in chapter 7. With four of those five brands or products, a campaign change had a striking and immediate effect on sales. The one apparent exception was Oxo, where the campaign change (to Katie) took more than a year to bring a noticeable effect on ex-factory shipments. I believe however that the campaign change worked immediately even here, but that its operation was obscured by special factors. The explanation is that the campaign had first to halt a decline in the brand's frequency of use, which had been responsible for a very gradual increase in household and retail inventories. The new campaign took time running these down, so that it did not work its way through into increasing ex-factory sales for many months. I am persuaded that this explanation holds for Oxo (a brand with an unusually large penetration and a high but skewed purchase frequency) because similar changes were accurately isolated when the brand showed a comparable weakening in the mid-1970s.

The reader will note then that the response of sales to advertising discussed in chapter 7 was in all cases both immediate and pronounced. The changes examined were all in the creative content of the campaign. However, examples of sales increases resulting from increased advertising pressure but no campaign change (those described in chapters 4, 8, and 9) also took place without delay, but the sales increases were generally of a much lower order. For instance, the average advertising elasticity of the eighty-four brands summarized in chapter 4 would require a 50-percent increase in a brand's advertising expenditure to bring about a 10-percent boost in sales. As explained in the earlier discussion, the extra profit yielded by such a sales increase would not be enough to fund the extra advertising in most cases.[2]

The reader should also be conscious that such analyses are more than elegant descriptions, or truth for its own sake. They are an important tool of management, part of the everyday working disciplines of a number of sophisticated marketing companies. A dramatic example I recently learned about concerned a major British advertiser, who was wisely dissuaded from reducing his advertising budget by a million pounds sterling, on the grounds of an econometric forecast before the event that the brand in question was highly advertising-elastic within the normal limits of advertising pressure, so that the proposed reduction would bring about a catastrophic drop in sales and profits. "The model suggested that the resultant sales loss would diminish profits by 1.8 millions sterling."[3]

Long-Term Effect of Advertising

The long-term effect of advertising can be demonstrated in at least four different ways.

First, there is the dynamic difference model described in chapter 4. This shows that in 70 percent of a substantial sample of observed cases, there is a linear causal relationship between a series of one-year changes in advertising pressure and a similar series of one-year changes in market share. This analysis enables us to do a number of things. For instance, we can predict the effect on market share of a quantitative change in advertising. We can quantify the advertising-related scale economies of the larger and more successful brands in a market: in the diagram describing the model, those whose regression line cuts the axes to the left of the point of intersection. It also enables us to evaluate the effect of a major campaign change on a year's sales.

Second, there is the technique of the shifting demand curve, which is also explained in chapter 4. Only brands that sell at different prices (in different areas or at different but adjacent time periods) can be analyzed in this way, but the statistical technique is simple to apply. The operational value of the method is that it can enable us to estimate the sales value (and marginal profit) yielded by the extra sales generated by a measured amount of advertising, and thus to quantify its productivity.

Third, there is the measurement of long-term advertising elasticity also referred to in chapter 4.[4] The calculation calls for a large number of market observations. It does however make it possible to estimate the value of repeat purchase of a brand, something that can be derived from a comparison of the long-term with the short-term advertising elasticities.

The fourth method is the pattern of different advertising response functions described at the end of chapter 8, with the more efficient brands occupying a higher position on the diagram describing the analysis. The higher position represents the larger marginal advertising yield of stronger brands, the result of their greater *overall* strength in the marketplace.

As with the techniques for short-term measurement, the long-term measures also have considerable operational value. There is however one point of difference. The short-term effect of advertising, insofar as it can be efficiently isolated, is a function of the advertising alone. The long-term effect, on the other hand, is the result of the advertising working in conjunction with the added values of the brand. Indeed the reason why the advertising has a long-term effect different from (and almost invariably greater than) the short-term effect is repeat purchase, to which the added values make a major contribution. In other words, a given dose of advertising yields smaller or larger volumes of sales, depending on the innate strength of the brands. Larger sales results accrue to brands with more added values, and the acquisition of such added values is a long-term activity.

This concept is different from the notion that advertising might work better on a long-term basis because people, when they see an advertisement for a brand, might be reminded of earlier ones for the same brand. Generally speaking, people, especially users of a brand, know much more about (and are more conscious of) the brand itself than the advertising for it, so that an advertisement should be regarded realistically as a reminder of the brand itself. This is because consumers spend much more time in the company of the brands they use than with the advertising for them. The relation between the brand and its advertising can be explained in philosophical terms by the "Politz Parable," which will shortly be recounted.

The methods described in this section relate to measurement of the advertising variable in isolation. If we wish to quantify the importance of the added values without any attempt to extract the explicit contribution of the advertising, there are two extremely simple techniques that will suffice.

First, we can estimate the amount by which a successful brand's price exceeds the average of its competitors. This often changes over time, an increase accurately describing a strengthening of the brand. I was recently reminded of an important British brand of which I once had first-hand experience, that had increased its price premium over the competition, from 10 percent to 30 percent over the twenty year period 1964–84.[5]

The second and equally simple device is the matched (blind and named) product testing described in chapter 2. This enables the relative contribution of added values over and above the brand's functionality to be isolated and quantified. The measure employed is the marginal number of consumers who discriminate in favor of the brand because of its added values, beyond those who choose it because of its bare functional performance.

Can Advertising Work on a Single-Exposure Basis?

There is decisive evidence that advertising *can* work on a single-exposure basis in many cases.

First, there is the experience of direct response, which if it works at all is effective on a one-exposure basis, because it works as a complete advertising stimulus. This evidence is not in dispute, and it is one of the few effects of advertising we know about with certainty.

Second, single exposures can be effective with other types of advertising, although the data in chapters 8 and 9 (which mainly concern packaged goods) are not extensive enough to enable us to make robust generalizations. There are seventeen cases excluding direct response. Of these, cases 9, 11, 15, and 17 (certainly for four of the brands examined in it) demonstrate that a first advertising exposure triggers a sales response. There is possibly also a first exposure response with a further eight:

Cases 10, 12, 13, and 14, where further progressive exposures yield diminishing returns.

Cases 2, 3, 4, and 5, where further progressive exposures yield increasing returns below the inflection point.

Among the seventeen cases, only two (cases 16 and 18) make it explicitly clear that the first exposure does *not* produce a sales response.

In addition to this evidence that advertising for packaged goods can often work with a single exposure, there are the informed opinions of a number of advertising practitioners. Here are six examples.

David Ogilvy, responding to a question based on my hypothesis that all advertising that works at all works from a single exposure, wrote: "I could give you two exceptions, but on the whole, I agree."[6]

Stephen King, responding to a similar enquiry, wrote: "I sort of agree with you about the short-term effect of advertising, but think that at least some of the arguments about the long-term effect are semantic."[7] He went on to develop this chapter's point, that the long-term effects of advertising stem from the increased value of the brand to the consumer, something almost invariably making the effect of advertising stronger in the long than in the short term.

Gus Priemer, manager of advertising services for S.C. Johnson, an executive with exceptional experience of the effects of media exposure, wrote: "My own evidence strongly suggests that the first ad exposure actually *can* stimulate a large proportion of the total *advertising response,* even when a product is using TV where the viewer is not in control of the communication vehicle."[8]

This conclusion parallels Michael Naples's: "Even one exposure in a four-week period can be powerful for a very large brand."[9]

Rosser Reeves's recommendation of media dispersion is an implicit statement of the same philosophy. An advertiser "might reach thirty million people—by and large, the same people—an average of three times a week. Or might it be wiser to reach ninety million people, say, once a week? The answer, of course, is—buy dispersion. Try to reach more homes, not the same homes. Try to reach more people, not the same people."[10]

My own experience, for what it is worth, confirms that for packaged goods, advertising can and often does work with a single exposure. The reader will remember the successful but unorthodox media buying practices of my pharmaceutical client described at the beginning of chapter 9.

Why Then Do We Need "Two Little Ads?"

This section is an amplification of the discussion in chapter 9 on the number of advertising exposures within a brand's purchase cycle needed to trigger a sales response. It also comments on the widely held belief that this number should be a minimum of two, and more probably three or more.

Let us accept for the sake of argument that more than two strikes are required to achieve the optimum sales effect, or even in some cases any sales effect at all. Evidence is provided by cases 2, 3, 4, and 5 in chapter 8, which all suggest the need for four, five, or more exposures for sales optimization. In chapter 9, cases 16 and 18 demonstrate that two or more exposures are necessary for *any* sales response.

Two lines of reasoning can be used to explain this phenomenon. They are separate and in some ways contradictory to one another.

First, there is the psychological theory stating that advertising needs multiple exposure to the consumer, if it is to work on her psyche. There is more than one expression of this theory, and the supporting evidence is respectable laboratory work on individuals' mental processes.

One of the more recent and persuasive of these expressions, which is associated with the name of Herbert E. Krugman, was intended to amplify the conclusions of a number of marketplace studies (including McDonald's) that there is a minimum level of exposure necessary for advertising to be effective. Krugman's unquestionably plausible theory is that three exposures are needed to do the following tasks, all of which, it is argued, are necessary if the advertising is to influence the consumer effectively:

1. To prompt the respondent to try and understand the nature of the stimulus, and to ask the question: "What is it?"

2. To prompt evaluation ("What of it?") and recognition ("I've seen this before.")

3. To remind (a stage which marks the beginning of disengagement). All the subsequent exposures function, in Krugman's theory, merely as repetitions of this third one.[11]

This work was underpinned by the extensive parallel experiments of Robert C. Grass of Du Pont, which were based on measures of respondents' attention to advertising, amounts learned, and generated attitudes. "Attention increases and maximizes at two exposures, while the amount of learned information increases and maximizes at two or three exposures." Moreover, "generated attitudes are much more resistant to satiation effects than the recall of learned information."[12]

My interpretation of how these theories work is that each advertisement exposure acts in effect as an exposure to the brand, so that the consumer is responding to three brand impressions rather than advertising impressions. This is a real distinction, and it is best explained by recounting a parable attributed to the distinguished market researcher Alfred Politz.

> There were once three rooms, each looking out over the same beautiful landscape. However, it was not possible to see the view as one entered any of the rooms; it was only possible to see the view reflected in a mirror. In the first room, this was a handsome eighteenth-century artifact with an elegant frame. In the second room, it was old and cracked. In the third room, the complete wall seen on entering the room was occupied by a mirror. When a man entered the first room, he saw a beautiful view reflected in a beautiful mirror. When he entered the second room, he saw a beautiful view reflected in a cracked mirror. When he entered the third room, he saw a beautiful view.

For "view," read "brand;" and for "mirror" read "advertising." My experience of brands has encouraged me to regard advertising in the same way as the mirror in Politz's third room. An advertisement enables us to see into a brand, but it need not draw attention to itself. A different but parallel thought is that an advertisement can be regarded as evanescent, but a brand as permanent.

The second line of reasoning is more compatible with the possibility of single-exposure effectiveness. In fact, the argument actually stems from the assumed possibility of advertisements working one exposure at a time. The idea is that the immediate effect of the single strike for one brand is sometimes blocked by the immediate effect of larger numbers of strikes for competing brands. The notion is expressed simply and clearly by McDonald, who uses it to explain the reason for the extreme type of S-shaped response function demonstrated by case 16 in chapter 9, with the first advertising exposure triggering a negative response. This point was discussed during my exposition of case 16, which included McDonald's reason why two exposures are necessary to achieve a positive sales effect—simply to break through the countervailing selling efforts of competitive advertising within the brand field.

This argument is strongly supported by Ad Tel (case 17). There the effectiveness of the first advertising strike proved greater for large brands (which have little competition) than for smaller brands (which have substantial competition). This case shows clearly that advertising for any brand has a greater effect on users than nonusers. Since the large brand has more users than the small brand, it follows logically that advertising for a large brand will, *ceteris paribus*, have more effect than advertising for a small brand.

Naples demonstrates, with a different but equally persuasive line of logic, the reasons why advertising has a greater effect for large brands than for small ones.[13] This argument can be related back to the argument in chapter 4, that there are scale economies with larger brands, which enable such brands to be supported with a share of market advertising a good deal below those brands' shares of market.

The reader will remember from chapter 4 the successful brand R, which in 1979 was supporting a 17-percent share of market with a 13-percent share of the market noise level. This brand should now be compared with the unsuccessful brand G, which was struggling to improve its 3-percent of the market with an 8-percent share of advertising. It is obvious that R's advertising is more productive than G's; the extent of this can be calculated by simple arithmetic:

$$17\%/13\% \text{ divided by } 3\%/8\%$$

the answer being approximately 3.5. In other words, R's advertising is three and a half times as productive as G's. The natural result of this (in Naples's words) is that "a large-share brand will reach [the saturation point] in fewer exposures because of its greater effectiveness per exposure. The result is, the response function changes shape from a straight line to a concave curve as the total possible increase in probability of purchase is compressed into a small range of exposure levels."[14]

Another aspect of the greater efficiency of the advertising of the large brand concerns the penetration supercharge described in chapter 5: the tendency of a large brand to have a higher frequency of purchase and repurchase than a small brand, with the accompanying tendency to greater brand loyalty. Although this can be described empirically (as I attempted in chapter 5), Michael Naples worked out the probability of the penetration supercharge from first principles. He concluded that the advertising is more efficient for a brand with such a scale advantage. "Occasional buyers for a large-share brand buy it a greater percentage of the time than do occasional buyers of a small-share brand. Which means the large-share brand faces less competitive forces against this group of buyers, so that each additional exposure has more relative weight in increasing their probabilities of purchase."[15]

Naples's view on the greater productivity of the advertising for large brands than for small is shared by one of the leading media researchers in

New York interviewed (in confidence) by my former student, George Sweda. This was an aside in an interview concerned with the agency's use of minimum frequency levels in its media buying policy.[16]

Two additional pieces of evidence suggest that the factor determining that the minimum frequency needed for a sales effect is the weight of advertising necessary to break through the competitive advertising in a market.

One relates to experience in different countries. It is interesting that the inflection point in two British cases (13 and 16) was at a low level of two or three opportunities to see. In the American cases in which an inflection point has been calculated (cases 2, 3, 4, 5, and 18), this was invariably at a higher level, in most cases at about five opportunities to see. I suggest it is likely that the higher level of competitive advertising in the United States has dictated that more frequency is required to break through it.

The second point relates to experience of different media, and is based on case 18. In this, the inflection points for radio advertising are significantly higher than those for television. I believe that this can be explained by the need for increased frequency to break through the high advertising clutter on radio, and also to compensate for the lower attention paid to radio than to television advertising.

Let us now reconsider the assumption made at the beginning of this section that more than a single advertising exposure within the purchase cycle is a practical requirement to achieve a sales response. We will also look at the two alternative theories: concerning psychological effects, and competitive advertising levels.

It is not easy to refute the psychological theories, which are well-founded and logically compelling. I hypothesize, however, that when they operate, the most important circumstance is people's unfamiliarity with the brand advertised. The main need for three exposures is therefore, during a brand's launch campaign, to achieve a basic cognitive effect—to increase consumer knowledge of the brand's functional and nonfunctional attributes. (A brand restage works of course like a brand launch. In it, it is necessary to expose the consumer thrice to the *changes* which have been made in the brand's functional properties.) The reader will also remember Krugman's other major theory, discussed in chapter 6, the low-involvement hierarchy. Krugman explains how learning leads to purchase, which in turn leads to development of favorable attitudes to a brand (learn—do—feel). I hypothesized in chapter 6 that the low-involvement hierarchy provides the best explanation of how launch advertising works for low-involvement goods (such as most FMCG). The reader should note the parallel between the two Krugman theories: they both operate, in my judgment, with brand launches, but not necessarily for ongoing brands.

An important element in Krugman's explanation of the psychological reason for the three-exposure effect is that the third exposure becomes a reminder about the brand, and that *all further exposures are in psychological terms mere repeats of this.*

In my opinion, it is logical to expect that if single exposures work for an ongoing brand, they will work as reminders, in Krugman's terms as repetitions of the third exposure, this third exposure having originally been made during the introductory phase of the brand's advertising. It follows from this that, if we can assume it to be unnecessary to add in any significant way to the consumer's knowledge of the brand, it is possible for *individual* advertising exposures during an ongoing campaign to trigger brand purchasing.

Krugman's explanation of the need for continuity of advertising is also important. People are in the market to buy a brand with varying degrees of irregularity. Continuous advertising is needed to catch them at the very moment they are ready to buy: a moment that cannot be predicted.[17]

The argument in this section leads to three hypotheses.

1. Single exposures have a demonstrable effect in the marketplace in many cases, particularly for larger brands. It follows that the psychological explanation that three exposures are required is not *universally* valid.

2. With continuous campaigns for repeat-purchase packaged goods, single exposures can be effective in psychological terms because they are in effect repeats of the result of the third advertising exposure (which itself took place at the time of the launch.)

3. Where a single exposure does *not* appear to work, McDonald and Naples plausibly argue that in effect it is being blocked or cancelled by the parallel stimuli of advertisements for competitive brands. This same explanation also holds for those brands for which the first exposure may work, but additional exposures work more strongly (demonstrating increasing returns below the inflection point). This effect takes place because additional exposures work better, as they become cumulatively heavier in relation to the competition.

How Can We Explain the Influence of Share of Voice on the Market Share of Individual Brands?

This question is elusive, but its answer is pregnant with clues to help us understand the processes of advertising.

Chapter 4 described a causal relationship between changes in advertising pressure and changes in sales, using the dynamic difference model. The changes in advertising pressure were measured as changes in a brand's share of total advertising in a market, in comparison with a normal percentage established by the brand's market share. The reader will remember the great care taken in the model to eliminate the possibility of contamination by the reverse influence of sales on advertising.

The purpose of the present discussion is to speculate on the reasons why (in 70 percent of real world cases) there should be a linear, fairly exact, and absolutely unmistakable relationship between these two variables, with causality from advertising to sales.

This notion of a brand's advertising measured as a share of total advertising in a market is useful as a mathematical, analytical tool. It is however misleading to expect it to help us understand how advertising works in human terms: as a stimulus to consumers to buy a brand. People see too little advertising for individual brands and even product fields to be aware of changes in the levels. Indeed, the reader must share my incredulity that consumers of a product will be in any precise way conscious of the relative amounts of advertising for different brands, and that they will respond to small changes in these proportions.

The way to make sense of the relationship between changes in advertising and changes in sales is to look upon an advertising campaign for a brand as a large number of individual advertisements. The brand with a larger share of the advertising in a market will therefore have more individual advertisements than a brand with a smaller advertising share. The ratio between the different numbers of advertisements will be more or less in line with the ratio of shares of total advertising.

This analysis suggests that people respond to advertising in a simple and direct way. They buy when they are reminded.[18] They respond to individual insertions. The brand with a large share of advertising has a schedule composed of a greater number of individual exposures, or stimuli to purchase, than a small brand. And if changes in relative advertising pressure lead to changes in sales of a brand, this is because there have been changes in the number of individual advertising stimuli for that brand in comparison with its competitors.

The argument in this section jibes therefore with other parts of this chapter. Advertising can and often does work on an individual single-exposure basis. And situations where it does not work may well be caused by a greater number of advertising stimuli for competitive brands.

A cleverer and more experienced advertising man than I recently described the impact of the individual advertisement on the consumer as akin to "hypnotism."[19] It would be a marvelous discipline if practitioners were forced to plan advertising as if it were capable of achieving such an effect. This is incidentally entirely compatible with my point in chapter 7, that all effective advertising works by encouraging the recipient to take a step toward the sender, this being the essential ingredient that enables advertising to achieve an emotional and intellectual engagement with its audience.

Operational Implications

I shall now hypothesize how this chapter's arguments and conclusions impinge on the ways in which we should plan and evaluate advertising.

Appropriation and Media Strategy

I am certain that the various measures of short- and long-term advertising effect described here are the best tools available to determine a brand's appropriation. In fact, without such measures, budgetary policy is likely to remain in the dark ages of myth and folklore. The calculation of the optimum appropriation is the individual activity that probably has the greatest influence on the short-term (and possibly also the long-term) profitability of a brand. I believe that fewer than 20 percent of major advertisers in the United States use the techniques described in this chapter to guide the formulation of their budgets, but the numbers of such advertisers are growing quite rapidly. This matter is concerned with the important subject of marketplace experimentation, which will be discussed in chapters 11 and 12.

The analyses of the short-term effects of advertising, in particular the calculation of response functions and the establishment of specific inflection points, enable us to plan the specific weight of media flights. As argued in chapter 9, it is brands of repeat-purchase packaged goods that tend to have S-shaped response functions; such brands require as much continuity as possible in their schedules because of the year-round nature of consumer demand. In media planning, the weight of the flight and the continuity of the campaign pull an appropriation in opposite directions. It follows that if the former can be minimized (which may mean optimized if the inflection point is low on the curve), then continuity can in turn be maximized.

Creative Planning

Since there is good evidence that advertising often works on a single-exposure basis, every advertisement should be planned to work on its own, with a special emphasis on its impact. In discussing lengths of spots and sizes of press space, the argument invariably concerns the trade-off between impact and frequency. Frequency should certainly not be increased if it carries the slightest danger of damaging impact in any significant way.

There is a strong argument for an advertisement to be as complete a stimulus as possible. Even when advertisements have a role as a simple reminder, they should not neglect any important parts of the brand's battery of functional and nonfunctional benefits. Different consumers need reminding about different brand benefits since the reasons for brand choice vary.

A strong case can be made that advertising should *say* more than much of it does at present. If this means reduced frequency because of longer spots, we should harden our hearts and face it. I believe it to be a grave mistake for an advertisement to tell an incomplete story on the fallacious assumption that an additional part of the selling story will be told by another different (but equally incomplete) advertisement in the campaign. If we persuade ourselves that every advertisement stands or falls as a complete independent stimulus, this (like the imminent prospect of the gallows in Dr. Johnson's well-known aphorism) should be a wonderful means of concentrating the mind.

Long television spots are, incidentally, not at all easy to execute efficiently. Look at old show reels from the days when sixty seconds was the normal spot length for American television advertising. The argument in the commercials all too often appears labored and repetitive. But the skills of using longer spots have been extensively developed in recent years—notably by European advertisers who use the cinema as an advertising medium.

Campaign Evaluation

Everything in this chapter confirms the points made about advertising research in chapter 6, and in particular the skepticism with which I treated the use of all types of recall testing, save in special and limited circumstances.

Consumers' ability to recall advertising has been studied longitudinally. A number of pieces of research have demonstrated that the rate of decay of such recall is rapid indeed: the result of failings in the human memory.[20] There is however a serious technical problem with such research. Unprompted recall can normally be demonstrated to fade rapidly, but awareness or recognition hardly declines at all, which means that the research used to measure changes in recall is imperfect, to say the least.[21]

An even more fundamental objection to the measurement of recall is that, since advertising can and often does work on a single exposure basis, it does not require knowledge of previous advertising to make it effective. It is consequently unnecessary and possibly counterproductive to measure such knowledge and incorporate it into operational policy, particularly media buying policy. Research into people's recall of campaigns has traditionally moved schedules into patterns of concentration at which serious diminishing returns have often operated.[22]

The Argument in Brief

This chapter evaluates and synthesizes arguments in earlier parts of this book. The hypotheses propounded here are the result of my reflection on a thin but consistent and suggestive data base. I have endeavored to answer four questions.

1. *How can we measure the short-term and long-term effects of advertising?*

Three methods of evaluating short-term impact and four methods of evaluating long-term impact have been summarized. The short-term effect of advertising (insofar as it can be accurately measured) essentially involves advertising as an isolated stimulus. On the other hand, the long-term effect reflects the overall strength of the brand, which tends to grow over time. The long-term advertising effect demonstrates how a given dose of advertising can operate with different degrees of effect for different brands because of differences in the strengths of their perceived functionality and added values.

The methods of evaluating the effects of advertising discussed here have great operational value in the determination of budgetary and media strategies.

1. *Can advertising work on a single exposure basis?*
2. *Why then do we need "two little ads?"*
3. *How can we explain the influence of share of voice (share of advertising in a market) on the market share of individual brands?*

In answer to these three questions, this chapter has demonstrated that advertising can work with a single exposure. There are, however, cases in which it is only possible to measure an effect on sales within the purchase cycle after the exposure of a minimum of two, or more commonly three or more advertisements. In explaining this phenomenon, the theory that three insertions are necessary to penetrate the consumer's psyche is the best explanation of how advertising communicates for unfamiliar new brands. With ongoing brands, however, single insertions operate as reminders (the equivalent of the third exposure in the psychological theories), and each can perfectly well work on its own. It is hypothesized that what prevents this from happening in many cases in the real world is the weight of competitive advertising: large numbers of individual advertising stimuli for some brands blank out the effects of single exposures for others.

The notion of campaigns as a collection of large numbers of individual advertising stimuli is, in my judgment, the best way by which we can explain the linear causal relationship between changes in a brand's share of advertising and changes in its market share.

The chapter as a whole provides additional insight into the nature of oligopolistic competition, specifically how given amounts of advertising effort can be nullified by the competition. It has also endeavored to show how a measurable effect in a competitive marketplace requires a manufacturer to outperform the competition, in this case in terms of advertising pressure, or more precisely by exposing larger numbers of individual advertisements.

Notes

1. Alfred Marshall, *Principles of Economics*, pp. 291, 302–15.
2. The analysis in chapter 4 was based on advertising elasticities estimated from a relatively narrow range of observations, so they are not generalizable over all advertising pressures. A parallel evaluation was carried out by Ogilvy & Mather, New York, based on an advertising response function derived from a construct called the Hendry model. In this, the extent of the projection outside the range of observations is undisclosed, but the model forecast that in a collection of actual cases, about a tenth showed that advertising could have been increased with a beneficial effect on profit. There were however more cases in which advertising should have been reduced, because profit would have been greater on the smaller sales volume.
H.R. Kropp, Stanley Canter, and Andrew Kershaw, *Determining How Much to Spend for Advertising—Without Experimental Testing;* and *Marketing Implications of Media Expenditures* (New York: Association of National Advertisers Research and Media Workshops, 1974 and 1971).
3. Stephen King (research and planning director of J. Walter Thompson, London), private letter to me dated May 22, 1984.
4. See also Nariman K. Dhalla, "Assessing the Long Term Value of Advertising," *Harvard Business Review* 56 (January–February 1978): 87–95.
5. King, private letter to me dated January 3, 1985.
6. David Ogilvy, private letter to me dated April 29, 1985.
7. King, private letter to me dated January 3, 1985.
8. Gus Priemer, "Are We Doing the Wrong Things Right?" *Media Decisions* (May 1979): 152.
9. *Effective Frequency: The Relationship between Frequency and Advertising Effectiveness*, p. 77.
10. Rosser Reeves, *Reality in Advertising*, pp. 124–25.
11. Herbert E. Krugman, "Why Three Exposures May Be Enough," *Journal of Advertising Research* (December 1972): 11–14; Herbert E. Krugman, "What Makes Advertising Effective?" *Harvard Business Review* 53 (March–April 1975): 96–103; *Effective Frequency: The Relationship between Frequency and Advertising Effectiveness*, pp. 24–26.
12. *Effective Frequency: The Relationship between Frequency and Advertising Effectiveness*, pp. 20–24.
13. *Ibid.*, pp. 76–78.
14. *Ibid.*, pp. 77–78.
15. *Ibid.*, p. 77.
16. George Sweda, *The Effective Frequency of Advertising*, unpublished Master of Science thesis (Syracuse N.Y.: Syracuse University, 1985), p. 109.
17. *Effective Frequency: The Relationship between Frequency and Advertising Effectiveness*, p. 26.

18. The reader will remember the evidence presented in chapter 4 that, for a majority of brands in a substantial sample of observed cases, the effect of advertising is a function of its quantity alone. Even the creatively weakest advertising can perform a simple reminder function for users of the brand.

19. David Ogilvy said this to me in private conversation in June 1985.

20. Hubert A. Zielske, "The Remembering and Forgetting of Advertising," *Journal of Marketing* (January 1959): 239–43; Hubert A. Zielske and Walter A. Henry, "Remembering and Forgetting Television Ads," *Journal of Advertising Research* (April 1980): 7–13.

21. Herbert E. Krugman, "What Makes Advertising Effective?": 99.

22. See, among others, Lois Underhill, "How Much Frequency is Enough?" *Media and Marketing Decisions* (November 1978): 74–134.

11
Advertising Appropriations and Some General Influences on Them

Before she had drunk half the bottle, she found her head pressing against the ceiling, and had to stoop to save her neck from being broken. She hastily put down the bottle, saying to herself "That's quite enough—I hope I shan't grow any more—as it is, I can't get out at the door—I do wish I hadn't drunk quite so much!"

This chapter concerns advertising budgets, in particular certain exogenous influences on the budgeting process. Budgeting is of extreme importance for most brands, for three special reasons.

First, over and beyond the budget's contribution to building a brand's sales in the short and long term, the budget itself has a special highly geared effect on a brand's profitability. In many circumstances, this relates to the budget's relatively large size in comparison with the brand's earnings. Any reduction in advertising, insofar as sales are unaffected in the short term, leads to an increase in the brand's immediate earnings equivalent to the advertising reduction, and this can sometimes make quite a dramatic difference to the profit ratio. The second factor to remember is that budgeting for the majority of brands is an inefficient procedure, because (as argued in chapter 10) most advertisers do not have the knowledge, skills, or interest to manipulate and evaluate their advertising with the intention of maximizing a brand's profitability at the margin. The third point about budgeting is less obvious. Budgets are influenced, in both directions, by a number of overall general forces and trends in the marketplace. This chapter examines them.

We shall consider certain specific pressures on a brand, and trends in advertising expenditures which result from these pressures. These are examined from a number of points of view: from that of all manufacturers taken as a whole, from the angle of certain product categories, from that of the firm, and from that of the brand.

Let me begin with some words of caution about a too facile interpretation of statistics and a too hasty extrapolation of statistical trends. The forward projection of trends, not only of sales but also of other types of statistical series, is in the majority of cases a ludicrously inefficient procedure, as anyone can see by studying—after the event—government projections of leading economic indicators.[1] A study of old marketing plans for branded goods is an even more instructive exercise; from my own experience, projections (certainly long-term ones) prove reasonably correct in only a tiny minority of cases.

The greatest problem is caused by the forward projection of what seem to be well-established trends by the worst technique possible: drawing a straight line into the future. This type of projection of airline traffic growth was made in the late 1960s, and led to capacity increases which have bedeviled the airline industry ever since.

Such a projection is based on the fundamental misunderstanding that a trend has a life of its own which causes it to continue in the same path. It is quite wrong to look upon trends in this way. In reality, a trend is the result of the interaction of a sometimes large number of variables: pressures, counterpressures, and constants. A change in one or a number of these can change a trend radically. In my example of the airline industry, the variables that had changed by the late 1970s included the passenger capacity of the industry (with the increasing need to sell even more seats to break even), the extent of the competition (particularly from new carriers with smaller overheads), the general economic climate (in particular increased cost pressures and reduced income growth), and finally and rather decisively, the cost of fuel. No projection of the future could have made any real sense if it had not attempted to disentangle these various factors contributing to the trend, and allocate some specific weight to each.

It is these difficulties that have led me, first, to devote attention to the underlying forces—some obvious but others much less so—that have together caused the statistical trends; and, second, to attempt to isolate the components whose interaction has brought these trends about.

Long-Term Trends in Advertising Expenditure

Note that for the first time, I am adopting a "macro" approach. When aggregated data have been presented in earlier parts of this book, they have been used to disclose general patterns as these might be typified by an average brand. We are now going to take a broader perspective, concentrating on overall trends in an attempt to uncover general forces that have influenced and are influencing different fields of advertising in different ways.

In any one year, the task of an advertising budget is finite: to contribute to selling a specific number of goods. (If in the year in question the advertising has boosted the brand's penetration, the advertising will almost certainly also have a long-term repeat-purchase effect.) However, if we compare one year with another, the absolute budget level necessary to achieve a stated sales effect could differ considerably. The simplest cause of such a variation is of course the inflation of media rates, with more or less continuous increases in the cost of the same media unit, reflecting both the general inflation in the economy and the variations in demand for different media. But the pressure of price inflation, which was of great importance during the 1970s, affects all aspects of a brand's advertising budget; it is a force at work, more pervasive than simply the cause of a diminution in the number of television spots that can be bought for a given dollar appropriation.

The commonest way of eliminating the influence of inflation on advertising trends is to compare ratios for individual years calculated from pairs of figures that have themselves been subjected to the same inflationary influences, thus cancelling the effect of inflation. The commonest example of this technique is to express advertising as a ratio of the Gross National Product (GNP). (Other indices of activity in the economy, for instance disposable personal income, could also be used, but the resulting statistics would not change the substance of the trends discussed in this chapter, which are derived from the GNP.) The necessary data are available from official sources, those on advertising having originated in the work of Robert Coen of McCann-Erickson.

Although there is a problem in comparing United States figures with those for other countries (because the coverage of American media is more broadly based than that in other markets), the American figures have been calculated in a consistent fashion from year to year, and are therefore comparable with one another.[2]

In figure 11–1, advertising has been plotted as a share of the Gross National Product for the sixty-six years, 1919–84. There are a number of remarkable features about this diagram.

1. The highest levels of advertising investments (generally above 3 percent of GNP) were recorded in the 1920s. In following decades, advertising expenditures have consistently been much lower. The ratio has never once exceeded 2.5 percent of the GNP since the early 1930s.

2. There is some suggestion of a cyclical pattern, but because of my reluctance to extrapolate trends in a simplistic way, I put no credence in the likelihood that it will repeat. Among the more obvious long-term shifts in the ratio are the lengthy and precipitous decline during the depression of the 1930s and the second World War, the climb during the postwar boom, the decline during the difficult business conditions of the 1970s, and the upsurge during the recovery of the 1980s.

3. The relationship between upward and downward GNP movements and similar movements in advertising can be explained by the crude principles that govern most advertising budgeting. Good sales send advertising appropriations up, and weak sales send them down. The aggregation of such policies leads to the normal directional relationship between GNP movements and advertising movements shown in figure 11–1.

4. The situation in the 1970s deserves special comment. Not only were

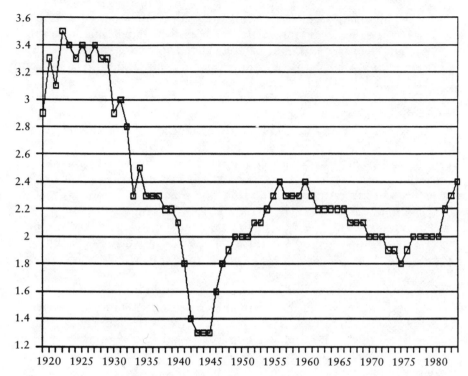

Figure 11–1. Advertising as a Percentage of Gross National Product, 1919–84.

Source: Statistical Abstracts of the United States (Washington, D.C.: U.S. Bureau of the Census).

business conditions generally difficult, but inflation caused manufacturers' incomes to lag behind their costs, a situation that put pressure on manufacturers' profitability. They naturally responded to this pressure on many occasions by making tactical reductions in their advertising budgets, thus exacerbating the downward pressure on advertising caused by slow trade.

5. The data illustrate two phenomena leaving unanswered questions:

a. Why was the post-1945 boom, which was generally much stronger than the boom of the 1920s, characterized by uniformly much lower relative advertising levels?

b. Although the post-1945 boom operated more or less continuously from the mid-1940s through the early 1970s, why did advertising start declining during the early 1960s?

I suspect that there may be the same answer or group of answers to both questions.

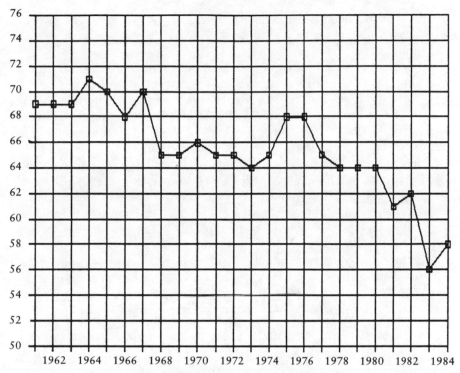

Figure 11–2. Packaged Goods Advertising as a Percentage of Total Advertising of 100 Leading Advertisers, 1961–84.

Source: Based on data published in *Advertising Age* and reprinted by permission.

The overall slope of the figures over the sixty-six-year span is negative. It is possible to draw a more or less straight line between the late 1920s, the mid-1950s and the mid-1970s. This unsophisticated device (which I am *not* recommending projecting) raises the suspicion that there may have been forces in the past both to dampen the long-term effect on advertising of increases in economic activity, and to exaggerate the effect on advertising of reductions in it. Moreover, I suspect that this slow and lengthy depression in expenditures has applied to some fields more than to others, and that the negative force has applied with particular strength to the repeat-purchase packaged consumer goods which are the concerns of this book.

There are no reliable and up-to-date figures for overall appropriation trends for FMCG, applying to brands of all sizes.[3] However, *Advertising Age*'s annual reports on the hundred leading advertisers cover a little over 25 percent of all advertising in the United States.[4] The reports are particularly valuable to this book because the data include advertising for the probable majority of the most important brands of packaged goods in national distribution.

My first analysis of the published data examines the share of total advertising expenditure for the hundred leaders that is accounted for by specific packaged goods advertisers. The calculations were rather laborious, but the picture which emerges in figure 11–2 is clear.[5] This diagram demonstrates that, over the run of the twenty-four years 1961–84, packaged goods advertising accounted for a slowly diminishing proportion of all advertising by the hundred leaders. Year by year the changes are small, but they account for a decline of more than ten percentage points, from approximately 70 percent during the early 1960s, to under 60 percent in the 1980s. These percentage movements, when applied to the actual amounts of money invested, account for changes in the absolute levels of advertising totalling hundreds of millions of dollars.

The next step in examining the trends was to concentrate on individual identified advertisers. My starting point here was to examine the single largest advertiser in the five most important packaged goods fields: soaps and cleaners, tobacco products, packaged canned and frozen foods, proprietary drugs, and soft drinks. In order again to exclude the effect of inflation, I concentrated on figures (which are comparable from year to year) for each manufacturer's advertising expenditure expressed as a percentage of sales. These data are found in table 11–1. Although there are large differences among their advertising-sales ratios, there is a remarkable similarity in the *trends* for all of them.

1. In every case, the expenditure ratio peaked in the mid-1960s (the earliest being 1964; the latest, 1967).

2. In every case, the ratio then began to fall, reaching its low point around the late 1970s (the earliest being 1974; the latest, 1982).

3. In every case, the ratio then began to recover, but for four of the five advertisers, the recovered level for 1984 is still well below the peak in the mid-1960s.

My next step was to isolate the twenty largest packaged goods advertisers from the 1984 list. Their 1961–84 advertising investments are summarized in table 11–2. The same patterns emerge consistently for all twenty advertisers: substantially the same trends as in table 11–1. These movements are also clearly evident in table 11–3, which was constructed from an extremely robust (although prematurely terminated) series of official figures from U.S. government sources. In this table, which covers approximately the same product fields as table 11–1, there is clear evidence of a decline in aggregate investments as a proportion of aggregate sales.

Table 11–1
Advertising as a Percentage of Sales for the Largest Advertisers in Five Major Packaged Goods Product Fields, 1961–84

	Procter & Gamble	*R.J. Reynolds*	*General Foods*	*Warner–Lambert*	*Pepsico*
1961	8.2%	3.3%	8.8%	21.4%	9.8%
1962	8.4	3.4	9.2	21.4	11.4
1963	10.4	3.5	8.4	25.0	15.7
1964	10.9	5.2	8.4	26.2	16.3
1965	10.9	4.1	8.7	16.8	7.7
1966	10.8	4.2	10.0	25.8	7.7
1967	11.1	4.2	9.8	18.3	6.3
1968	10.0	4.1	9.4	11.6	5.1
1969	9.2	3.8	8.5	17.0	4.8
1970	8.3	3.4	8.6	15.6	4.7
1971	7.8	2.5	7.8	15.1	4.2
1972	7.0	2.6	8.6	14.6	not available
1973	6.3	2.6	8.1	14.6	4.4
1974	7.3	2.3	6.9	14.3	3.3
1975	7.9	2.3	6.8	13.9	3.9
1976	8.4	2.4	7.6	15.3	3.5
1977	5.7	2.6	5.6	7.9	3.5
1978	5.9	2.8	6.2	7.3	3.6
1979	5.7	2.9	6.5	6.8	4.2
1980	5.7	2.9	6.2	6.8	3.9
1981	5.6	2.7	5.5	8.0	3.7
1982	5.8	4.1	5.2	9.1	4.1
1983	8.3	6.2	6.2	19.0	5.9
1984	8.5	6.6	6.5	23.0	6.4

Source: Based on data published in *Advertising Age* and reprinted by permission.

Note: Beatrice Foods is not included in this analysis because insufficient data are available for this advertiser, which became the third largest in the United States as a result of mergers during 1983.

The patterns are unmistakable, although the differences in the ratios between the maxima and minima appear not to be large, which creates a misleading impression, because when small percentage differences are applied to large totals, the absolute differences that emerge can represent dollar amounts of a startling size, as seen in table 11–4. In constructing this table, I started with the data from the twenty largest packaged goods advertisers analyzed in table 11–2. I then excluded the three advertisers (Bristol–Myers, Col-

Table 11–2
Advertising Decline and Recovery, 1961–84: Advertising-Sales Ratios of the Twenty Largest Packaged Goods Advertisers

Advertiser	Peak in Early Period (Percentage and Year)	Trough in Later Period (Percentage and Year)	1984 Ratio (Percentage)	Change, Peak to Trough (Percentage Points)	Change, Peak to 1984 (Percentage Points)
Bristol–Myers	39.9% (1963)	5.7% (1981)	8.2%	−34.2	−31.7
Colgate–Palmolive	23.7 (1965)	4.9 (1981)	11.0	−18.8	−12.7
Unilever	21.2 (1961)	6.7 (1981)	11.0	−14.5	−10.2
PepsiCo	16.3 (1964)	3.3 (1974)	6.4	−13.0	− 9.9
Am. Home Products	17.2 (1961)	4.8 (1980)	12.0	−12.4	− 5.2
Coca-Cola	12.3 (1965)	3.1 (1980)	7.5	− 9.2	− 4.8
General Mills	9.3 (1965)	3.1 (1974)	5.6	− 6.2	− 3.7
General Foods	10.0 (1966)	5.2 (1982)	6.5	− 4.8	− 3.5
Revlon	15.2 (1961)	4.5 (1981)	11.9	−10.7	− 3.3
Warner–Lambert	26.2 (1964)	6.8 (1980)	23.0	−19.4	− 3.2
Procter & Gamble	11.1 (1967)	5.6 (1981)	8.5	− 5.5	− 2.6
Anheuser–Busch	7.1 (1963)	1.8 (1974)	5.6	− 5.3	− 1.5
Philip Morris	6.8 (1965)	2.7 (1973)	5.7	− 4.1	− 1.1
Kellogg's	12.6 (1965)	4.4 (1980)	11.7	− 8.2	− 0.9
Pillsbury	7.9 (1964)	3.8 (1980)	7.3	− 4.1	− 0.6

Dart & Kraft	3.2 (1961)	1.4 (1980)	3.8	− 1.8	+ 0.6
Johnson & Johnson	7.3 (1966)	4.4 (1975)	8.0	− 2.9	+ 0.7
R.J. Reynolds	5.2 (1964)	2.3 (1974)	6.6	− 2.9	+ 1.4
H.J. Heinz	5.1 (1967)	1.8 (1975)	8.5	− 3.3	+ 3.4
Ralston Purina	2.8 (1961)	1.6 (1973)	8.6	− 1.2	+ 5.8

Source: Based on data published in *Advertising Age* and reprinted by permission.

Note: For inclusion in the above list, each advertiser had to be included among the hundred leaders during most of the years in question. Because of recent amalgamations, Beatrice and Nabisco Brands have been excluded.

Table 11–3
Ratio of Active Corporation Advertising Expenditures to Receipts, by Industry, 1961–75

	Food & Beverages	Tobacco	Chemicals	Retail Trade
1961	2.4%	5.2%	3.7%	1.5%
1962	2.5	5.3	4.0	1.5
1963	2.5	5.6	4.1	1.5
1964	2.6	6.1	4.4	1.6
1965	2.6	5.8	4.3	1.5
1966	2.4	6.1	4.2	1.6
1967	2.5	6.0	4.2	1.5
1968	2.4	5.9	4.0	1.5
1969	2.4	5.4	4.0	1.5
1970	2.3	5.3	4.0	1.5
1971	2.3	4.3	3.7	1.5
1972	2.2	4.2	3.5	1.5
1973	1.9	3.7	3.3	1.5
1974	1.8	3.7	2.9	1.5
1975	not available	not available	not available	1.5

Source: Statistical Abstracts of the United States (Washington, DC: U.S. Bureau of the Census). Data are based on federal tax returns.

gate—Palmolive, and Unilever) who made the most extreme drops from their maximum and minimum advertising-sales ratios, for fear that some of these extremely pronounced differences might have been the result of unexplained statistical eccentricities.

The seventeen more "normal" advertisers are analyzed in table 11–4. This table examines the expenditure implications of a hypothetical situation in which each advertiser's 1984 expenditure ratio was the same as at its peak during the 1960s. As can be seen, this assumption would have meant that most of these seventeen advertisers would have spent tens if not hundreds of millions of additional advertising dollars in 1984; this despite the fact that in every case the absolute expenditure in 1984 was a record high in absolute terms. The difference between the 1984 actual expenditures and what these seventeen advertisers would have spent at their peak advertising to sales ratios, would have aggregated to a net total of more than $1.5 billion.

So far this analysis has demonstrated that:

—In the very long term (the period since the first World War), advertising has shown an overall declining trend relative to the GNP, despite short-term upward movements;

Table 11–4
What Selected Large Packaged Goods Advertisers Would Have Spent in 1984 If They Had Maintained Their Peak Advertising-Sales Ratio

Advertiser	Change in Ratio, Peak to 1984 (Percentage Points)	1984 Ratio (Percentages)	1984 Actual Expenditure ($ millions)	Change in 1984 Expenditure if Spending Had Been at Peak Ratio ($ millions)
PepsiCo	−9.9	6.4	428	+$664
Am. Home Products	−5.2	12.0	412	+ 178
Coca-Cola	−4.8	7.5	343	+ 219
General Mills	−3.7	5.6	283	+ 188
General Foods	−3.5	6.5	450	+ 241
Revlon	−3.3	11.9	205	+ 57
Warner–Lambert	−3.2	23.0	440	+ 61
Procter & Gamble	−2.6	8.5	872	+ 266
Anheuser–Busch	−1.5	5.6	364	+ 98
Philip Morris	−1.1	5.7	570	+ 110
Kellogg's	−0.9	11.7	209	+ 16
Pillsbury	−0.6	7.3	318	+ 26
Dart & Kraft	+0.6	3.8	269	− 43
Johnson & Johnson	+0.7	8.0	300	− 26
R.J. Reynolds	+1.4	6.6	678	− 143
H.J. Heinz	+3.4	8.5	227	− 91
Ralston–Purina	+5.8	8.6	429	− 289

Source: Based on data published in *Advertising Age* and reprinted by permission.

—Since the early to mid-1960s, packaged goods advertising specifically has accounted for a gradually declining share;

—The poor trading conditions and inflation of the 1970s contributed to this decline but were not its exclusive cause, because

—The decline began some years before 1970 in every specific instance;

—When business conditions improved in the 1980s, the recovery brought expenditure ratios to well below the peak of the 1960s in perhaps three–quarters of the cases.

In summary, for a long period of time there may have been a subtle, almost undetectable, but nevertheless continuous and perhaps irreversible declining trend, which operates with particular force on packaged goods advertisers. This trend is connected perhaps with cost pressures or management policies. If such influences can be isolated, we can begin to forecast whether they are likely to continue. Such forecasts are likely to have operational implications for advertisers and agencies represented in the various markets for repeat-purchase packaged consumer goods. The last part of this chapter and much of chapter 12 concern such operational implications.

A Discussion of Underlying Causes

Executives directly concerned with setting and implementing advertising budgets for consumer brands in competitive markets are accustomed to planning regular annual increases in the nominal or money value of these budgets. A combination of pressure from oligopolistic competition and normal media inflation provides a firm and continuous although not always powerful upward pressure. More extreme inflation has the opposite effect, for reasons connected with a squeezing of profit, but this phenomenon of the 1970s represents an extremely exceptional circumstance.

This natural upward pressure is in almost all circumstances supported by advertising agencies, mainly because they tend to be philosophically optimistic and instinctively favor growth strategies, but also partly because of considerations of self-interest in the cases of those agencies still compensated on the commission system. Dubious research data based on recall testing also commonly flash alarm signals that the brand urgently requires increased frequency—and therefore extra advertising expenditure.

Evidence in this chapter suggests strongly that in the medium and possibly also the long term, upward pressures that lead to increases in the nominal or money value of budgets appear much less effective when the trends are measured in real terms (that is, after accounting for inflation, and in particular when the appropriations are expressed as a share of the advertiser's sales value). It is obvious that some countervailing forces are at work—I believe that there are at least two, although they are probably not of equal importance. The first applies to all advertisers, especially packaged goods manufacturers who sell to the grocery trade, most particularly the weaker manufacturers. The second force has been especially important in its influence on larger advertisers in all fields.

Cause 1. *The Growing Power of Retailers*

The first factor, which is the easier to demonstrate and possibly the more important in its operation to date, is a very gradual change in the marketing world's balance of power between manufacturers and retailers. This trend is a result of the growing concentration and strength of the retail trade, which evolved in Europe before the United States, which is why it appears more in the European than in the American professional literature.[6] In various European countries, powerful nationwide chains of stores are a common phenomenon. There has also been a considerable strengthening of the retail trade in the United States, but on a regional rather than national basis. An important empirical study by Schultz and Dewar provides convincing evidence based on official statistics, concerning growth of retail concentration in all categories of trade, not just food stores. In the authors' opinion, "[W]e're only just beginning to see its true impact."[7]

Studies by McKinsey of the American market demonstrate that the inflation and price controls of 1972–74 clearly resulted in a relative strengthening of retailers in comparison with manufacturers.[8] This resulted from manufacturers being allowed to increase their list prices; they lifted them to high levels, but discounted to a greater degree than ever before. This amount of discounting of manufacturers' brands has now become normal, and has resulted in a relative shift in revenue and profits from manufacturers to retailers.

The pressure of retail buying power had led to a general increase in retail discounts, both for manufacturers' labels and also for store brands and generics (which manufacturers have been increasingly forced to produce for the retail chains, because of the latter's strength). I am certain that such increases have in the main been funded by reductions in manufacturers' expenditures on all aspects of branding, including both research and development, and consumer advertising. This reduction has been met by some increases in retailers' expenditures on their own advertising, which have been partially funded by their improved discounts. This means that manufacturers have become relatively less important and retailers relatively more important as advertisers.

Table 11–3, taken from government statistics based on tax returns, confirms that the share of sales applied to advertising in the period up to 1975 was falling for food and beverages, tobacco, and chemical manufacturers, but was constant for the retail trade. Table 11–5 applies retail advertising figures to the total volume of advertising expenditure. Here we see the retail share of total advertising rising progressively from 20.2 percent in 1961 to 25.9 percent in 1975. These figures, based on an enormous sample of advertisers, demonstrate quite decisively what has been going on.

Although they are based on a smaller sample, *Advertising Age* figures of advertising expenditures by the hundred leading advertisers point in a similar direction. There are very few retailers among this group of the largest advertisers in the country, but their share of the total volume of expenditure has risen progressively. As can be seen in table 11–6, there was only one retailer (Sears, Roebuck and Co., number 12 on the list) among the hundred leading

Table 11–5
Summary of Retail Advertising Trends, 1961–75

	Total Corporation Advertising Expenditures ($ millions)	Total Retail Advertising Expenditures ($ millions)	Retail Advertising as a Percentage Share of Total Advertising Expenditures (%)
1961	$ 9,563	$1,929	20.2%
1962	10,391	2,221	21.4
1963	11,032	2,370	21.5
1964	12,058	2,668	22.1
1965	13,310	2,829	21.6
1966	14,534	3,149	21.7
1967	15,018	3,240	21.6
1968	16,235	3,619	22.3
1969	17,690	4,050	22.9
1970	18,089	4,155	23.0
1971	18,981	4,565	24.1
1972	21,351	5,399	25.3
1973	23,021	5,878	25.5
1974	24,640	6,396	26.0
1975	26,606	6,898	25.9

Source: Statistical Abstracts of the United States (Washington, DC: U.S. Bureau of the Census). Data came from federal tax returns.
Note: After 1975, the method of analyzing data was changed. Later figures cannot be provided on a comparable basis.

Table 11–6
Retail Advertisers among *Advertising Age's* Hundred Leaders, 1961, 1984

	Expenditure ($ millions)	1961 Rank	Advertising-to-Sales Ratio (%)	Expenditure ($ millions)	1984 Rank	Advertising-to-Sales Ratio (%)
Sears, Roebuck	$47	12	1.1%	$747	3	2.1%
K Mart	not recorded among 100 leaders			554	9	2.7
J.C. Penney	not recorded among 100 leaders			460	11	3.5
Levi Strauss	not recorded among 100 leaders			122	67	6.4
Cotter	not recorded among 100 leaders			64	98	3.9

Source: Based on data published in *Advertising Age* and reprinted by permission.

advertisers in 1961. In 1984, there were five retailers, all with healthy advertising-to-sales ratios, with the largest, again Sears, placing third.

This chapter has exclusively concerned advertising directed at the consumer. The relative declines in the advertising expenditures of packaged goods manufacturers have not been accompanied by reductions in their sales promotions, which are activities directed more toward the retail trade. Expenditures on promotions have probably been maintained in real terms and possibly increased in recent years, although estimation in this field is a notoriously difficult procedure.[9] Much sales promotional expenditure represents subsidies paid directly by manufacturers to retailers, and it is therefore another manifestation of the trend toward a transfer of the income and profits generated by manufacturers' brands from the manufacturers to the retail trade.

Since all this movement of resources between parties in the retail chain is a matter of relative bargaining power, it follows that larger manufacturers have been able to withstand it slightly more effectively than small manufacturers. This opens an interesting direction of enquiry (which must be pursued on another occasion) into any connection which might exist between the increasing strength of retailers and increasing concentration in manufacture. The second cause of the overall reduction in packaged goods manufacturers' advertising expenditures relates to such a concentration.

Cause 2.   Economies of Scale in Manufacturers'
Advertising

It is axiomatic that large manufacturers become large because they manage to achieve, as they grow, scale economies in all aspects of their businesses: factory production, purchasing, marketing. It would be surprising if there were no scale economies associated with advertising. I am not referring here simply to the media discounts available to large advertisers, nor to the massive bargaining power of these advertisers in media negotiations, although these both contribute to large manufacturers' ability to expose their campaigns at sometimes huge reductions in cost below card rates. (Indeed, the data in tables 11–1, 11–2, and 11–4, which are based on card rates, almost certainly consistently exaggerate the advertisers' actual expenditures.)

The most important advertising-related scale economy of large brands is the ability of such brands to be supported year after year by advertising investments below the norm suggested by those brands' shares of market. In other words, the financial benefit of such a scale economy is manufacturers' ability to reduce advertising without losing market share, the process described so tellingly by Ackoff and Emshoff in their descriptions of the budget reduction programs for Budweiser beer.[10] Readers who think that the Budweiser experience is an exception in the world of packaged consumer goods should refer again to the evidence in chapter 4 that in many markets, large brands can be supported by relatively low advertising budgets. (Although in absolute terms these are the largest budgets in the market, they tend to be the largest by a smaller margin than their market shares would suggest.)

This matter is connected with the fairly well-established fact of consumer purchasing behavior discussed in chapter 5: brands with high levels of consumer penetration and market share benefit from an above-average purchase frequency, or penetration supercharge. This factor of scale imposes a ceiling on the advertising investments put behind many large brands. It is, of course, a highly selective matter, applying only to a few brands, but these are the more important ones, so that the influence of this downward pressure on budgets is greater than it might at first glance appear.

Another point about these large brands also sets top limits to the advertising investments behind them. Manufacturers of large brands and their advertising agencies are the ones who carry out the most extensive econometric investigations of advertising response functions, with the discovery that, as a general rule, there is an early onset of diminishing returns to increments in advertising pressure within the brand purchase cycle.

Empirical studies, such as those discussed in chapters 8 and 9, have made it plain that this is a realistic description of the eventual path of sales response in all normal circumstances. Probably for the majority of brands of packaged goods in normally competitive markets, diminishing returns will be at or near the level of three opportunities to see in the purchase interval. In crude terms, this suggests an optimally effective use of television at a level of 200 gross rating points; this indicates that if the purchase interval is monthly, such a national schedule could be obtained for a rather modest television budget of under $10 million.

At least two pieces of evidence covering collections of brands demonstrate that substantial numbers of them have advertising budgets *above* the optimum.[11] Such discoveries can be expected of course to lead manufacturers to reduce their expenditures.

Implications for the Future

The prolonged advertising expansion following the second World War led to a vast growth in the absolute size of the advertising business, although (as we have seen) the relative size of the industry was smaller than it had been in the 1920s. Nevertheless, the twenty years following 1945 were unparalleled in their optimism; but this sunlit advertising boom was clearly losing impetus long before most people realized. Since the cause of the decline that began in the mid-1960s was not during those early years the result of a flagging economy, other influences must have begun to operate. I have little doubt that it is about this time that there came into operation (without observers noticing them) those other factors analyzed here: the growing strength of retailers and the discovery by a minority of important advertisers that they could reap the scale economies of their large brands by reducing advertising expenditures on them, which was allied to the discovery from econometric analysis that high pressure soon results in diminishing returns.

It is possible that certain other factors played a role. Distinguished advertising practitioners with whom I have discussed the content of this argument have mentioned a slowing of new brand activity and a subtle change in the nature of oligopolistic competition, with many markets moving in a promotion-oriented direction in which brands would lose their added values. But in my judgment, these factors have not been as important as those I have isolated here.

With the onset of the troubled 1970s, the interruption in the growth of the Gross National Product added its own weight to depress advertising expenditure. The strong economic revival in the present decade is causing a reversal again, although advertising as a percentage of GNP took until 1983 to reach the 1961 level and has not progressed much beyond it.

The downward pressure on advertising has applied especially to the important category of packaged goods, although it may have had a somewhat wider application (for instance, to the automotive category). But it has clearly not applied universally, not having affected retail advertising (for the reasons discussed), direct response, or classified advertising. Nevertheless, the packaged goods category is individually the largest single one, accounting for more than a third of the grand total of advertising expenditure of all types; this proportion is on its own sufficiently large for a decline in it to have exercised a demonstrable influence on total advertising expenditure.[12]

I believe strongly that the various causes of the downward pressure are unlikely to weaken in the future, and they might well grow stronger. This means that the advertising industry, media and agencies in particular, should brace themselves for a future more austere than the past.

As far as the media are concerned, there continues to be a shift in advertisers' expenditure from other media to television, whose share of advertising expenditures (in "measured media") as illustrated in table 11–7, has gone up from 27.8 percent in 1970 to 34.5 percent in 1984. Radio has held its own, but newspapers and magazines have suffered a severe loss of market share. It is impossible at the moment to forecast the effect of cable television on television's total share of advertising dollars, but it is unlikely to be beneficial. The downward pressure on advertising budgets discussed in this chapter does not offer much optimism about future prosperity to any of the media, least of all the print media.

Nor does the future offer attractive prospects to advertising agencies, except for large agencies whose billings are dominated by television expen-

Table 11–7
Distribution of Advertising Expenditure by Media, 1970–84 ("Measured Media" Only)
(percentages)

	Newspapers	Magazines	Television	Radio	Outdoor
1970	44.1%	16.2%	27.8%	10.1%	1.8%
1971	45.6	15.8	26.0	10.6	1.9
1972	45.9	14.9	26.8	10.5	1.8
1973	46.1	14.4	27.1	10.5	1.9
1974	45.8	14.2	27.8	10.5	1.8
1975	45.7	13.3	28.5	10.7	1.8
1976	44.5	13.1	30.2	10.5	1.7
1977	44.1	13.7	30.1	10.4	1.7
1978	43.5	14.0	30.8	10.1	1.6
1979	43.8	14.0	30.7	9.9	1.6
1980	43.0	13.7	31.4	10.3	1.6
1981	41.8	14.0	32.0	10.7	1.6
1982	41.0	13.3	33.2	10.8	1.7
1983	41.4	12.8	33.7	10.5	1.6
1984	41.2	12.8	34.5	10.0	1.5

Source: *International Journal of Advertising* (3, 1, 1984) *Advertising Age* (May 6, 1985). Reprinted by permission.

ditures, agencies that have of course grown as television has gained in market share at the expense of other media. But again, the influence of cable systems on the monolithic mass audiences of the networks will have a direct bearing on the future of these agencies, especially if they continue to be remunerated by commission. The movements discussed in this chapter will provide a strong impetus to the change already under way for agencies to be remunerated by fees, a subject to be discussed in chapter 12.

Despite the (perhaps temporary) special position of television, both the media and the agencies will suffer to some extent from the downward pressure discussed in this chapter, which will to an extent inhibit advertising from sharing in the growth of the economy, even with growth as strong as that of the 1980s. And any decline in the real value of advertising resulting from a slowing of growth or a return of recession will be made worse.

There remain two other interested parties: advertisers and consumers. For these, the effect of the downward pressure on advertising is by no means devoid of benefits.

First, the advertisers. The reader will have noted that the pressure of retail competition has operated against all manufacturers (although it is rather more effective against the weaker ones). As a consequence, it has caused a decline in the real value of all manufacturers' advertising budgets to a greater or lesser degree. But the unexpected result is that brand shares in most markets have not been influenced in any significant or consistent way. What manufacturers have discovered is that they are able to support their brands at a lower advertising cost than before, a serendipitous effect and one of the pieces of evidence suggesting that the determinant of the effect of advertising volumes on market shares is not the absolute amount spent by each advertiser, but rather each advertiser's share of the total amount spent by all advertisers. The likelihood that manufacturers can apparently support their brands effectively at reduced advertising expenditures if their competitors do the same is something of material interest to all manufacturers,[13] and should provide an impetus to further serious econometric studies of advertising's contribution to sales.

Finally, what do the trends discussed in this chapter mean to the consumer? Taking a broad view, a reduction in advertising, if this results in no reduction in its effectiveness, must denote an increase in economic efficiency, which must be in the general interest. And if the savings are not added to manufacturers' profits (as they were when advertising budgets were reduced as a result of the removal of cigarettes from the television screen in 1971), then the benefit must be passed on to somebody else. This chapter has pointed to these savings being substantially passed from manufacturers to retailers in the form of extra discounts. And if, as most certainly has happened, a proportion of these profits has in turn been passed to the public in the form of lower prices (a result of competition between retailers), this has clearly benefited us all as consumers. It is a movement directly in the public interest, and an excellent and topical example of the operation of the "invisible hand."

The Argument in Brief

This chapter has analyzed long- and medium-term trends in total advertising expenditure, and has concluded that since the 1920s, there has been a subtle, almost undetectable, but nevertheless real downward pressure on advertising appropriations. This has applied particularly to FMCG.

There is clear evidence that with a majority of larger brands in such fields, advertising expressed as a percentage of sales value progressively declined between the mid-1960s and late 1970s, with only a partial recovery in the 1980s. For such brands, there are substantial differences between the sums actually spent in 1984, and what would have been spent if the peak advertising-sales ratios of the 1960s had still applied. These differences might be described as "lost" expenditures; for a sample of seventeen of the largest packaged goods advertisers, such sums total more than $1.5 billion.

Whenever advertising budgets are established, there are forces which press them upward. The three strongest are psychological attitudes engendered by oligopolistic competition between manufacturers; normal inflation; and the influence of advertising agencies, especially those still remunerated by the commission system. But these influences have obviously proved less effective in the long term than the countervailing negative influences, of which two are of considerable (although not necessarily equal) importance.

These influences are, first, a gradual change in the balance of power between the manufacturing and retail sector, because of the latter's growing strength. The second cause is connected with the behavior of large advertisers. They are increasingly learning how to benefit from the scale economies accruing to their brands by reducing advertising expenditures on them. They are also the types of advertiser accustomed to carrying out econometric investigations, which always demonstrate the eventual onset of diminishing returns to incremental advertising pressure, something obviously inhibiting increases in advertising budgets.

There is no reason to suppose that these causes of downward pressure will become less important in the future. The result will be a dampening of the positive effect of economic revival on advertising expenditure, and an added impetus to the negative effect on advertising of an economic downturn.

These prognoses do not offer optimism to media proprietors or to advertising agencies working on the commission system. The forward thrust in these businesses has in recent years been confined to television, but the emergence of cable competition may weaken this thrust in the future. However, the ability of advertisers to support their brands with reduced advertising expenditures so long as their competitors do the same offers increasingly attractive opportunities for them to reduce their operating costs and thus to withstand better the pressure from retailers, which has led in the past to a syphoning of margins from manufacturers to retailers. Insofar as a proportion of these margins is passed to the consumer in the form of lower prices (a move forced by the pace of retail competition), this movement is strongly in the public interest.

Notes

1. "The Faulty Foundations of Social Security," *Wall Street Journal* (April 25, 1983) shows a rich and typical example of imperfections in forecasting. The base data were simple demographics. The article shows that the projection of even these turned out to be hopelessly wrong.

2. The point about the lack of comparability of advertising estimates from the United States and other countries is convincingly made in the analyses of international trends in advertising expenditures prepared by J. Walter Thompson and published in the *International Journal of Advertising* 1, no. 1 (January–March 1982); 2, no. 1 (January–March 1983); 3, no. 1 (January–March 1984). Mathematical errors in figures referring to the United States in the first of these issues were corrected in subsequent ones.

3. An estimate made in 1966 put the total of food plus what was rather misleadingly called "homogeneous package goods" as approximately 36 percent of all advertising. Julian L. Simon, *Issues in the Economics of Advertising* (Urbana, Ill: University of Illinois Press, 1970), pp. 269–71.

4. Based on estimates in *Advertising Age* (May 6, 1985: 47, and September 26, 1985: 16.)

5. The data relating to packaged goods advertisers are based on an individual examination of each of the one hundred leading advertisers. In most years, the packaged goods advertisers comprise those in the following *Advertising Age* categories:

All those in "soaps and cleaners," "tobacco," "toiletries and cosmetics," "pharmaceuticals," "gum and candy," "wine, beer and liquor," and "soft drinks."

The majority in "food."

None in "automotive," "airlines," "communications and entertainment," "retail chains," "electronics and office equipment," and "telephone equipment."

In every case, each advertiser's list of brands was studied. In the vast majority of cases, the advertiser could be cleanly categorized into "packaged goods" or "other." The actual advertisers appearing in the list vary to some degree year by year, but naturally the leading organizations in most categories return every year. The data are calculated from published "card" rates of media prices; larger advertisers are of course likely to pay significantly below these. However, this factor should not affect too seriously the comparability of the advertisers analyzed here, because they are all likely to benefit from similar scale economies in media purchasing.

6. Stephen King, *Crisis in Branding* (London: J. Walter Thompson, 1978.)

7. Don E. Schultz and Robert D. Dewar, "Retailers in Control: The Impact of Retail Trade Concentration," *Journal of Consumer Marketing* 1, no. 2: 81–89.

8. Thomas W. Wilson, Jr., *Achieving a Sustainable Competitive Advantage* (New York: Association of National Advertisers, 1982); Nancy Koch, *The Changing Marketplace Ahead and Implications for Advertisers* (New York: Association of National Advertisers, 1983).

9. See estimates of sales promotion expenditures in *Advertising Age* (August 22, 1983): M30–31.

10. Russell L. Ackoff and James R. Emshoff, "Advertising Research at Anheuser—Busch (1963–68)," *Sloane Management Review* (Winter 1975): 1–15.

11. David A. Aaker and James M. Carman, "Are You Overadvertising?" *Journal of Advertising Research* (August–September 1982): 57–70; H.R. Kropp, Stanley D. Canter, and Andrew Kershaw, *Determining How Much to Spend for Advertising— Without Experimental Testing* and *Marketing Implications of Media Expenditures*

(New York: Association of National Advertisers Research and Media Workshops, 1974 and 1971.)

12. See note 3.

13. This statement must not be construed as a recommendation to collusion between competitors. The point is that if all manufacturers are subjected to the same pressures in the marketplace, they are likely to respond in the same way.

12
How to Develop and Expose Better Advertising

"Consider your verdict," the King said to the jury.

"Not yet, not yet!" the Rabbit hastily interrupted. "There's a great deal to come before that!"

This chapter is devoted to agency practice, the field in which I spent my professional career. I have much cause to be grateful for the knowledge and professional satisfaction, not to speak of the financial and other rewards that it gave me. However, toward the end of my time in it, my feelings became rather ambivalent, as they have remained to a considerable degree. If one tries to observe the advertising scene from a detached and essentially technical point of view, it is difficult not to be impressed, and to respect profoundly the originality and understanding demonstrated by many of the campaigns being exposed for FMCG and other goods in advertising-intensive product fields, the fields in which campaign development is the most difficult art. Nevertheless, if one knows how difficult it normally is to develop such campaigns, and if one adopts a broader point of view, it is hard also not to conclude that there are specific ways in which advertising practice could be improved, in both the United States and other countries.

Advertisers and agencies, if they heed the points in this book, will not be overoptimistic about growth prospects for their businesses. Most major brands of repeat-purchase consumer goods are positioned in stationary markets and occupy substantially stationary positions in such markets. Advertising budgets are in many cases not increasing in real terms (indeed probably falling in the long term) for the reasons discussed in chapter 11. New brand activity remains as hazardous as ever, and available scientific tools have been of little help in making it less so. When companies are forced, by need for growth, into areas outside their traditional expertise, failure too often dogs them. Recently such need for growth has also led to numerous major company acquisitions and mergers. But since most consumer goods markets are already controlled by a sometimes overlapping network of oligopolists, there is clearly a top limit to the possibility of individual firms' further expansion by these means.

It follows that there is great need for us to increase the efficiency of our marketing and advertising efforts. The most obvious expression of this would be to improve the productivity of campaigns, to maintain or increase their yield despite reductions in the investments behind them. To bring this about, advertisers and agencies need a change of attitude regarding their advertised brands. They need to wean themselves away from the objective of volume growth, and to direct attention to profit growth from volumes that are not themselves increasing.

It is obvious that any pronounced increase in the efficiency of advertising is also unlikely to take place without either a change in existing methods or else a significant growth in what we know about advertising and its effectiveness. Developments of this sort normally take place only rarely in the real world. Nevertheless, we need a quantum increase in both the effectiveness of our methods and the amount of our knowledge, and these are the matters that I shall address in this chapter.

In it, I am making two specific proposals: more market experimentation and closing the gaps in our knowledge. The first has as its immediate and direct objective an improvement in advertising efficiency. My second suggestion is equally important, but its influence is more indirect, and will be manifested only in the long term. But the best clients and agencies—like the best organizations generally—plan for a long-term future.

First Recommendation: The Case for More Market Experiments

By way of background, I shall describe how advertising campaigns are planned and written in agencies today, and also—an important separate stage in their progress—how eventually they are exposed publicly. To my knowledge there has been no searching appraisal of this process, probably because it is considered so normal that no alternatives have been thought of, let alone experimented with. The picture I shall paint is impressionistic, because agencies are numerous and vary considerably in the detail of their organization, yet my portrayal approximates the overall situation.

When a new campaign is developed for a brand every three or four years (sometimes more often), the starting point is appropriately an extensive examination of the advertising strategy. This is most often carried out by the agency, but there are substantial client inputs and much debate. On the client side, three or more layers of management may be involved in these discussions, and the most important recommendations have to be processed progressively through all of these groups.

The advertising strategy is generally drawn up on the basis of judgment supported by quantitative and qualitative research, but in some respects it almost always falls short of the ideal. This is partly because the research on which it is based is variable in quality, the advertising research in particular relying heavily on recall. At a more fundamental level, the procedure is bedevilled by the large gaps in our general knowledge of how advertising works in both psychological and marketplace terms. As a result, most strategies, while they are neither completely ill-directed nor grossly deficient in detail, tend to be rather jejune and to lack the subtlest insights. As one example of this, target groups are almost always defined in the simplest demographic terms; and demographic measures are, as I argued in chapter 7, the *least* useful way of defining target audiences for creative (as opposed to media) planning.

The unmistakable impression made by most strategies is that they are not so much a critically important tool for the development of campaign ideas, as a frame of reference or a checklist drawn up with the intention of helping to sell a campaign.

When the strategy has been agreed upon (although it has not been unknown for the strategy to be at least marginally adjusted *after* the development of the creative ideas), the agency creative group produces a range of different proposals, which are expressed, with television campaigns, either in scripts, storyboards, "animatics" (storyboards shot on videotapes), or experimental commercials; and, with press campaigns, in layouts of different degrees of finish. Ideas are normally presented in rough form for the first presentations. They are now subjected to discussion and qualitative research, sometimes in progressive stages using the "focus group" technique to test creative hypotheses by exposing them to groups of consumers. This is done with the intention of homing in on one of the alternatives, which then becomes the agency's recommendation, and which is in turn sold to the client.[1]

The final campaign idea is normally converted into finished advertisements which are rich with expensively acquired production values. It is then subjected to simple standardized quantitative research (normally testing for day-after-recall plus some superficial persuasion measures) before being widely exposed to the public.

Problems with the Procedure

This way of planning campaigns has been accepted pragmatically by agencies. Much of its efficiency stems from the fact that agencies have adapted their organizations to make it work: to increase the operating efficiency of this whole process of problem evaluation—idea generation—elimination of alternatives—sale of the favored campaign. I suggest that agencies have accepted the system and encouraged its growth without asking any fundamental questions about it.

It seems to me that the system has four characteristics that are all far short of desirable.

In the first place, despite a superficial appearance to the contrary, the system is not really concerned with generating a wide range of creative alternatives. It is really concerned with finding one alternative; the elimination of the others becomes a tool for selling this selected one. Creative groups in agencies are sometimes cruelly realistic about this procedure when they label the rejected alternatives "client fodder." The reason the agency favors a single creative route may be that the route has been its favorite from the beginning, even before the various stages of qualitative research. Agencies are generally organized to have a single creative group responsible for a brand; and it is a fact of nature that such a group (which normally comprises a pair of people who work together all the time, or—less often—a small, cohesively organized body of people dominated by one individual) will nearly always decide that one single alternative is best. Moreover the clients, most of whom have a professional orientation toward selling, generally expect that there should be no ambiguity or uncertainty about what the agency is selling *them.*

The effective restriction of serious creative exploration would not matter if the development of creative ideas were more like the evolution of strategy, a "vertical" process which tends to lead in a single direction. But on the contrary, the creative process is mentally a lateral and "bisociative" one concerned with the pursuit of entirely unexpected connections, and the number of creative alternatives that can be produced in answer to a given strategic problem or opportunity is often very large indeed. To discriminate between this large number of alternatives is not nearly as easy or foolproof as it might appear. Much bathwater is thrown out. One wonders about the babies that might still have been in it.

With one brand with which I was personally concerned, the agency produced and presented a total of forty-seven alternative campaign ideas, the work of a number of creative groups in three countries. All these alternatives were finally reduced in qualitative testing and discussion to *one* single idea, which was actually tested in the market. In fact, the whole project was mainly concerned with demonstrating to the client the agency's enterprise, hard work, and internationalism—considerations that may be important, but have little to do with the brand and its advertising. If the sole object of the exercise had been to find a new campaign for the brand, it would have been at the very least highly desirable to experiment in the marketplace with more than one creative alternative.

The second characteristic of the system is that it is heavily judgmental. The judgment is often supported by methodologically flimsy qualitative research. "Sheer conventional group discussions which often masquerade as qualitative research but are little more than reportage—running the risk of portraying consumers as rational and worthy, and stunting the creative process."[2] In the absence of research, decisions are made on the basis of background knowledge, and gut feeling. My own experience (which is neither narrow nor of short duration) is that such judgment can be extremely fallible. And this is amply confirmed by the investigation of Bogart and his colleagues that experts are not at all good at evaluating the important aspect of campaigns: their selling ability. A sample of "83 advertising decision makers (company brand and advertising managers, agency account executives, creative, media and research men) in New York, Boston, Cincinnati, Detroit and Los Angeles . . . could not predict which ads would sell more of the brand."[3]

As an aside, we *know* that with direct response, there are huge differences in the pulling power of different advertisements, which are normally only different creative expressions of the same strategy; but direct response practitioners admit that it is highly unlikely that subjective evaluation will detect these differences in effectiveness. This is why they rely so heavily on experimental market place exposure.[4]

The imperfections of human judgment are serious in all events, but what makes the matter even more worrying is that campaigns are commonly judged by six or more people, all of whom have strong opinions and are empowered to require or at least request modifications. In few circumstances does this procedure lead to an improvement in a campaign; on the contrary, in many cases it leads to disastrous erosion and distortion of the original concept. Some clients are worse than others; indeed some have such a bad reputation that the best creative people will not work on their business. (I wish I were at liberty to name names!)

The system has (to my personal observation) become progressively worse over the past twenty or thirty years. Indeed agencies today are less concerned with idea generation than with idea evaluation, and less involved with creation than with mere dialectic.

These serious criticisms bring me to the third fault with the system. For a complex of interrelated reasons, there has been a gradual change in the internal balance of advertising agencies from the creative function to the account executive function. It is rare today for there to be fewer than four layers of account executives working on major brands. These are people who judge and can demand modifications to campaigns even before they reach the echelons of executives on the client side.

This fattening of the account executive function was partly in response to client requirements. (Agencies commonly believe that they should match each layer of a client's marketing organization to reinforce the overall client—agency relationship by providing a "safety net" if the account executive at one level loses the confidence of his or her client.) It was also much encouraged by the extreme profitability of larger accounts, which stemmed from the size of the agency's commission income from them. This executive loading mostly took place in the prosperous 1950s and 1960s, but there is little evidence that in the austere 1970s, agencies made many attempts to reduce their executive layers.

There has indeed been a move from another direction to *increase* the number of noncreative people in agency account groups: the widely discussed arrival of the account planner, the specialist in the consumer viewpoint and in consumer research, whose job is to establish within the agency the strategy for a brand. This function is common in British agencies,[5] where it appears to have been set up to compensate for weaknesses in the training of European account executives, "Partly because account men were rarely competent to [handle data] but more dangerously because, as my own account man experience had shown—clients on the one hand and creative direction on the other hand made one permanently tempted to be expedient. Too much data could be uncomfortable."[6] However, there has been a very slow adoption of the system in the United States, partly because of the financial pressures that have assailed American agencies, and partly because of the greater professional competence of American account executives. The account planning function is a valuable one; the dispute is about who should carry it out: account executives or account planners. To date, the system is used in one small but influential agency (Chiat/Day), and it has been implemented experimentally in two of the leading agencies on Madison Avenue.

The fourth problem with the system is that it imposes delays. The lead time from the beginning of campaign planning to final public exposure is commonly a year. It is also extremely expensive in management time.

A Lesson from Direct Response

There is one centrally important point about this category of advertising. Since the results can be so easily traced, the *efficiency* of direct response advertising, and by extension the efficiency of the advertising agencies handling it, can be easily established and carefully measured. Not only can the results of the advertising be simply quantified, but (with a little more difficulty) so also can the agencies' contribution to the profitability of their clients' businesses. The scientific basis for direct response is so strong that people engaged in other types of advertising cannot afford always to ignore its lessons. Rather, in my opinion they should work on the assumption that they can learn something from direct response unless there are facts to prove the contrary.

Quantification is in the bloodstream of direct response advertisers and their agencies, and it is their main device in maximizing the effectiveness of their efforts. Measurement here means changing on a test basis all the main advertising variables (one at a time) and counting and costing the resulting response coupons.[7] This approach has on occasion been transferred into other fields of advertising by experienced practitioners who believe in the principle of marketplace testing. One such exponent is David Ogilvy: "Test your promise. Test your media. Test your headlines and your illustrations. Test the size of your advertisements. Test your frequency. Test your level of expenditure. Test your commercials. Never stop testing, and your advertising will never stop improving."[8]

I should be extremely interested to know how closely this admirable advice is followed today at Ogilvy & Mather. But I am frankly skeptical, as much if not most of this agency's business is in packaged goods. To test what are in so many cases detailed variations by use of techniques available in direct response advertising is easy; but in the world of repeat-purchase merchandise sold via the retail trade, there is the widespread belief that the relentless type of detailed testing of element after element that is the norm with direct response is in practical terms almost impossible.

This view should not however be accepted as final. Remember the lesson of the Oxo case in chapter 7: by shrewd contingency planning, the client and agency were used to the procedure of testing campaign alternatives, and this stood them in good stead when the brand's main campaign showed serious signs of faltering. What the client and agency had repeatedly done was to implement in the marketplace alternatives to the national campaign. They had exposed and punctiliously evaluated (by a number of different criteria) the results of the alternatives, something simple and inexpensive with direct response, but complex and costly—although certainly not impossible—for other types of advertising.

The point made by the Oxo case is that even in the world of repeat purchase, the procedure of market experimentation has great value (and even greater rarity value). Such experimentation is much more difficult than with direct response, so the number of tested alternatives must be restricted. But even one is greatly better than none; and six might be six times as good as one, depending of course on what is tested and how carefully the testing is carried out.

An Actionable Proposal

A properly conducted market experiment requires the following conditions:

1. A significant alternative in the marketing mix (the variable to be tested);
2. A control, which is the normal ongoing marketing mix;
3. A reasonable sized, representative, and self-contained test area;
4. Effective media that are comparable in the test and control areas;
5. Time (in most cases, at least two years);
6. An evaluation procedure, which as a minimum should include (for the tested brand and its competitors):

   Continuous usage and attitude measures;
   Continuous consumer panel data, with the routine possibility of tab-

ulating all the consumer behavioral measures described in chapter 5;
Retail audit data;
Continuous quantitative and qualitative evaluation of competitive
advertising.

Such a program is routine for market tests of new brands. It is more
unusual for experiments with ongoing brands, although in view of the potential rewards of such procedures, the reluctance (or rather inertia) of marketing managements to implement or even consider such programs is difficult to
understand.

I shall now describe my recommended program for major established
brands. The purpose of such a program is twofold: first, to explore in a practical way a number of marketing variables, some of which might be the keys
to future protection and growth for the brand; and second, to have creative
alternatives prepared and tested in the event of serious problems with the
national advertising campaign.

I believe that at any one time, the marketing management of a major
brand, if it is properly to exercise its responsibility to that brand, should have
in the field at least six programs, each of which should be run for two years.
These can be differently phased, so that for instance in any single year, three
market experiments can be in their first year, while three others are in their
second year. Routine experimentation of this sort should be as much in the
bloodstream of manufacturers of repeat-purchase goods and their advertising
agencies as it has always been in that of direct response practitioners.

The specific things which deserve such market experimentation will depend on the brand and its competition. A typical program for the sorts of
brand I was mostly concerned with during my professional career would be
as follows:[9]

Area 1: Campaign *A* (the ongoing national campaign); 20-percent media downweight.

Area 2: Campaign *A;* 10-percent price increase.

Area 3: Campaign *A;* 20-percent promotional downweight.

Area 4: Campaign *A* (perhaps adapted); improved formulation.

Area 5: Campaign *B;* other variables constant.

Area 6: Campaign *C;* other variables constant.

The control for all these experiments would of course be the national
marketing mix used in all areas outside the test regions. For these, the United
States is extraordinarily rich in its size and diversity. Each test area need not

in normal circumstances comprise more than four cities, so that the test areas (approximately twenty-four cities in toto) would account for no more than a significantly minor share of the country as a whole.

Although such a procedure offers enormous advantages over the type of hand-to-mouth and opportunistic marketing so widely practiced with even large and well-established brands, a program like this does have two major problems.

The first is that market tests and experiments, which are rather a public activity, invite competitive retaliation. This is a fact of life—nothing can prevent it. But never in the past has this vulnerability invalidated the principle of test marketing, although retaliation can of course increase the difficulties of interpreting the test results. If my recommendation concerning ongoing market experimentation were to be accepted on any scale, this would of course mean a substantial increase in the total volume of testing, and a resultant increase in the difficulty of effective retaliatory activity. Indeed, in the celebrated Budweiser case (an extremely complex and prolonged series of market experiments), published evidence does not reveal any consistent competitive retaliation at all.

The second problem with the sort of experimental programs I am proposing is obviously their cost, the seriousness of which cannot literally be minimized. I shall however suggest a way in which it might be *viewed:* in relation to a brand's aggregates.

The advertising production, market research, and management time costs for the market experiments should be estimated and compared with the overall marketing costs for the brand. This will provide a more rational perspective than appears at first glance. For example, if the advertising production costs for two new campaigns to be tested in different areas total $500,000 (or $250,000 for each of two years), this total would account for a significant but not outrageously disproportionate share (2½ percent) of the overall above-the-line advertising budget for a $10-million brand. Viewed in this way, the costs seem at least to be sensibly evaluated against a broad total picture of the brand.

The reader should not forget that the scale economies of large brands are capable of yielding millions of dollars per year in advertising savings. It is only prudent that manufacturers should plough back some of these savings into their ongoing brands (and not just their new ones), so that planned steps can be taken to continue indefinitely their extreme profitability. Profit is also "seed money" for a prudent company.

Without being privy to any inside information, I am fairly certain that Charmin, Crest, Crisco, Ivory, and Tide enjoy significant advertising-related scale economies. And if I were asked to comment on the remarkable company that manufactures them (and others with similar strengths), I should have little hesitation in saying that the efficiency of Procter and Gamble's marketing operation comes, first, from its emphasis on highly competitive functional performance for its brands; second, from its ability to nurture its older brands without any disastrous long-term erosion of their sales and profits, allied to an active response to first signs of such erosion; and third, from its ability to employ the profits yielded by their scale economies to operate experimentally in the marketplace—both with these older brands and also with a continuous stream of new brand introductions.

I believe that the recommendations in this chapter and implicitly throughout this book will be treated with less skepticism in Cincinnati than in the head offices of certain other manufacturing companies in the United States and abroad. I should also add that I never personally worked on Procter and Gamble business, although I have made a consistent effort for many years to study its operations from the outside: by drawing conclusions about its policies by scrutinizing its actions.

The Division of Labor between Advertisers and Their Agencies

If the proposals in this chapter were to be implemented at all widely, agencies would, I believe, be forced back to a much greater concentration on constructing advertisements—the sort of role they adopted so successfully for many decades after emerging from space brokerage a hundred years ago.

As a complement to this, I visualize that clients should adopt the leading role in planning and evaluating market experiments. These would of course greatly add to the store of knowledge about their brands, so that marketing would become a more efficiently planned activity. Specifically, these experiments could provide a more scientific basis than is at present available for drawing up a brand's budget and media strategy. The increase in the sharpness of the division of labor between clients and agencies should also provide natural benefits in terms of increased operational efficiency, in the way predicted by classical economic theory. They are likely however to bring about some changes in the internal structure of agencies, which may not be popular in some agency circles.

If the agency of the future will be expected to produce for its client not one campaign, but three or more, all to be exposed in the marketplace, it is unlikely that such a change could be implemented with the old system of one creative group per brand. Agencies' most likely routes would be to have a much faster rotation of creative groups on individual accounts; to employ more roving troubleshooting groups in addition to the regular ones; or to make much more use of freelance talent than is done at present.

However, in all events, it seems inevitable that agencies' creative staffs should occupy a higher proportion of the total than they now do. This proportion varies at the moment between 25 percent and 30 percent, depending on the agency. Viewed objectively, this is remarkably low, considering the importance of the creative product in any agency operation, especially since this general creative category covers a total of about twenty functions, some of which are peripheral to the central creative process. (For instance home economics, packaging, and proofreading are often included with the creative).

It is of course likely that agencies will in time be able to make savings in the size of their client contact departments, especially as the emphasis of agency work changes more toward the production of ideas, and away from an endlessly extended evaluation of them. It is also likely that a widespread move away from remuneration based on commision, toward fees based on time of staff, will force reductions in the layers of account management (as clients are made aware of their cost).

Implications for Agency Compensation Systems

Perhaps a discussion of the commission system of agency remuneration is unnecessary since the system is being abandoned at a noticeable rate. But two of its specific imperfections deserve comment.

First, the system in essence penalizes efficiency. As the productivity of advertising increases—for instance as brands benefit from advertising economies of scale—it should be possible to work with smaller appropriations. Advertising can work like a rapier, although it is only too often used as a bludgeon. What is the incentive to an agency working on commission if more effective work on its part leads to a reduction in its income? The commission system is an obvious impediment to operating experimental programs of budget reduction. Indeed, it is a handicap to any form of experimentation involving high costs in agency staff time but low returns in commission income. The agency for Budweiser beer was—perhaps understandably—only prepared to cooperate in the marketplace tests of advertising pressure—tests which were eventually to prove so beneficial to the brand—after Anheuser-Busch had made special arrangements to maintain the agency's income.[10]

Second, the commission system is intended, in the last analysis, to ensure that the scale economies of agency operation are retained by the agency. This is frankly resented by many clients.[11] It led, during the prosperous 1950s and 1960s, to a crude overstaffing of agencies which had long-term ill effects. It has also, in my judgment, led to much abrasiveness in the relations between clients and agencies. Indeed, I believe that price competition between agencies might be a more comfortable as well as a more efficient system.

A fee system means that with very large budgets, the client pays the agency less. But if there are extensive labor-intensive experimental programs, the agency is protected against losses. Moreover, by its flexibility, it encourages necessary changes in agency organization. In Sweden, where the commission system effectively broke down in the 1960s, agencies changed their nature in a short period of time. Agencies spearheaded a considerable creative revival, which coincided with a decentralization into small, self-contained units (a trend followed in other countries). A rather dramatic decline in the older full-service agencies was partially brought about by the growing number of younger thrusting ones. I am convinced that these evolutionary changes were encouraged by the change in the method of agency compensation, but this is of course a major reason for established agencies in the United States to resist the complete abandonment of commission.

However, the pressures of change are affecting even the staunchest of the old guard. In fact, enquiries conducted among members of the Association of National Advertisers show the proportion of advertisers who work with their agencies on a pure or modified commission system to have come down from 83 percent in 1976, to 75 percent in 1979, and to 71 percent in 1982. Furthermore, in 1982, over a quarter of that 71 percent departed in some way from the rigidity of the 15-percent level, leaving the proportion of clients who work on an unamended 15-percent commission as low as 52 percent.[12] Indeed, I know of only one major agency which holds the line on a uniform 15 percent for all its clients. The movement to change already exists; it just needs an increased impetus behind it.

Second Recommendation: How to Close Some of the Gaps in Our Knowledge

A recurrent theme in this book is the paucity of our knowledge about advertising. It is not that we know nothing, but the gaps in our knowledge are formidable, particularly if we accept my point that there are no absolutely generalizable patterns about how advertising works. (The absence of such patterns is one of the few things we know pretty well for certain.) The amount we know about the extent of the variations and their causes is however much flimsier. In summer 1985, I carried out a piece of consultancy which involved making a formal inventory of the state of advertising knowledge. I concluded that we had certain knowledge of only 35 percent of the total corpus of what could or should be known.

The four areas of enquiry with which I have been most concerned in this book are all related in some ways to one another:

1. The response to advertising, including short- and long-term effects of absolute amounts of pressure and the effects of incremental pressure.
2. Advertising and the human mind: how advertising operates on people.

Psychological theories are plentiful, but despite their intellectual attractions, they are almost devoid of empirical support.

3. The creative process: idea generation, and why and how some campaign ideas are more effective than others.

4. Ways of researching advertisements and advertising campaigns, and in particular research techniques to forecast the success of new brands.

I am convinced that advertising will never come near to being a scientific subject, despite the claims of some of its protagonists, unless our knowledge of these relative unknowns greatly increases in extent and depth. The vast amount of research (much of it subtle and thought-provoking, but much more, unfortunately, unidimensional and repetitive) is hardly intended or used to fill these gaps in our knowledge, for two reasons. First, much of it is too similar to what has been done before in terms of problems tackled and methodology, to push forward the frontiers to any extent; and second (an even more important point), it is no one's job to synthesize it and use it for the broader purpose of adding to the general store of what we know. The problem is of course compounded by the extreme care taken to avoid the publication of expensively acquired proprietary data.

This situation should be a source of disappointment to everyone in marketing and advertising. In effect it seriously hampers any serious attempts to extend the amount of our general knowledge. Many people do in fact regret this, and unfair criticism is lavishly distributed. For instance, advertising academics are attacked for their seeming inability to carry out fundamental research. (On the other hand, some people believe that academics should concentrate more on practical, day-to-day brand and market problems, much as commercial researchers do.)[13] The critics would be wise however to give some thought to the nature of advertising knowledge, and the methods of enquiry available to researchers to extend it. A number of people contend quite wrongly that the study of advertising resembles the study of natural science, in that basic research is in some way a foundation for applied research. This view, as it applies to various pure and applied scientific disciplines, has been expressed with admirable lucidity by a scientist of distinction, the late J. Robert Oppenheimer:

[B]asic research: that is, research that is aimed primarily at increasing our understanding and our knowledge, without too direct a thought of what use this will be in practice. That this is typically a university function is true in the natural sciences; it is true in the mathematical sciences; and I believe it is even more true in those areas, let us say, of anthropology, psychology, and economics which are becoming subject to research.[14]

With due deference to this most distinguished observer, I question his conclusion regarding the social sciences. And if by extension a similar conclusion were to be made about the study of advertising, I believe it would be unambiguously wrong.

My reason for this disagreement is quite simple. Most worthwhile advertising research must in my judgment be inductive; it must be based on the study of the particular, which will help us to understand parts of the marketing process for certain brands and (to quote Chapter 1) "provide the hope (although not the firm expectation) that a general theory might eventually be built up to explain the whole." This progress from the particular to the general is of course what McDonald is talking about in his comparison of the study of advertising to entomology.

If my line of reasoning is correct, it would explain why there may indeed be validity in the common view held by advertising practitioners that there has been little worthwhile research into advertising carried on at universities.[15] The reason is simple: the only fundamental place in which research into advertising can possibly be carried out is the market. The method of enquiry must be the punctilious and extensive examination of particular brands, marketing situations, and advertising campaigns; and the primary (although not the sole) source of data must be the consumers of the brands under examination and their competitors. Universities lack the financial resources to fund studies of this type, which are rightly seen as the province of the custodians of brands: manufacturers and their advertising agencies.

Advertising people know from first-hand experience (as is clear from the cases in this book) that the inductive principle is well established in the advertising field; indeed, it is the method by which we have acquired most of our worthwhile knowledge of advertising. The trouble is, however, that the amount that has been done, or rather the amount released for objective study of underlying conditions, is very small in relation to the amount necessary for the formulation of anything like robust general hypotheses, let alone principles.

There are three reasons for this. First, not enough market experiments have actually been carried out, although the pace is increasing. Moreover, if manufacturers listen to what I have to say in this book, it will increase more rapidly in the future. Second, not enough experiments have been released for examination, for reasons of confidentiality. Third—a big reason—is that it has been no one's job to carry out what some people would consider the laborious tasks of analysis and synthesis. What has been grossly lacking is a body of people with the skills, time, and interest to begin to build an edifice out of what at the moment is a small number of bricks; and then (an even more important task) to persuade people to make many more bricks available.

The reader may by now have guessed what I visualize to be the true role of advertising research as it should be carried out at univerisities: to take individual brand studies and to evaluate them in the mass in order to detect, hypothesize, and eventually enunciate general principles; and to examine the extent and the characteristics of variations and exceptions. A certain amount of work of this sort has already been carried out by the various professional organizations in the marketing field, notably the Advertising Research Foundation, the Association of National Advertisers (ANA), and the Marketing Science Institute. An admirable example is the ANA's *Effective Frequency* discussed in chapters 8 and 9. But the total amount of such work done to date is tiny in comparison with what needs to be done; and the research which has been undertaken by these important bodies has been done in the main by people who have full-time commercial careers which make extreme demands on their time and energy, so that my comments should not be construed as critical of their work.

For reasons connected (but not solely connected) with the lack of other suitable expertise, I believe that universities have a great deal to offer such research programs. In fact, critics of universities' advertising work would be wise to consider four of academia's advantages.

To start with, universities have brainpower. There are full programs in advertising in ninety-one state and private universities and colleges in the United States.[16] Each faculty has a number of instructors and often also a body of energetic graduate students. The standard of education among the faculties is generally high.

Second, most academics are objective. They are generally not proponents of any single philosophy or method, which can narrow the thinking of employees of many manufacturing concerns, advertising agencies, and research companies.

Third, academics have a priceless amount of time. Research, intellectual speculation, and plain thought are a central part of their job; and the amount of uncluttered time for these activities is the most striking (and delightful) feature of academic life as it is experienced by someone like myself who has adopted it after a career as an advertising practitioner.

Fourth, and not least, is something more intangible but very important indeed: what Oppenheimer calls "the fructification of the classroom," something which a person who has not experienced it first-hand cannot fully understand.

> The experience of the student is to be puzzled, not to understand, to be confused, and gradually to find some sensible order, to get a new idea, to find out that what he had been thinking was wrong; this is a typical experience for the man engaged in research, and it is a typical experience for the student, and this is one point of harmony. . . . One finds that although it is not possible to give a theoretical argument why research and education

should occur in the same place, a man himself by uniting these two functions will make it manifest that it is a good idea.[17]

Indeed the relentless demands of advertising research resemble those of the small handful of outstanding students in the academic's classes, especially if the teacher has successfully taught them a healthy skepticism, an unwillingness to accept received wisdom without testing it first.

This chapter's proposal, that manufacturers should greatly increase the number of market experiments they conduct for their brands, must be decided on its own merits—by its perceived contributions to the health and progress of those brands. In my opinion, these contributions are likely to be considerable indeed. My proposal about using cases individually and in the aggregate to add to our store of general knowledge about advertising is a separate but related matter. If manufacturers accept my first proposal, the amount of material available for general study will be greatly increased, and this is our starting point.

The advertising industry is the only body with the interest in and resources to acquire this knowledge and then (an equally important consideration) to release it for analysis and synthesis. A good deal of case-by-case data collection takes place at the moment (although this is far short of what is needed), but there is no evidence that the industry yet realizes what would be gained if there were a first class series of studies of the existing corpus of information, let alone what could be done if we had much more data to start with.

My proposal that universities have a real role to play in these studies is made cautiously, but with some knowledge of their capacity and intellectual horsepower. The work would incidentally involve the industry in little financial outlay over and beyond the marketplace experiments that would naturally account for the most substantial proportion of the cost of any broad empirical evaluation program.

During my years as an advertising practitioner and academic, I have been both excited about what we do know about advertising (no matter how little), and frustrated by what we do *not*. From talking to present and former colleagues, I do not think that these feelings are untypical, which makes me optimistic that at least a few of the things I have said in this book may not fall on deaf ears.

I began this book with the intention of using it indirectly or directly as a teaching aid. In retrospect, I can see that I have also had some fun writing it. But I am ending the manuscript with an attempt to reach you, the reader, who may have some sympathy with what I have been trying to say and also the interest and energy to turn thoughts into deeds. Will you respond to my call to action? Will you realize both your responsibility and your capacity to extend the frontiers of our knowledge? Will you accept my suggestions as constructive, practicable, and relatively inexpensive to put into action? Will you employ your professional authority and your talents to support what I am saying in a practical way? And will you please act now. I should very much like to hear from you.

The Argument in Brief

This chapter began by emphasizing that advertisers and agencies will probably have to continue to operate with stationary markets, stationary brands, and advertising budgets that may be falling in real terms. It then addressed the fundamental problem of how to increase advertising's productivity—its ability to augment profits, despite static sales and declining (real) advertising investments. The chapter argued that success can only be made possible with changes in the methods of planning advertising and increases in our store of knowledge.

There was an analysis and critique of the general method of campaign development in major agencies in the United States. In brief, the system puts less emphasis on idea generation than on the processes of idea evaluation, and the selling of campaigns to clients. A strong recommendation was made to embark on much more creative experimentation than is common at present, with evaluation by more extensive programs of marketplace testing of alternatives. The chapter recommended that, for major brands, there should at any time be at least six ongoing market tests of variations in the marketing mix. Such testing programs will only be enthusiastically endorsed by agencies when they have substantially abandoned the media commission system.

A second recommendation related to the poverty of our knowledge of the various processes of advertising. A formal study recently revealed that we have reasonably firm knowledge of a mere 35 percent of the actual or potential corpus. The advertising industry should take serious steps to augment this store of knowledge. Advertisers and agencies should be persuaded to make proprietary market data available to universities for them to analyze and synthesize, with the object of seeking general patterns and generating hypotheses about how advertising works in a variety of circumstances. This would be a practical example of how advertising can be studied using the principles of entomology, a notion introduced in the first chapter of this book.

This book has attempted to sound the tocsin—to alert advertisers and indeed the whole advertising industry to the pressing need to study their profession in a serious way, so that it can begin to justify the scientific pretensions of so many of its protagonists.

Notes

1. Stephen A. Greyser, *Cases in Advertising and Communications Management*, 2d ed., pp. 3–22, 373–401. Two described cases dealing with the Northwestern Mutual Life Insurance Company illustrate well the processes of creative development, research, and elimination of alternatives.

2. Two skilled practitioners of qualitative research, Judie Lannon and Peter Cooper, express this view in "Humanistic Advertising: A Holistic Cultural Perspective," *International Journal of Advertising* 2, no. 3: 211.

3. Leo Bogart, B. Stuart Tolley, and Frank Orenstein, "What One Little Ad Can Do," *Journal of Advertising Research* (August 1970): 12.

4. See an excellent empirical statement of this principle by well-known British practitioner of direct response Graeme McCorkell, "When Experts Can Get It Wrong," *Campaign* (February 15, 1985): 55–56.

5. For a detailed description of British practice, see *Account Planning* (London: Institute of Practitioners in Advertising, 1981).

6. Stanley Pollitt, "How I Started Account Planning in Agencies" in *ibid.*, pp. 24–28.

7. Greyser, *Cases in Advertising and Communications Management*, pp. 447–72. This provides an excellent example of the technique in action. The advertiser was *The National Observer*.

8. David Ogilvy, *Confessions of an Advertising Man*, p. 86.

9. Many if not most television schedules include spot as well as network transmissions. Media downweighting in an area would naturally involve cutting back the spot advertising exclusively to achieve the necessary overall reduction. With somewhat more difficulty, an experimental downweighting could be implemented with the use of the split-cable TV mechanism. The latter device is also suitable for testing campaign alternatives.

10. Russell L. Ackoff and James R. Emshoff, "Advertising Research at Anheuser—Busch 1963–68," *Sloane Management Review* (Winter 1975): 13.

11. Evidence of this is provided by a number of investigations by the Association of National Advertisers, for instance, *ANA Member Practices and Views on Advertising Agency Compensation* (New York: Association of National Advertisers, 1967).

Such dissatisfaction appeared as long ago as the early 1930s, at least on the part of larger advertisers. James Webb Young, *Advertising Agency Compensation* (Chicago: University of Chicago Press, 1933), p. 156.

Recent evidence collected by the Association of National Advertisers demonstrates that although certain advertisers have moved to reduce their agencies' compensation, others have moved to increase it. In both cases, the fee system was thought to offer greater flexibility. William M. Weilbacher, *Current Advertiser Practices in Compensating Their Advertising Agencies* (New York: Association of National Advertisers, 1983), pp. 38–46.

12. William M. Weilbacher, *Current Advertiser Practices in Compensating Their Advertising Agencies*.

13. Herbert J. Rotfeld, Spencer F. Tinkham, and Leonard N. Reid, "What Research Managers Think of Advertising Research by Academics" in *Proceedings of the*

1983 Convention of the American Academy of Advertising (Lawrence, Kans.: University of Kansas, 1983): pp. 52–57.

14. J. Robert Oppenheimer, "The Relation of Research to the Liberal University," *Freedom and the University* (Ithaca, N.Y.: Cornell University Press, 1950), pp. 97–98.

15. Rotfeld *et al.*, "What Research Managers Think of Advertising Research by Academics": 54.

Thirty leading advertising agencies with which I have been in personal contact have confirmed and added to the conclusions of this investigation.

16. Don E. Schultz, "Advertising Education: Where It Is, Where It's Going", in *Advertising Age Yearbook* (Chicago: Crain Books, 1982), pp. 37–50.

17. Oppenheimer, "The Relation of Research to the Liberal University," pp. 101–2.

Index

Achenbaum, Al, 221
Ackoff, Russell L., 201, 257
Ad Tel split-cable market, 216, 232–233
Added values, 6–7; augmenting, 34, 83; building, 84; embedded in name, 57; long-term effects of advertising and, 229; low-involvement hierarchy and, 144, 20, 29–34; maintenance of position and, 157; measuring contribution of, 32; most important, 30–31; non-functional, 32–33; pack and, 52
Adstock, 149
Advertisements: content of, 237–238; form versus content of, 176–177
Advertising: brain wave activity related to types of, 144; building added values and, 52; continuity of, 2–3, 235; direct and indirect, 161, 221–222; direct response, 146, 188, 189–190, 229–230, 270–271; dispersion versus concentration of, 188; downward pressure on, 258–261; factors contributing to growth of, 22; of growing brand, 83–92; historical growth of, 23–26; to increase volume of usage, 175–176; intensiveness of, 7–8; "investment" level of, 84; long-term effects of, 34, 225–229; measuring increments of, 186; method of influence of, 141–145; print, 24, 196–198, 212–213; recall of explicit and implicit copy for, 139; recommendations to increase knowledge about, 276–281; reduction associated with rise in

sales, 201–202; reinforcement, 144, 157; role of, factors influencing, 125–126; short-run effects of, 95–96, 225–229; single-exposure, 229–231; size of field, 8; trial and reinforcement, 144
Advertising agencies, 8; compensation systems of, 275–276; effect on budgets, 254; role of, 274–275; shift to account executive function in, 269–270
Advertising appropriations: calculation of, 237; general influences on, 243–262; for restaging, 158, 159
Advertising elasticity: long-term, measurement of, 228; price elasticity and, 94; short-term, computation of, 227
Advertising elasticity coefficient, 84
Advertising expenditures: long-term trends in, 244–254
Advertising pressure: diminishing rate of yield and, 183–205; frequency and, 209–223; for restaging, 159–160; tracking studies, 149–150
Advertising recall, see Recall
Advertising research: concerns with, 131–132; conducted by universities, 278, 279–280; marketing test evaluation system, 164; recommendations for, 276–281; role at universities, 279–280; roles of, 140
Advertising Research Foundation, 134, 279; conference held by, 159
Advertising response functions: economies of scale and, 202–204;

About the Author

John Philip Jones was educated at Cambridge University (graduating with Honors B.A. and M.A. in Economics). He spent his professional career on the international side of the advertising agency business, most of the time managing the advertising of brands like those discussed in this book. He worked for J. Walter Thompson for twenty-five years: mostly in London, but also in Amsterdam and Copenhagen, before coming to Syracuse, N.Y. in January 1981. Professor Jones is a member of the faculty of Syracuse University and Chairman of the Advertising Department of the Newhouse School of Public Communications. He is also a University Senator, member of the Chancellor's Panel on the Future of the University, and Editor-elect of the *Syracuse Scholar*.